IMAGES
of America

ENNIS

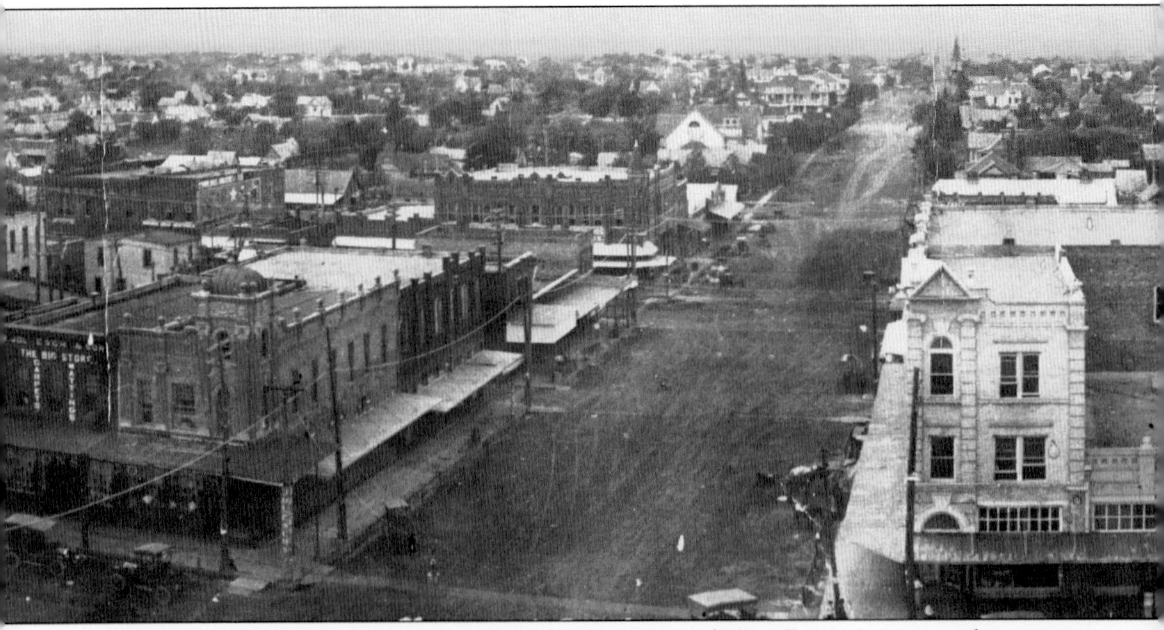

Many once referred to this intersection at Main Street and West Ennis Avenue as the entrance to the city. At each corner were majestic structures—the Jolesch and Sons Dry Goods Store to the left and the Moore Building to the right. The streets were yet to be paved, horses still roamed the streets, church bells tolled within blocks of the avenue, and as one travelled down the avenue, homes could be seen everywhere. Ennis had come into its own.

ON THE COVER: The Ennis High School graduating class of 1923 numbered 46. Many would stay in Ennis, marry, and raise families. Many too would leave; some returned, yet others did not. Pictured here before their graduation, with the Passenger Depot in the background, they gathered together knowing they would soon be going their separate ways. They appear ready to take on the world. Some, in their own way, did. (Courtesy of Telfair family.)

IMAGES
of America

ENNIS

Laurie J. Wilson, Peggy Holland Rankin,
Ellis County Czech Heritage Society,
and Ennis Heritage Society

ARCADIA
PUBLISHING

ISBN 978-0-7385-5859-2

Published by Arcadia Publishing
Charleston SC, Chicago IL, Portsmouth NH, San Francisco CA

Printed in the United States of America

Library of Congress Catalog Card Number: 2008932140

For all general information contact Arcadia Publishing at:
Telephone 843-853-2070
Fax 843-853-0044
E-mail sales@arcadiapublishing.com
For customer service and orders:
Toll-Free 1-888-313-2665

Visit us on the Internet at www.arcadiapublishing.com

This is dedicated to those who knew us and those who didn't but believed in what we were doing and opened their photo albums, dug out their boxes, searched their memories, and allowed us to tell this story.

Contents

ACKNOWLEDGMENTS

There are several individuals who helped this project come together in numerous ways. Their assistance, ideas, patience, and support have been immeasurable. They did fact-checking, helped get releases signed, gathered photographs, edited, proofread, and did so much more. Our heartfelt thanks go to Randy Bigham, Retha Bigham, Norma Black, Paula Campo, Victor Havel, Dorothy Kudrna, Mary Ann Lamkin, Lucy Mikula, Georgie Vrla Morales, Gina Rokas, Mike and Mary Ann Sibley, David and Michelle Slovak, Eric Strong, Ray Telfair, Ben Tucker, and Susie Wilson.

There are those who have made the stewardship of preserving the documents, including photographs, of our city's history a priority. Their foresight and understanding that preserving these pieces of our history is an invaluable gift to future generations has humbled us on more than one occasion. Our sincere gratitude goes to the late Tia Atwood, Jimmy and Ginger Boon, Elaine Gallagher, Charles and Mary Helen Gentry, Sugar Glaspy, David Hopkins, Steve Howerton, Sylvia Laznovsky, "Conductor" Bill Martz, Ann Peeler, Jim and Helen Templin, the Ellis County Czech Heritage Society, the *Ennis Daily News*, the Ennis Heritage Society, the Ennis Public Library, the Ennis Railroad Museum, the Ennis Sokol Museum, and all those we have yet to meet that have been guardians over the history of our community.

The Ennis Public Library and its entire staff provided constant assistance and a willingness to support this project from the very beginning. We thank each of them for their interest and support, including Charlene Ballard, Jessica Diaz, Ray Lowry, John Miller, Michael Sibley, Lisa Slaughter, Karen Witte, and Evelyn Young.

We thank every single person who trusted us with their photographs; without them, this project would not be what it is. All unattributed photographs are courtesy of private donors.

We also want to express our appreciation and gratitude to our editor at Arcadia Publishing, Kristie Kelly, who never faltered in her expert advice and support of this project.

We especially thank our families; without their love, support, and understanding, we could not have done this.

INTRODUCTION

The story of Ennis and her people has often been one of overcoming obstacles. In April 1875, much of the small business area of Main Street was either severely damaged or completely destroyed by fire. They rebuilt. Over the years, some of the brick buildings began to crumble because of the weakness of the bricks, which they believed was due to the soil from which they had been made. Again they rebuilt. The city battled several obstacles in obtaining the Houston Texas and Central Railroad roundhouse, machine shops, and district headquarters, yet they persevered and found success. All along the way, generations of Ennis residents have shown resilience and determination and passed those qualities on to their children. In the late 1920s and into the 1930s, the Ennis High School yearbook was not published for many reasons, including a strained economy from lower cotton prices and the continued effects of the Great Depression. In 1939, the senior class decided to change that. They took on the task themselves, publishing the first yearbook since 1926.

Ennis was established in 1872. The Houston and Texas Central Railroad came through and made its mark and, in the minds of many, made Ennis. It was named for Cornelius Ennis, an early Houston and Texas Central Railroad official and mayor of Houston.

There had been a scattered population in the Ennis area prior to the railroad, but many more settlers began to arrive with the rail. Between 1874 and the mid-1880s, the population grew from around 300 to 3,000. Many of these new settlers came from the war-torn states of the Southern United States. Others came from war-ravaged countries, including the area that would one day become Czechoslovakia. All came to build something more and better than what they had left behind.

The 1870s and 1880s were difficult times for Ennis pioneers. The city began with just a handful of buildings, and what is now the downtown area was then all of Ennis. Homes, small and few, were built where stores would be found just a decade later. The large Rowe Cotton Gin and Grist Mill took up much of the block where the U.S. post office has now stood for almost a century. McKinney Street, south of Ennis Avenue, was a great spot for fishing, as streams from McEnnis Pond crept up almost to the avenue. Churches were built within blocks of each other, and with most less than four blocks from the railroad, people often walked to services. Porches were not just for decoration; they were often the center of neighborhood gatherings and frequently cooler than being inside during hot summer months. Land near what was the first Ennis High School on North Gaines Street was still mostly considered a rural area.

Business lots could be purchased for $50 to $800, depending on whether there was a building on it. Early accounts of life illustrate the fortitude required of those who set up business here. One account tells of a young man's desire to help build Ennis, how he came into town in 1878 selling fruit trees, heard a band playing at the train depot, and decided this would become his home. He made a trade to obtain inventory and set up shop in a small wooden building, where the Jolesch Store would later be established at the southwest corner of Ennis Avenue and Main Street. The new store owner then found 34 bullet holes, in a building that couldn't have been more than a couple of years old, from what he referred to as recent trouble. But this man, W. G. Giddings, stayed, as did many others despite the hardships.

Although lots for residential homes could be purchased for as little as $50, there was no running water, no sewer service, and only a handful of stores from which to get needed goods. For the first decade, the majority of residents lived in boarding homes, where privacy was often provided only by hanging a piece of cloth. Safety was a prime concern. Fire caused tremendous damage, and several newspaper reports detail numerous shoot-outs and times when residents had to take to their homes for safety because of the danger of going outside.

In 1891, the Houston and Texas Central Railroad contracted to make Ennis its Northern Division Headquarters. This provided numerous jobs at the newly built roundhouse, machine shops, and division headquarters. This prosperity continued through the 1890s as the business sector of the town grew steadily, the schools were considered among the best in the state academically, and the residential areas continued to expand.

The first decades of the new century were ruled by cotton. Thousands would fill the streets on "trade days" to buy and sell this commodity. By 1930, "Where Railroads and Cotton Fields Meet" became the official chamber of commerce slogan. Cotton prices had plunged in the years after World War I, yet by 1930 the community had established nearly 205 businesses. Among these businesses were a cottonseed oil company, a creamery, two ice companies, and two printing companies. Despite some hard economic times, the businesses in Ennis, many of them family owned and run, persevered.

And the community began new traditions. In 1951, the Ennis Garden Club established its first Bluebonnet Trails, which has grown to over 40 miles of trails that highlight the spectacular beauty of the state flower—bountiful in the official Bluebonnet City of Texas, as designated in 1997. The National Polka Festival, now a yearly event in Ennis, began in 1967 and has grown continuously over the decades, bringing thousands of visitors to the city for a weekend of "a little bit of Czechoslovakia."

The contributions many of the first settlers made in those first decades were numerous and costly, both physically and financially. Many came here to build more than homes, businesses, or family farms. Their visions spanned generations, for ultimately they were building a community that would last far beyond their own lifetimes. There have been families who passed homes from one generation to the next, families who bought land over the course of their lives to farm and then to pass on to the generations to come, and businesses that remained in the same families who began them a century ago. Even now, there are reminders of some of the businesses long gone, yet what identified them remains. Ennis National Bank, Banner Insurance, Castellaw Drug Store, J. M. Calhoun, and W. L. Maroney can still be seen in the names that grace their buildings, remembrances of what once was.

For centuries, it has been the practice to pass down stories from one generation to the next. This practice includes stories of family, customs, and community. In the course of preparing this story of Ennis, several publications on the area as well as local newspaper issues from the late 1800s through the 1900s have been researched. The authors have also been privileged to speak with many Ennis residents who have shared their stories. Images of America: *Ennis* is a celebration of where Ennis has been and for all that is yet to be.

One

Early Years

In 1880, A. H. Rowe, owner of the Rowe Cotton Gin, became the leader of the bucket brigade. He also provided the building at McKinney and Baylor Streets to house the first firefighting equipment as well as use of the nearby water tank. The Ennis Fire Department was formed in November 1884. Fire was a very real threat to the new community, and an organized effort to control the danger was a recognized necessity. J. Baldridge was the first fire chief. Some of the first major fires included the Ennis High School in 1893, St. Joseph's Catholic Church in 1902, and the King Hotel in 1926. Volunteer fireman Fred J. Ferris died from injuries in the line of duty in 1910. The first members of the volunteer fire department are pictured; at the lower right-hand corner is Ben (last name unknown), the first paid employee in 1899. His responsibilities included caring for the horses and getting the horse-drawn pump to the scene of a fire. (Courtesy of Ennis Public Library.)

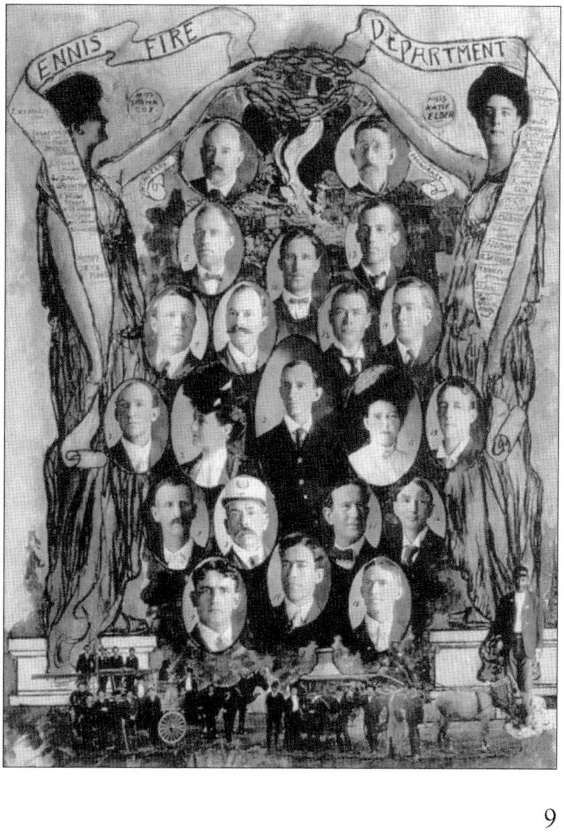

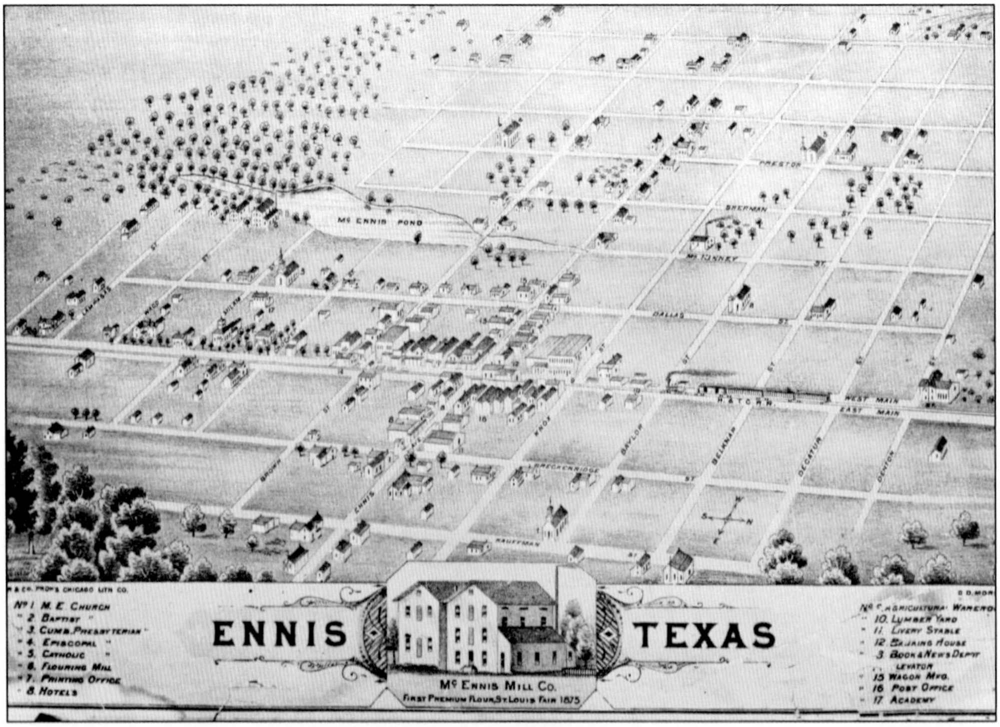

An early view of Ennis around the mid- to late 1870s is pictured here on this early map of the city. The short legend accompanying the map highlights what was considered important for the time: churches, the post office, hotels, and the first businesses within blocks of the railroad. The McEnnis Mill Company, pictured at the bottom of the map, won first prize for premium flour at the St. Louis Fair in 1875. (Courtesy of Ennis Public Library.)

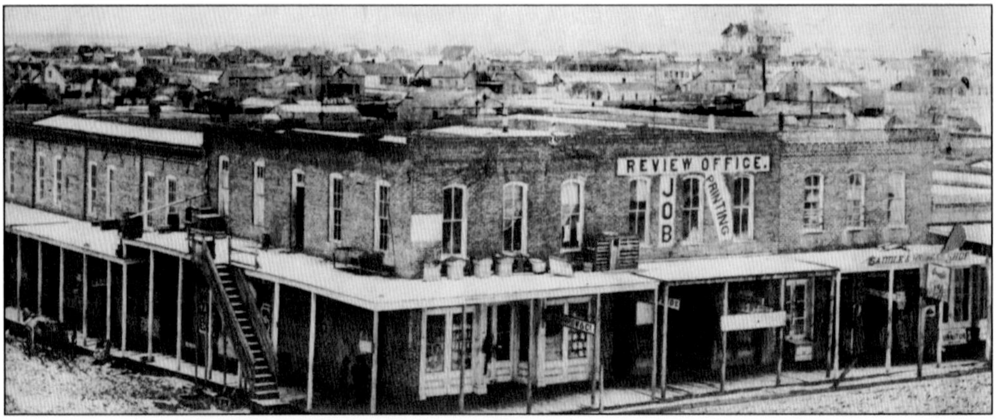

Businesses continued to provide increasing services to the growing population of Ennis. Stores along the 100 block of South Main Street in 1883 included the T. H. Marrow Company at the Brown Street corner pictured here, and to its right was the Saturday Review Newspaper and Printing office, established in 1875. Next to it stood the Soapes Saddle and Harness Shop, established in 1876. (Courtesy of Ennis Public Library.)

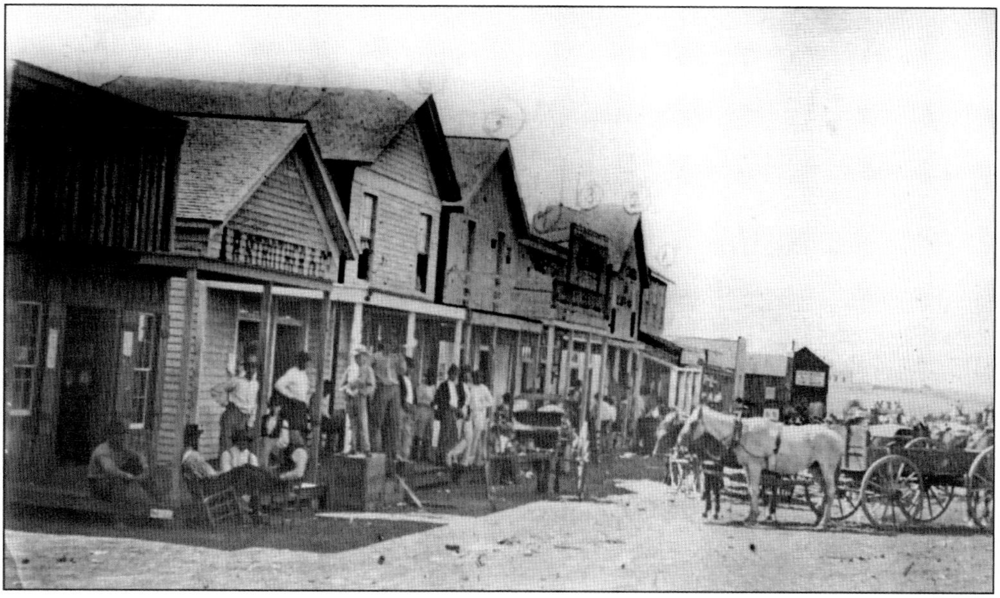

Ennis began with a small cluster of stores to the west of the railroad, including A. R. Strothers, pictured to the left, in early 1875. Strothers was one of the earliest dry goods stores built in Ennis. (Courtesy of Mary Ann Novy Lamkin.)

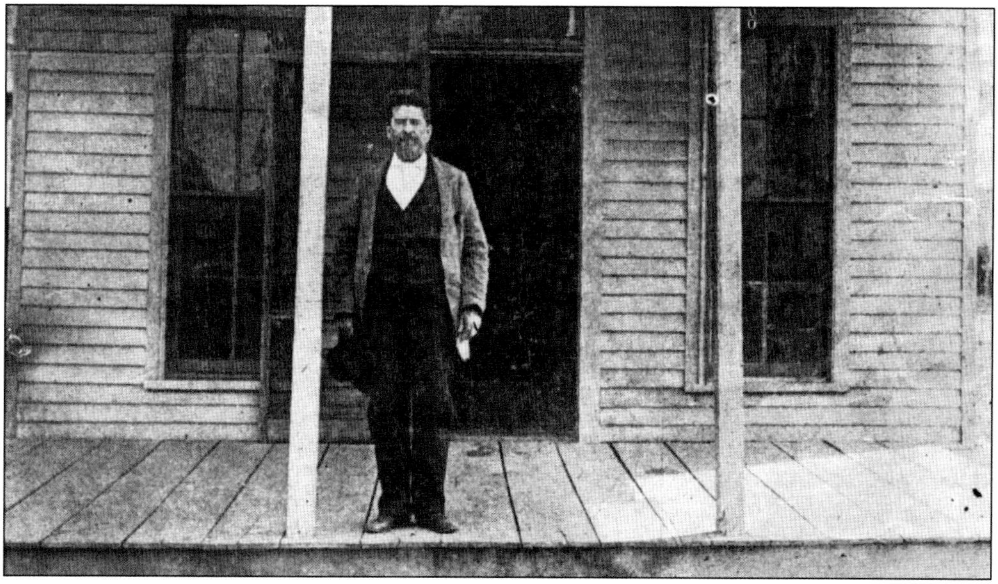

G. G. Higginbotham was mayor of Ennis in the early 1880s. Mayor Higginbotham is pictured in front of the mayor's office, which he donated the land to be built on. Directly behind the mayor's office at that time was the city jail. (Courtesy of Ennis Public Library.)

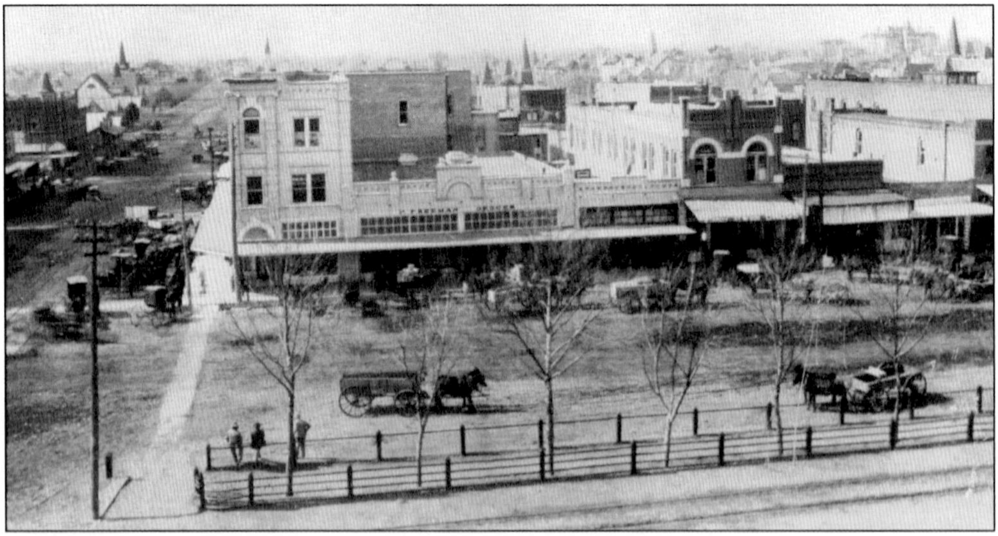

From the very beginning, music has played an important role in the culture of Ennis. One of the earliest known bands was the Ennis Specialty Band. Their first known concert performance was in 1888. Members included one of the first dentists in Ennis, Dr. T. S. Riggs; an Ennis mayor, George Higginbotham; editor of the *Ennis Weekly Local*, W. C. Perry; and co-owner of one of the first furniture stores, C. P. Kendall. Pictured below, from left to right in front of the first depot, they are W. C. Perry, T. L. Cunningham, C. P. Kendall, George Higginbotham, Ed Brown, Will Keach, Dr. T. S. Riggs, Frank Rust, Jim McCoy, J. W. Walker, and unidentified. The scene along North Main Street pictured above may have been similar to what the Ennis Specialty Band saw as they posed for their photograph. (Both courtesy of Ennis Public Library.)

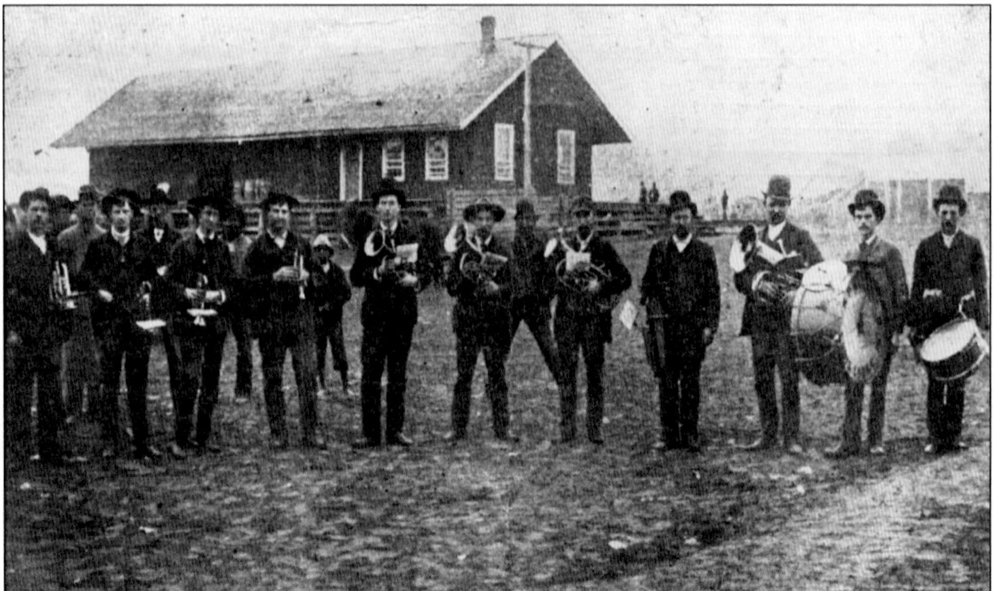

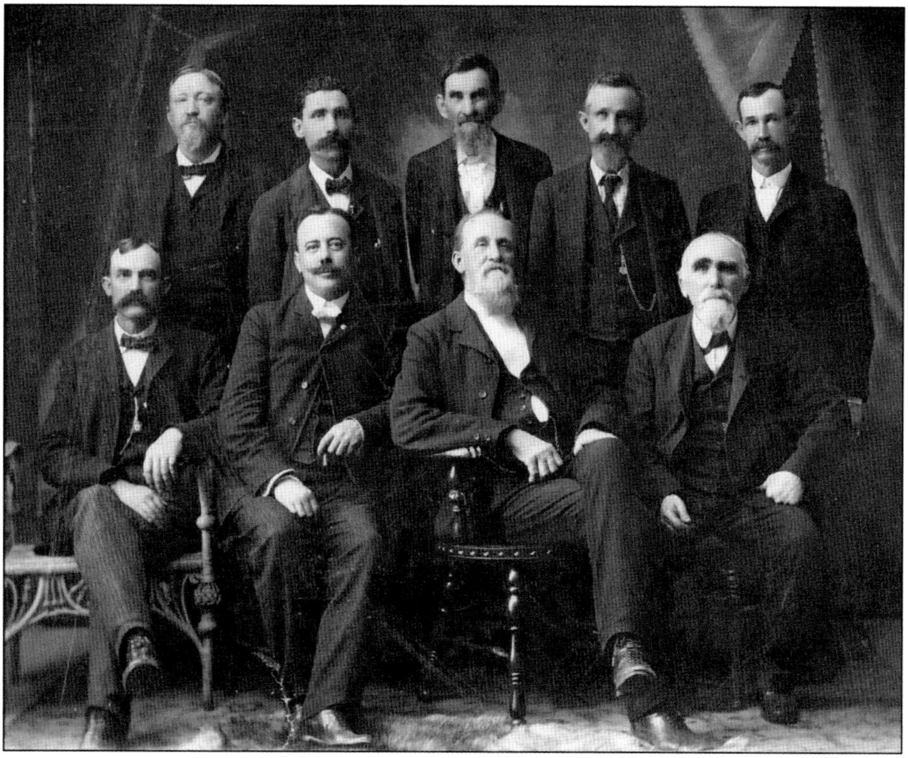

The Ennis City Commission of 1902 included V. W. Neal, C. B. Lewis, J. A. Pace, I. T. Allen, F. C. Stevenson, Ed Overhiser, J. F. Craig, M. B. Moseley, and C. M. Banner. Pictured above, many of these city commissioners served a number of roles in their efforts to further the living standards of those they represented. Commissioner Allen served on the school board; Commissioner Overhiser was a strong advocate for a better water supply for the city; Commissioner Pace owned land, a grocery, and a dry goods store; and Commissioner Banner served as both city secretary and city tax assessor and collector for many years. Included in their responsibilities was to bring more people and businesses to Ennis, such as Mr. Wyatt, who is pictured below in his small cotton oil mill grocery in 1898. (Above, courtesy of Ennis Public Library.)

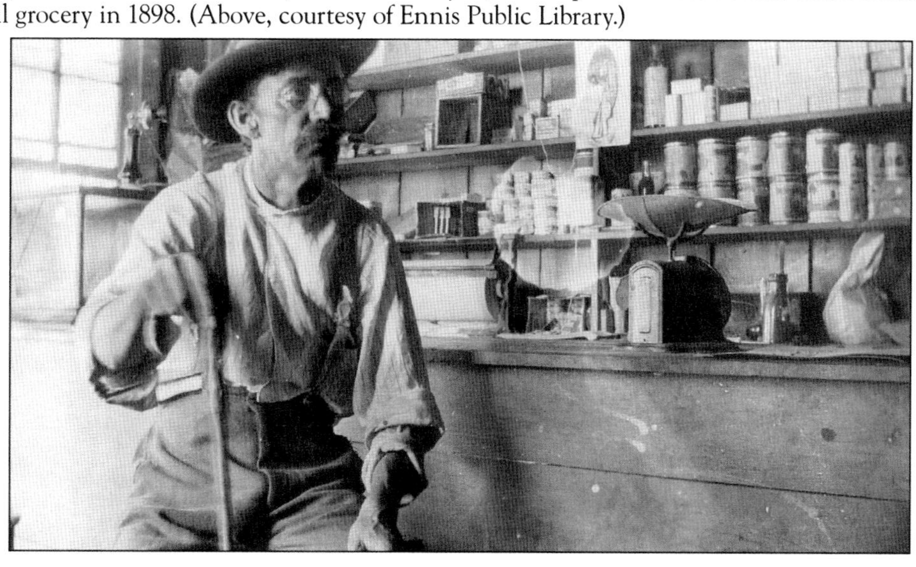

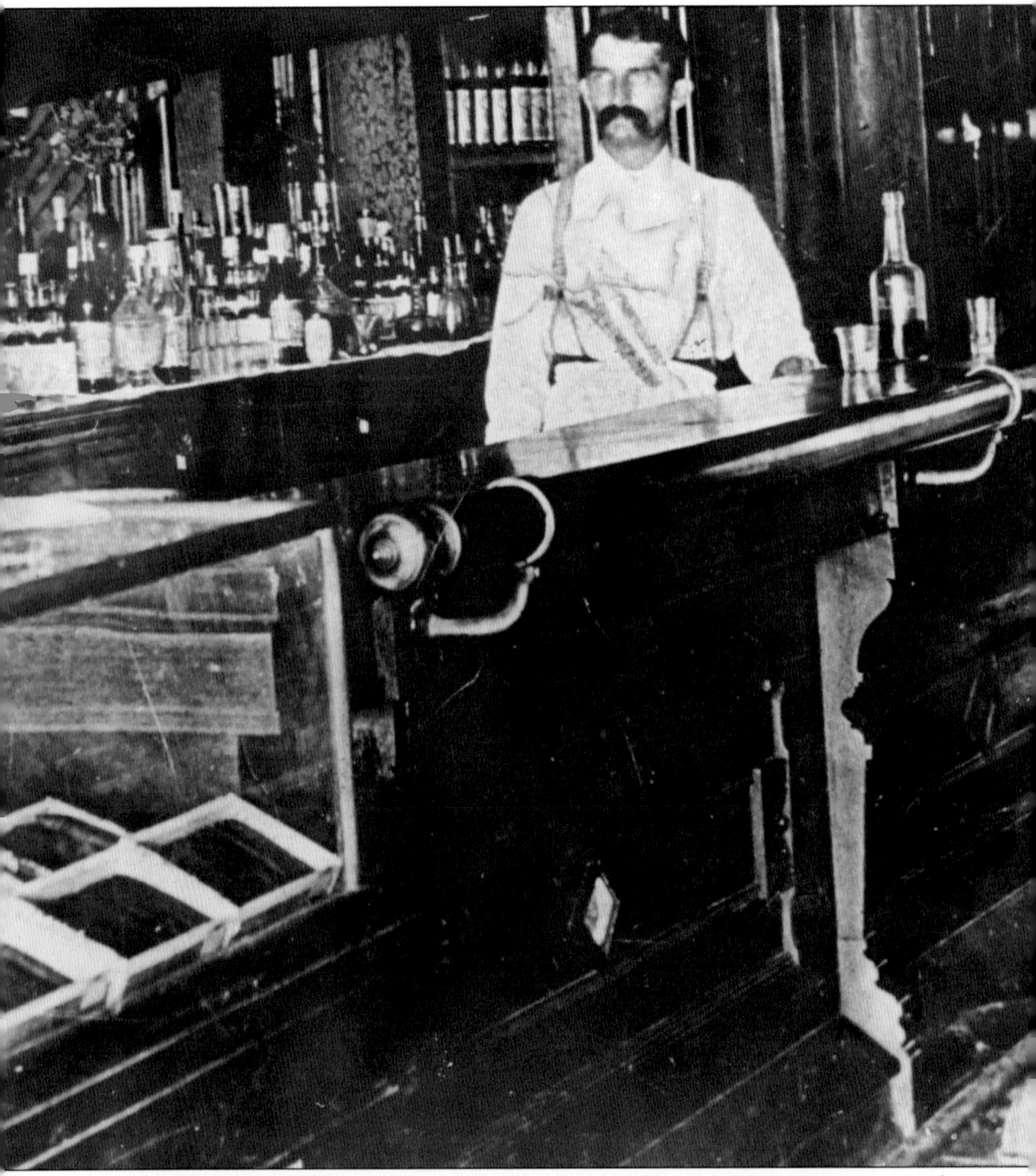

In the words of some of the earliest settlers of Ennis, the early years of the town were ones where the "Old West" element was rampant. One such element was the large number of saloons, as many as 13, that could be found throughout the city. Often they were located in the back of a building behind the main storefront business. In 1892, William Nesuda's Saloon was located behind Skroh's Grocery Store on Northwest Main Street near Baylor Street. William Nesuda is seen in his bar in the early 1890s. (Courtesy of Dorothy Kudrna.)

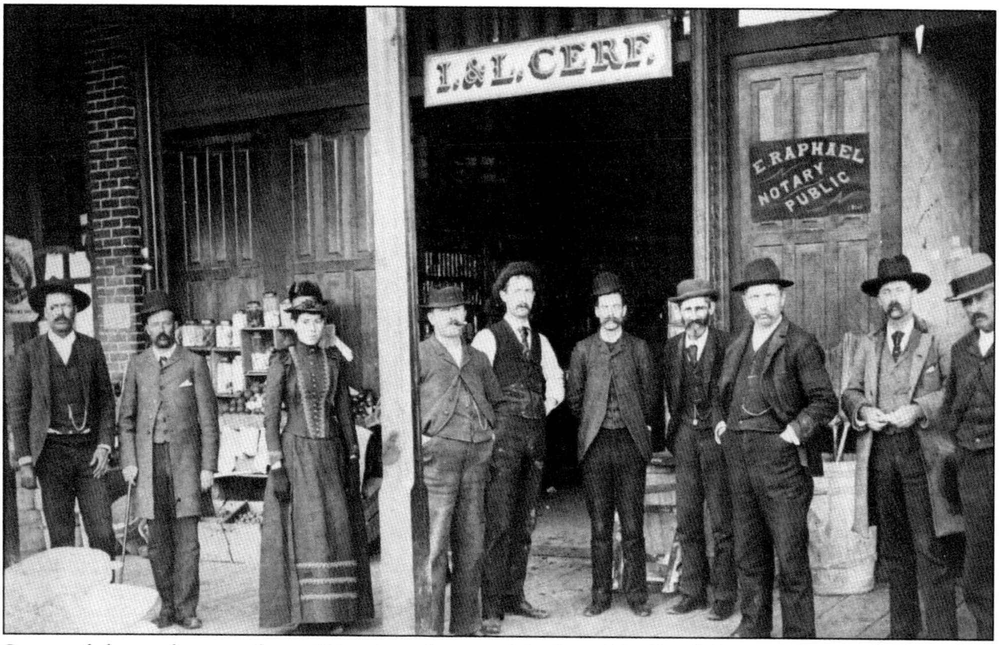

Some of the earliest settlers of Ennis gather outside I. and L. Cerf Grocery Store in the 1880s; from left to right are Will Dodson, Dr. T. S. Riggs, Mrs. Tom Mullican, L. Cerf, E. Raphael, A. Meyer, A. G. Cox, I. Cerf, Rodger Haynes, and Bill Pitts. Leon Cerf arrived in Ennis in 1876 and bought John Chancellor's grocery business. His brother Isidore later joined him in the business. (Courtesy of Ennis Fire Department.)

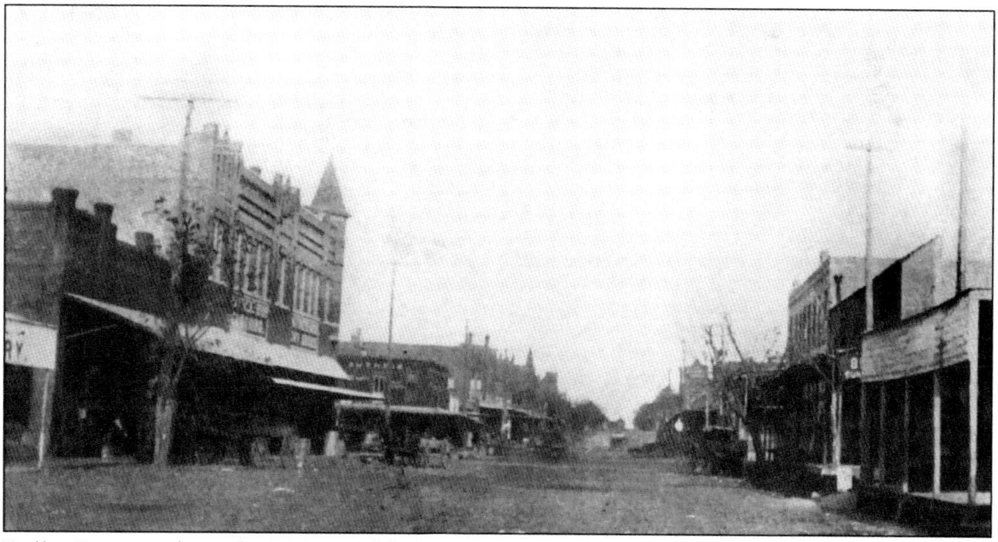

Dallas Street in the early 1900s was filled with merchants. Looking north from Brown Street, the Matthews Brothers Dry Goods Store is at the left with the large and impressive turret. Directly across Ennis Avenue from it was the Glover and Guthrie Drug Store. Seen along the right-hand side of the photograph are covered wood sidewalks, which provided shelter from the sun and rain.

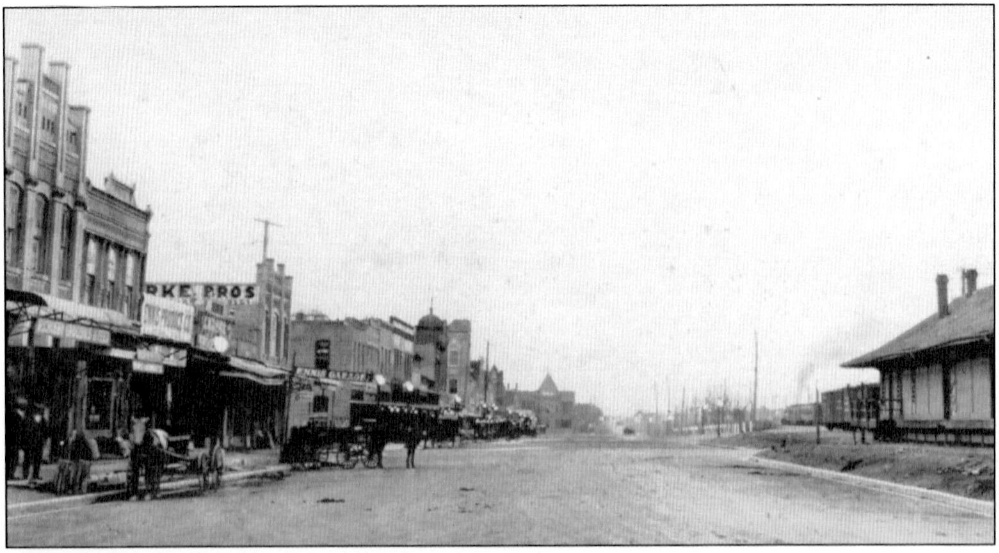

In 1872, Theo Kosse, a civil engineer, was given the task of mapping out the town. Most streets were made 80 feet wide, but the railroad was given a reservation of 300 feet, making Main Street, running along each side of the rail, one of the widest Main Streets in the United States. The view above from the 200 block of South Main Street (west of the railroad looking north) illustrates the width of the west side. The freight depot is visible at the right side of the photograph. As the town grew, so did the need for many services such as seen below in Looney's Barber Shop around 1900. Robert Looney later worked at the Commercial Barber, located at 103 North Main Street. (Above, courtesy of Ennis Fire Department; below, City of Ennis.)

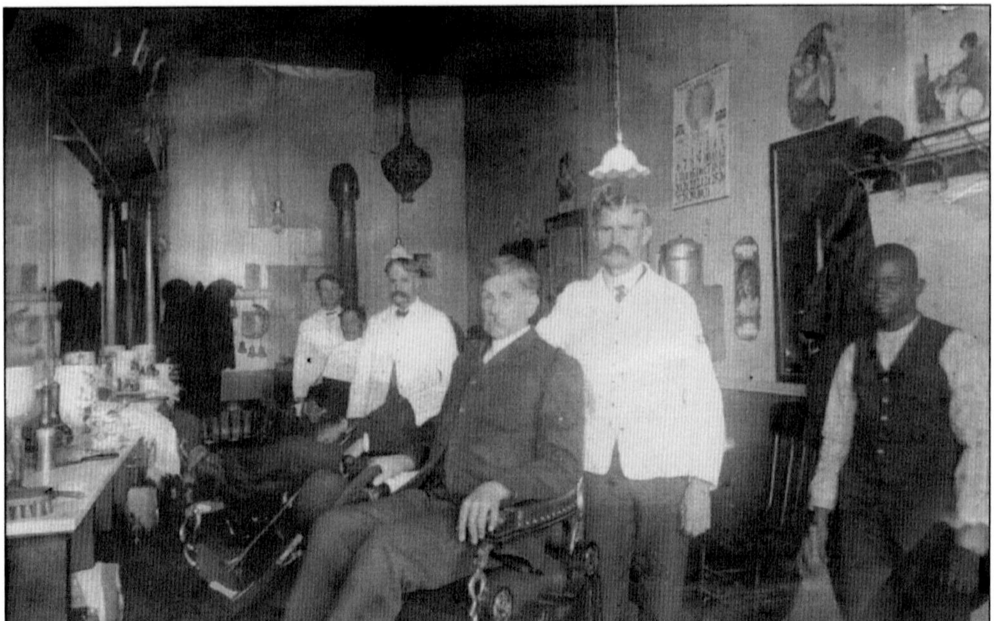

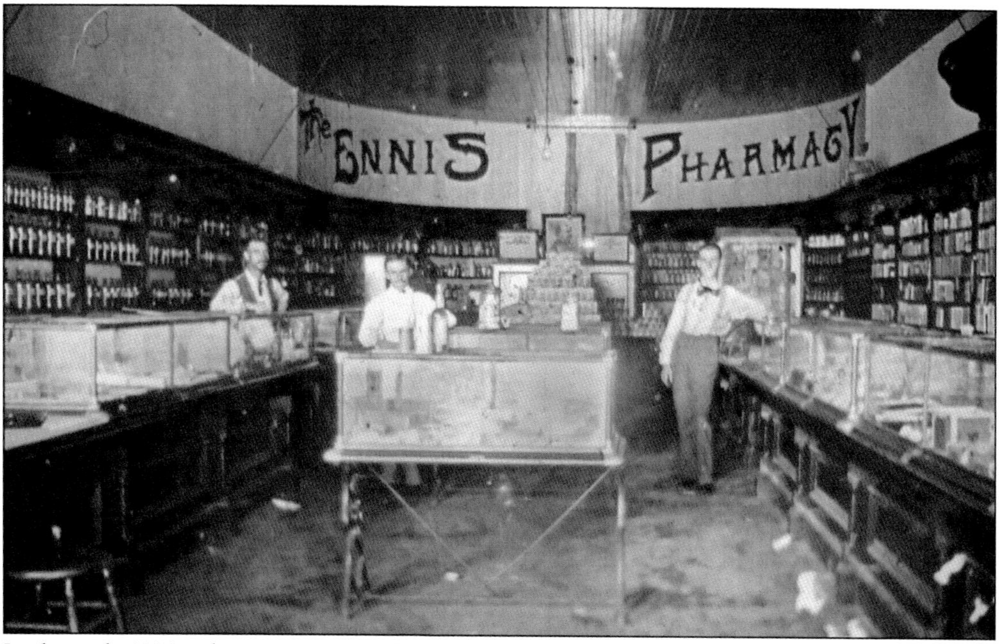

In the early 1890s, pharmacist E. E. Glover bought Oliver and Calhoun Drug Store and renamed it Ennis Pharmacy. Glover sold the pharmacy in 1901 to start another venture. Later, around 1911, J. M. Collins and J. E. Fisher purchased the store. It was located for many years on northwest Main Street between the Thomas Shoe Store and the Ennis Candy Kitchen. (Courtesy of Ennis Heritage Society.)

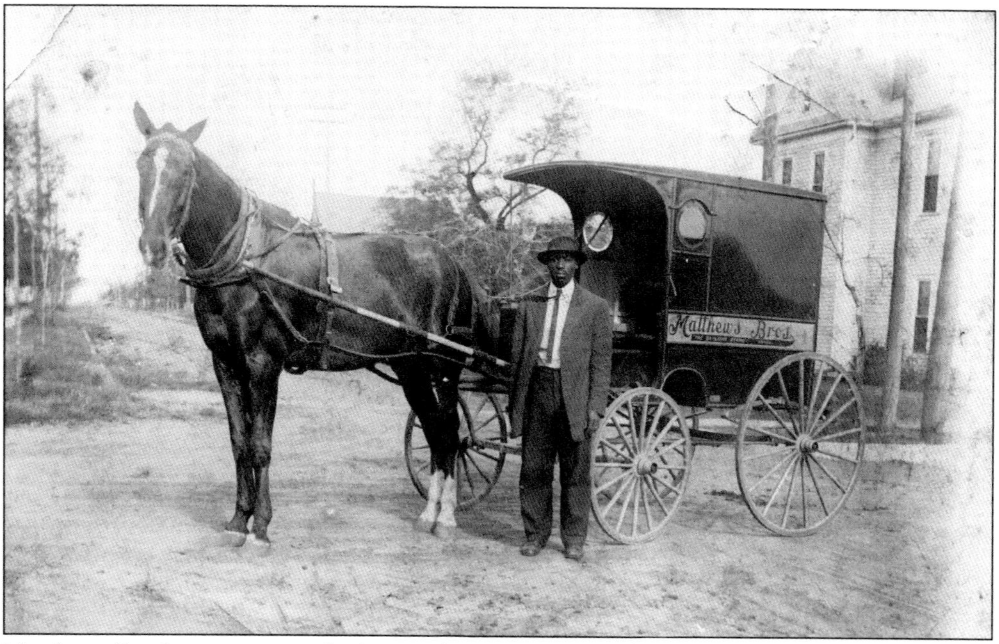

Matthews Brothers was an early dry goods store in Ennis, located at the southwest corner of Ennis Avenue and Dallas Street. Matthews Brothers was among the stores that provided delivery services to its customers. Clarence D. Jones, pictured here with the buggy he made deliveries in, worked for the company for many years. (Courtesy of Loretta Davis.)

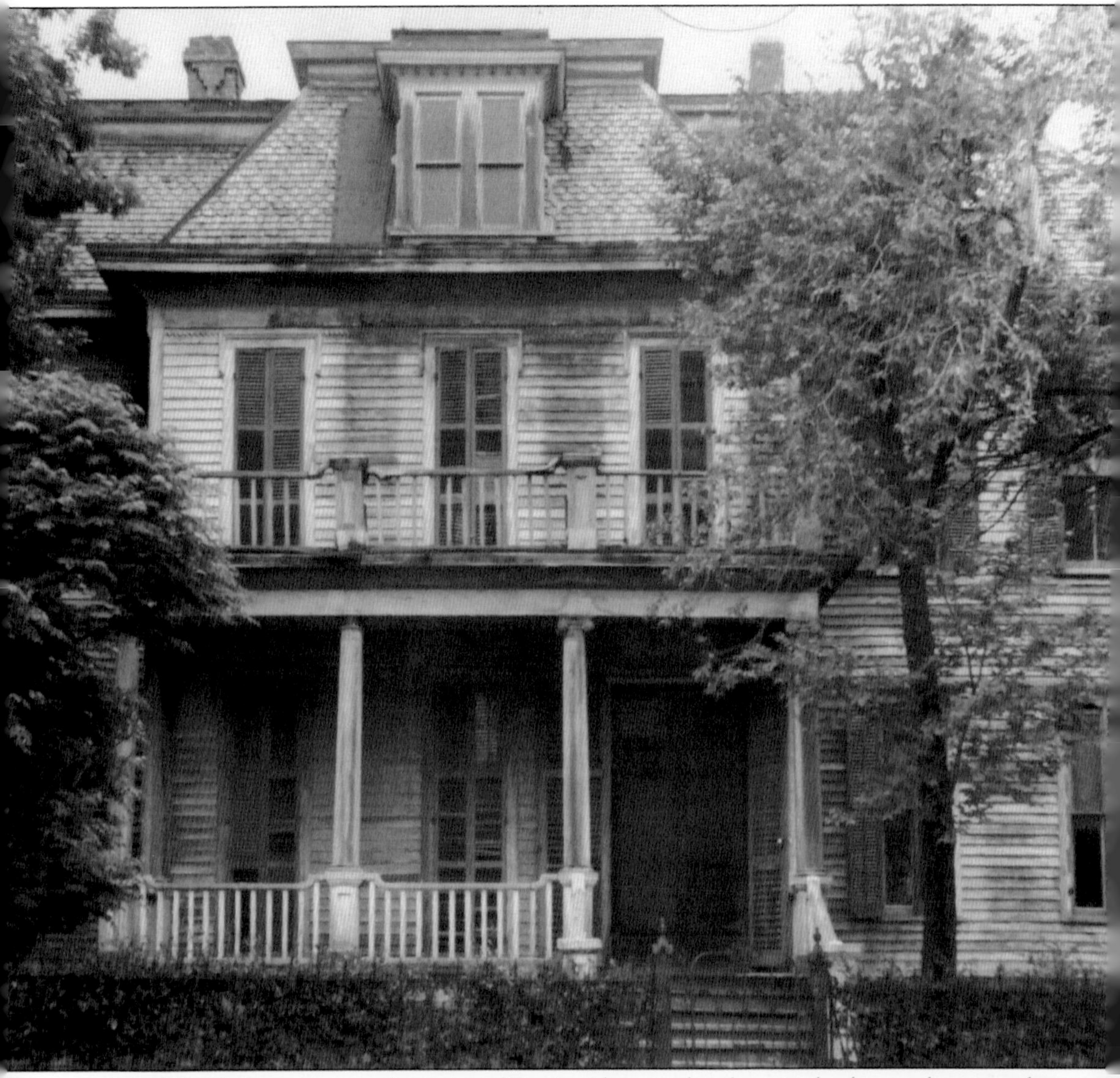

Joseph Baldridge was an early settler of Ennis. Along with other city leaders at that time, he led the successful effort to bring the railroad roundhouse and machine shops to Ennis in 1891, which would provide hundreds of jobs to the area. He was a member of the committee that travelled to Houston to meet with railroad officials, with whom they reached an agreement that the Houston and Texas Central Railroad would build a roundhouse, machine shops, and the northern division headquarters in Ennis. The city agreed to pay the railroad a bonus of $25,000 and 90 acres of land. Baldridge donated $3,000 of his own funds to achieve this, feeling strongly that the contract would positively impact the city's future. His family home, built in 1883 on West Belknap Street just blocks from the railroad, is pictured around the 1950s. When the city won the railroad contract, Baldridge sold his home to Col. L. A. Daffan, the incoming division superintendant to the railroad. (Courtesy of Ennis Public Library.)

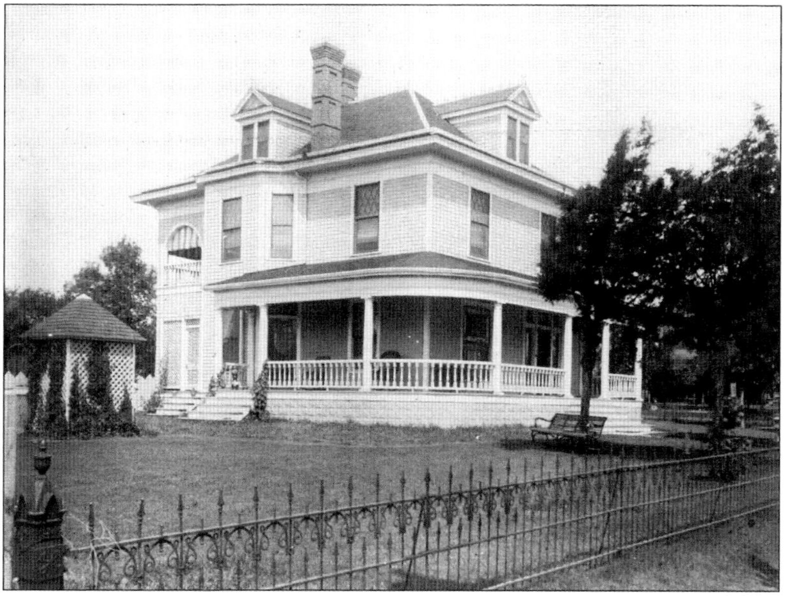

The Telfair home was built in 1902 by John Spier Telfair, a conductor with the railroad since the 1890s, on the site where members of St. Joseph's Catholic Church first met. Telfair's home was designed by Hix McCanless with many of the Victorian features of that time. (Courtesy of Telfair family.)

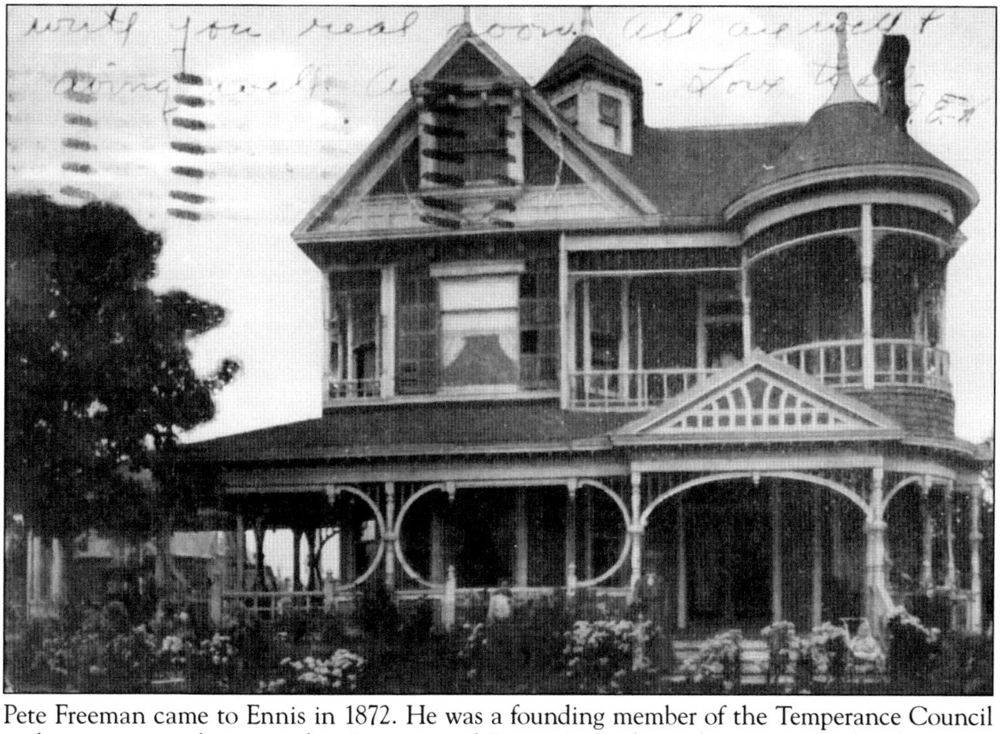

Pete Freeman came to Ennis in 1872. He was a founding member of the Temperance Council and was active in bringing the Houston and Texas Central Northern Division headquarters, roundhouse, and machine shops to Ennis. He married the daughter of Col. Joe Rushing, who established the *Evening Argus Newspaper* in 1873. Freeman's 1895 home is pictured as it once stood at 307 North Dallas around 1912.

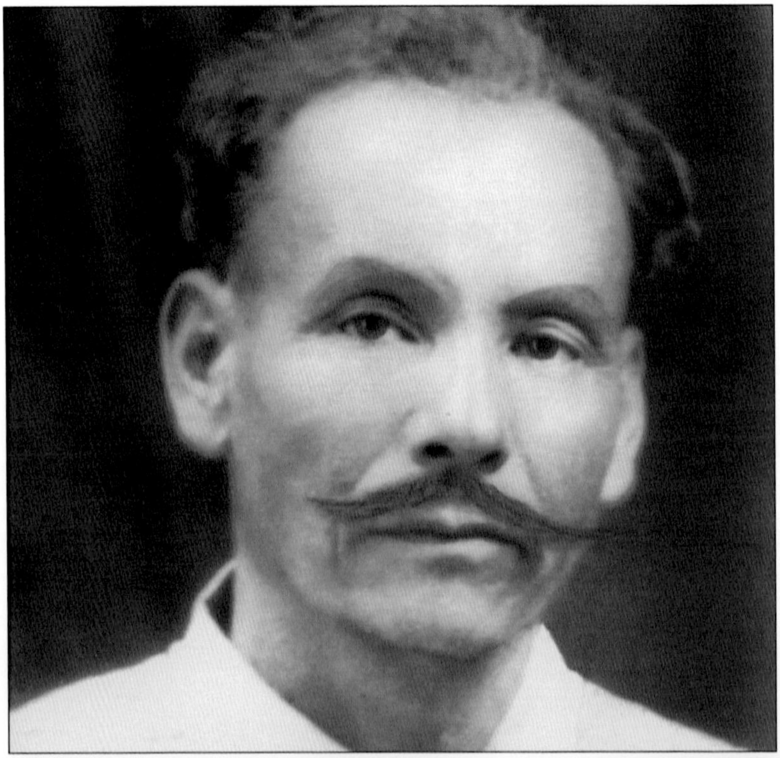

Many of Antonio Santos's descendants still call Ennis home. A farmer, Antonio emigrated from Mexico to the United States and arrived in Ennis in the mid-1890s. He later met and married Christina Esquivel of Ennis, and they raised their family here. (Courtesy of Gilbert Santos.)

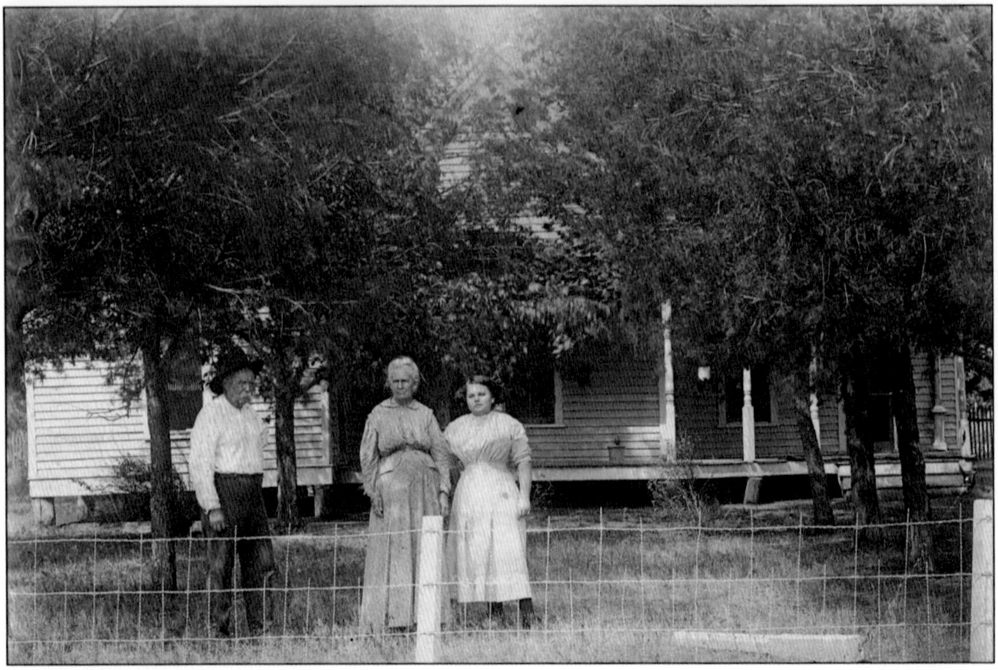

Brooks Wakefield Barnes was a native of Tennessee and served with the Confederate army before moving with his family to Ennis in the early 1880s. Brooks is pictured in front of his home on North Kaufman Avenue, along with his wife, Eugenia Gant Barnes (center), and relative Willie Ruth Barnes (right).

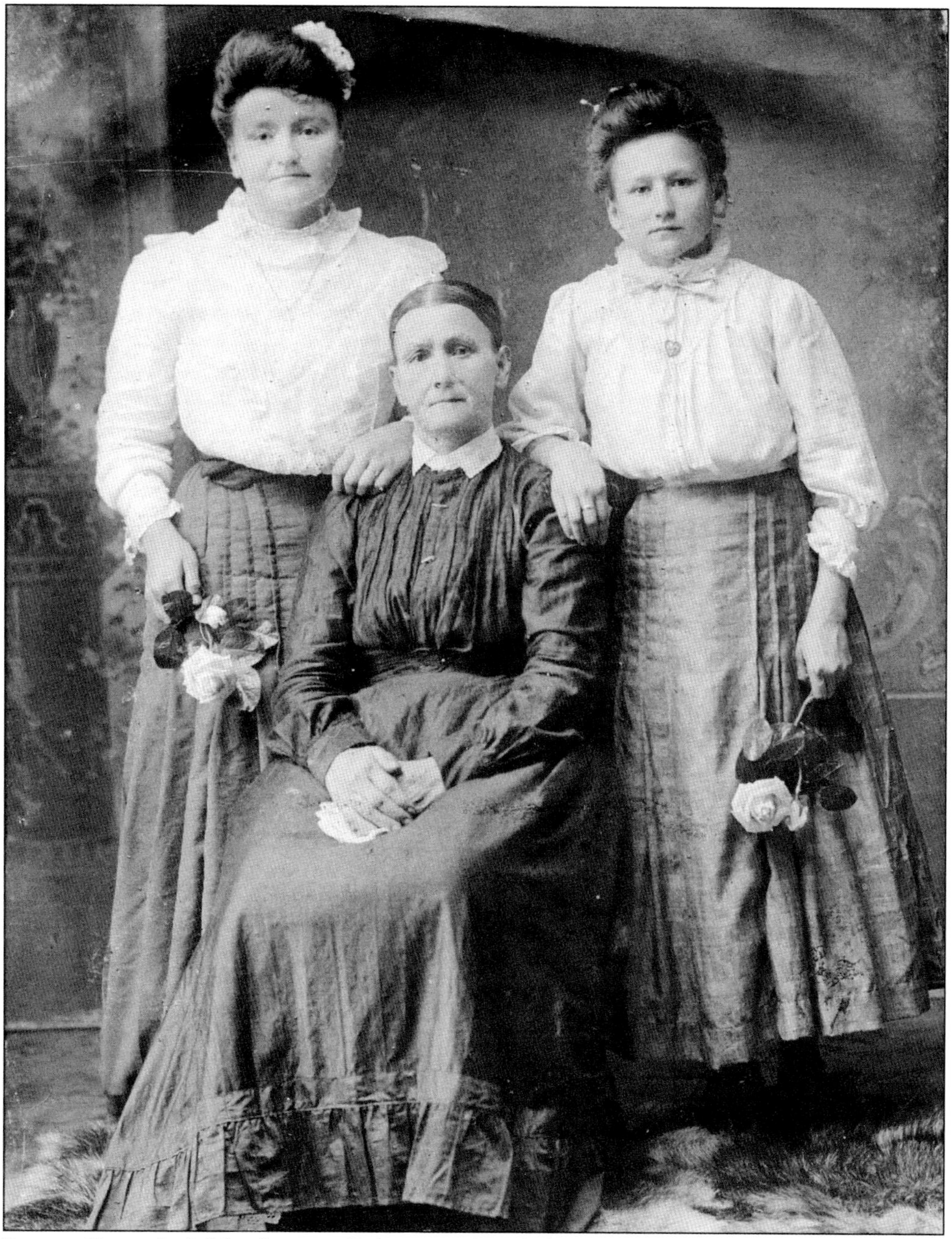

Frances Cervenka left her home in Bohemia and settled in Ennis in the 1880s. Known as Fannie to family and friends, she is pictured here (seated) with her daughters, standing from left to right, Mary Luksa and Carrie Bobalik. (Courtesy of Mary Ann Zmolik Sibley.)

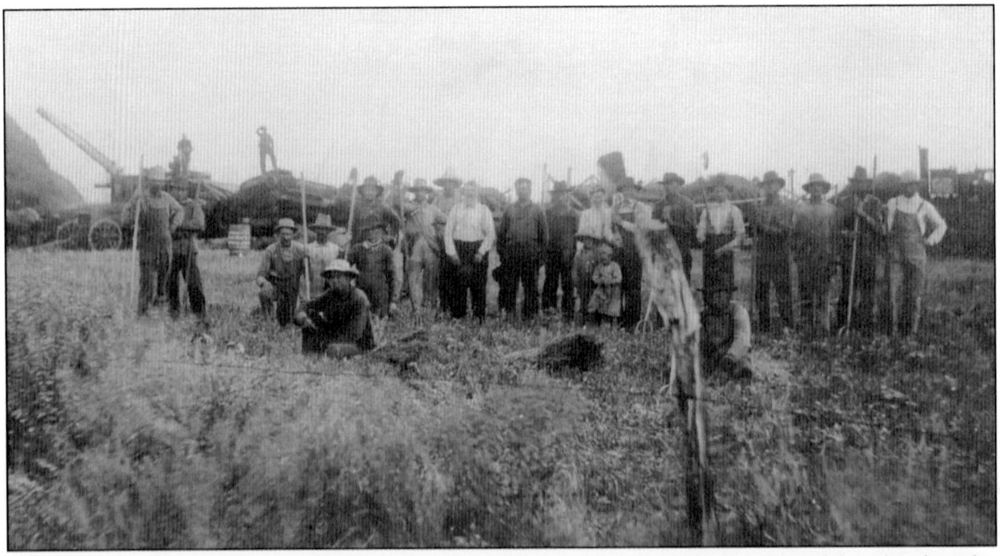

John Novy Sr. brought his family to Ennis in 1878 from Missouri. He purchased farmland to the east of Ennis and is pictured here in the center, wearing a white shirt, at his farm in the early 1900s amidst family and farmworkers. (Courtesy of Mary Ann Novy Lamkin.)

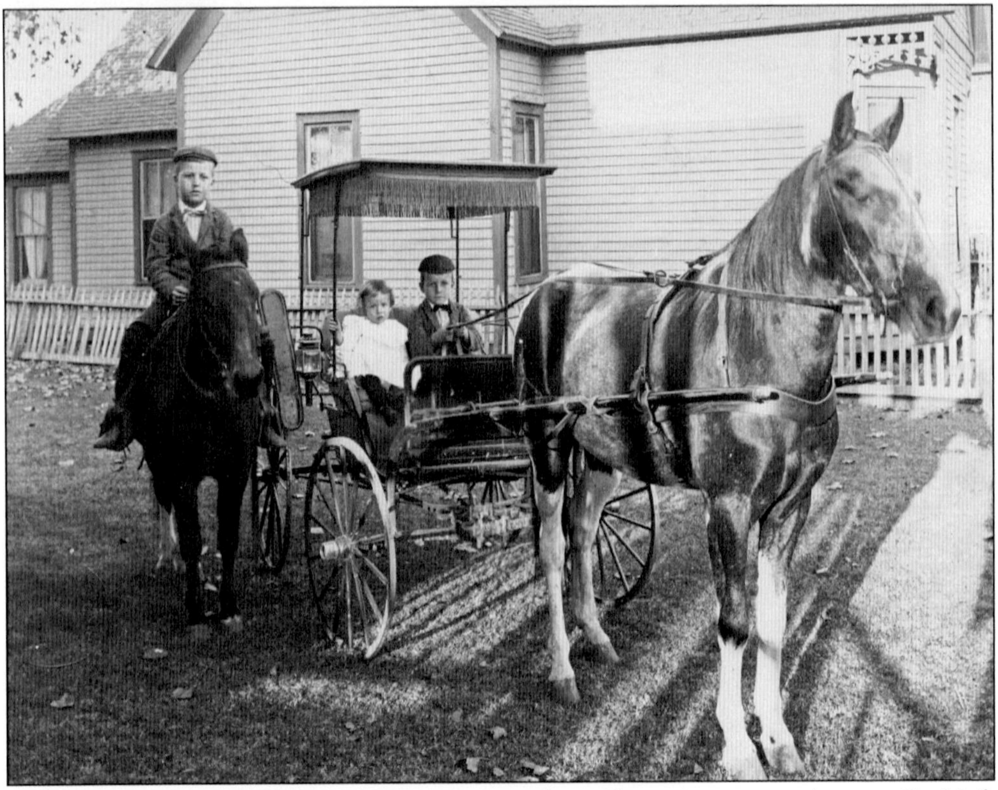

Horses and horse-drawn buggies were a common sight in Ennis during its early years. For Neil, Shaddy, and Bobby Mims, horses were a way of life. Their father, Lon Mims, owned a livery stable. The Mims children are pictured here in the yard of their home around 1900. (Courtesy of Ennis Public Library.)

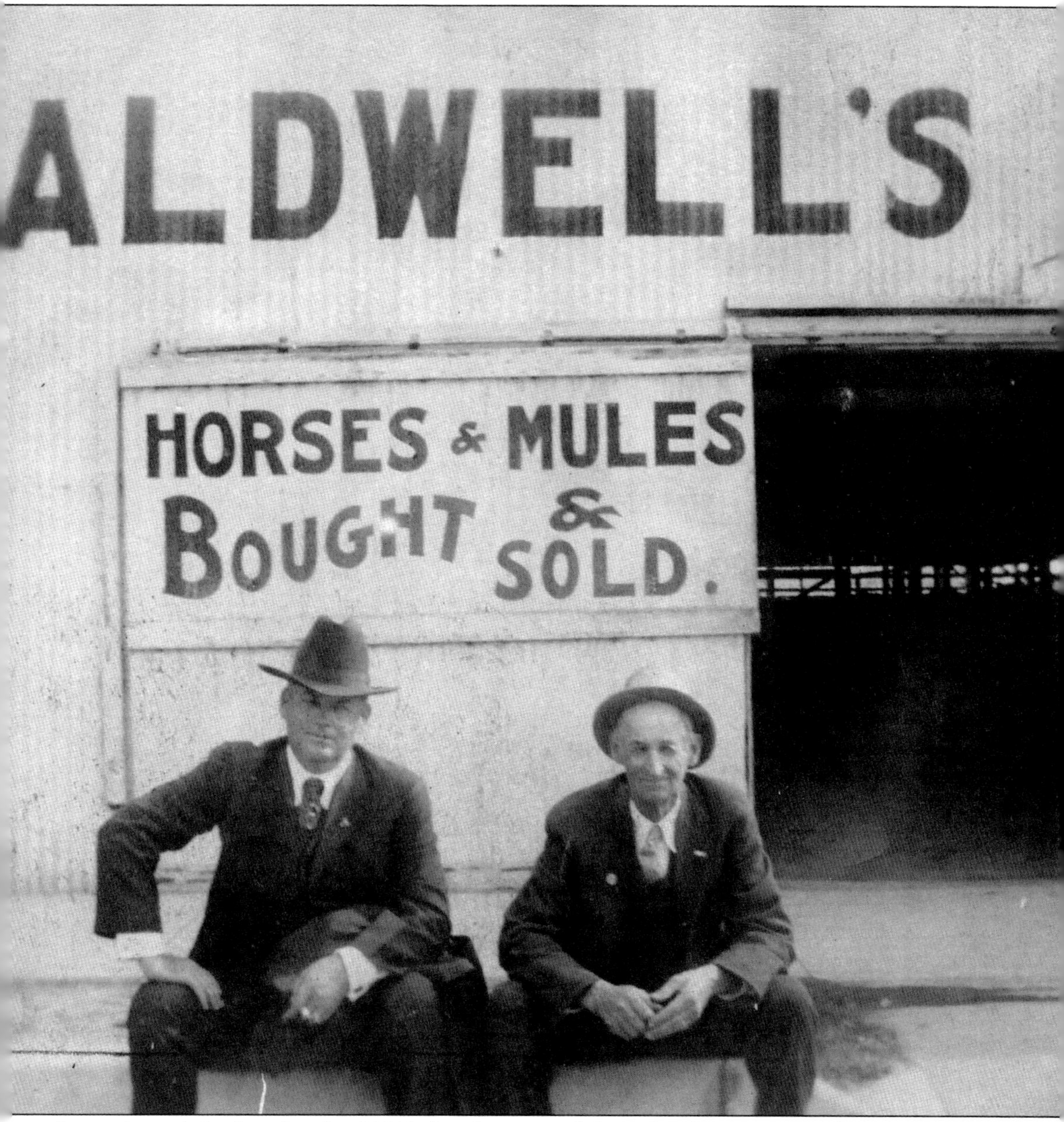

It wasn't until the first decade of 1900 that the automobile made a big impact on the young city of Ennis. Horses and mules were the mode of transportation for many up until World War I. There were several mule barns, or livery stables, along the streets of Ennis, including the Mims Mule Barn and the Caldwell Mule Barn. John Caldwell and his father, Albert, owned and ran the mule barn on the west side of the business district on Ennis Avenue before it gave way to the residential area. (Courtesy of Mary Ann Novy Lamkin.)

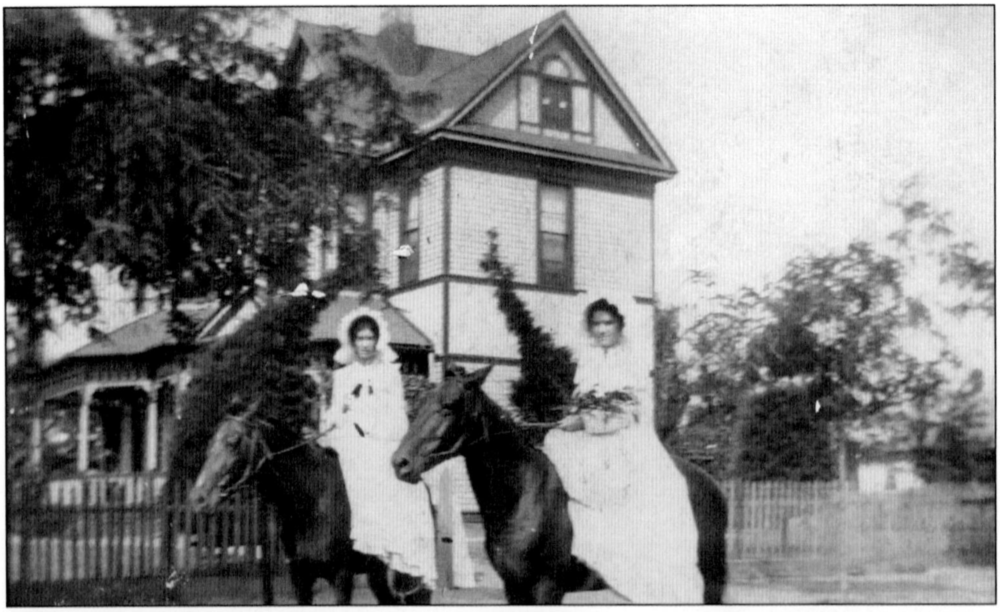

Many residents kept their own horses, as Ethel McCarty (left) and Lena Banner may have. McCarty's father was Thomas L. McCarty, one of the first agents to sell land lots in Ennis. Banner's father was C. M. Banner, who owned one of the first insurance companies in the city. (Courtesy of Ennis Public Library.)

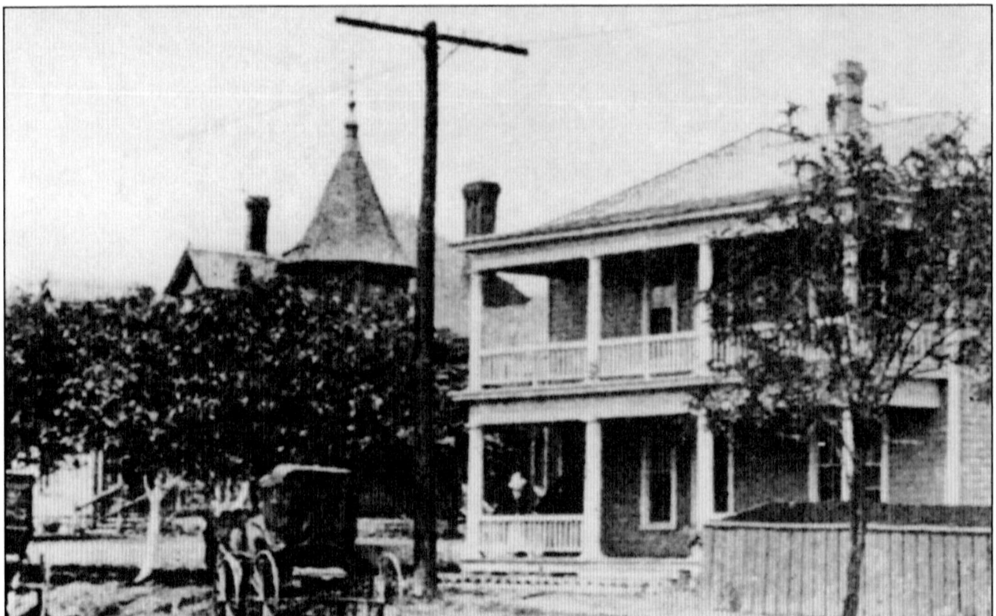

Pictured at 406 West Baylor is the private medical infirmary that Dr. R. A. McCall, a pioneer doctor of Ennis, built on the back of his home at North Preston and West Baylor Streets to provide needed medical care to his patients. Mrs. Mabel Percival was one of the first nurses to work at the infirmary. (Courtesy of Ennis Public Library.)

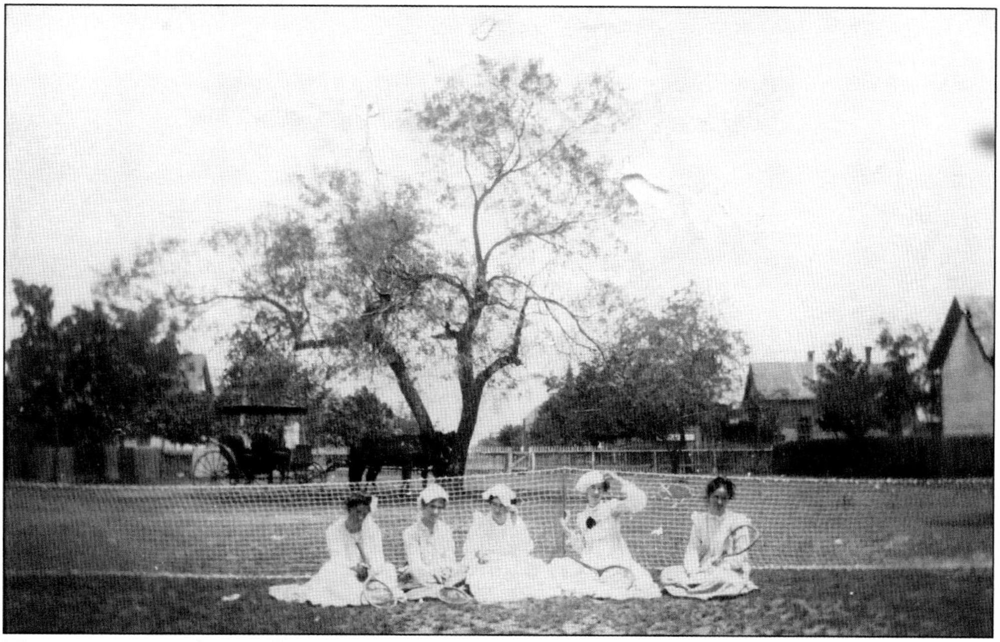

There were many forms of entertainment for early Ennisites, including ice skating on McEnnis Pond, horse racing, social events at Stallworth Hall, dancing at Kirschner Hall or Rowe Hall, and badminton. These young women relaxing after a game are, from left to right, Della Lattimer, Ethel Crumley, Stella White (the future Mrs. Jack Rowe), Ethel McCarty, and Lena Banner. (Courtesy of Ennis Public Library.)

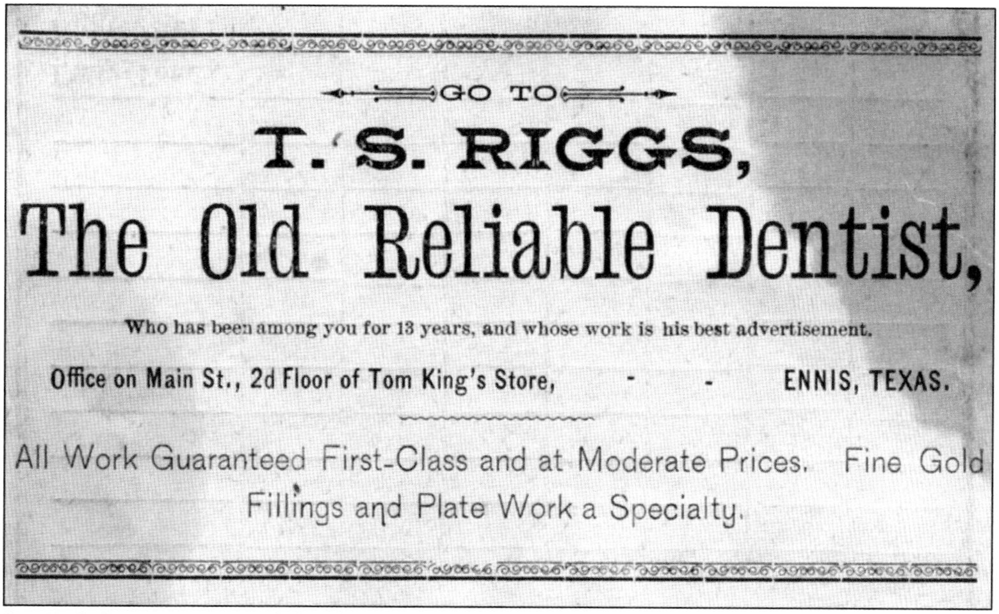

Dr. T. S. Riggs was one of the first dentists in Ennis, establishing his dental practice in 1875, and continued treating patients through the early 1900s. Riggs promoted himself as the "oldest dentist" in the county as seen in the 1888 advertisement above. His home, originally on North Preston Street, was later moved around to face West Denton Street and is one of the oldest homes in the city.

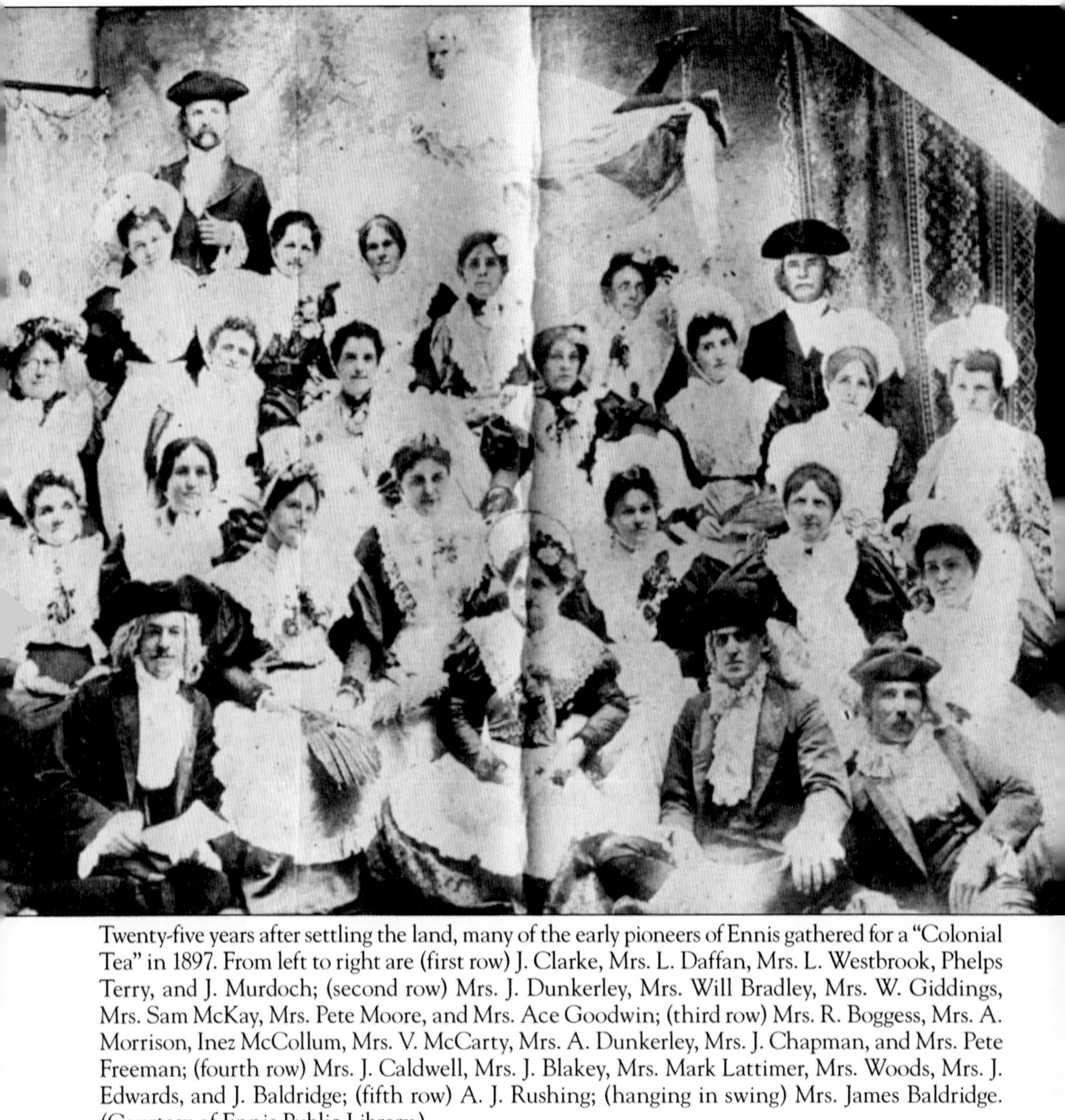

Twenty-five years after settling the land, many of the early pioneers of Ennis gathered for a "Colonial Tea" in 1897. From left to right are (first row) J. Clarke, Mrs. L. Daffan, Mrs. L. Westbrook, Phelps Terry, and J. Murdoch; (second row) Mrs. J. Dunkerley, Mrs. Will Bradley, Mrs. W. Giddings, Mrs. Sam McKay, Mrs. Pete Moore, and Mrs. Ace Goodwin; (third row) Mrs. R. Boggess, Mrs. A. Morrison, Inez McCollum, Mrs. V. McCarty, Mrs. A. Dunkerley, Mrs. J. Chapman, and Mrs. Pete Freeman; (fourth row) Mrs. J. Caldwell, Mrs. J. Blakey, Mrs. Mark Lattimer, Mrs. Woods, Mrs. J. Edwards, and J. Baldridge; (fifth row) A. J. Rushing; (hanging in swing) Mrs. James Baldridge. (Courtesy of Ennis Public Library.)

Two

Building a Community

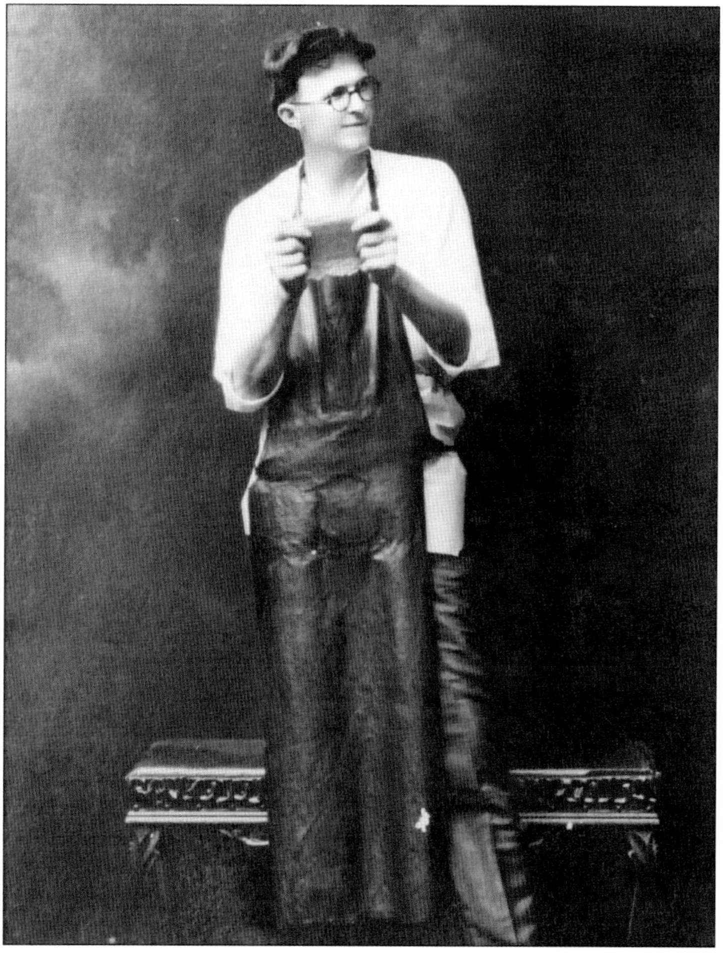

Photographer Henry Anthony Maresh, pictured in the early years of his career, settled in Ennis after his marriage to Bessie Valek in 1913. He spent decades chronicling the lives, the families, and the community of Ennis, Texas. His motto was "Portraits That Live." His first studio, which he bought from Harper Studio in 1916, was on the second floor of 111 West Ennis Avenue. He later relocated his studio to 108 West Ennis Avenue. (Courtesy of Mary Ann Novy Lamkin.)

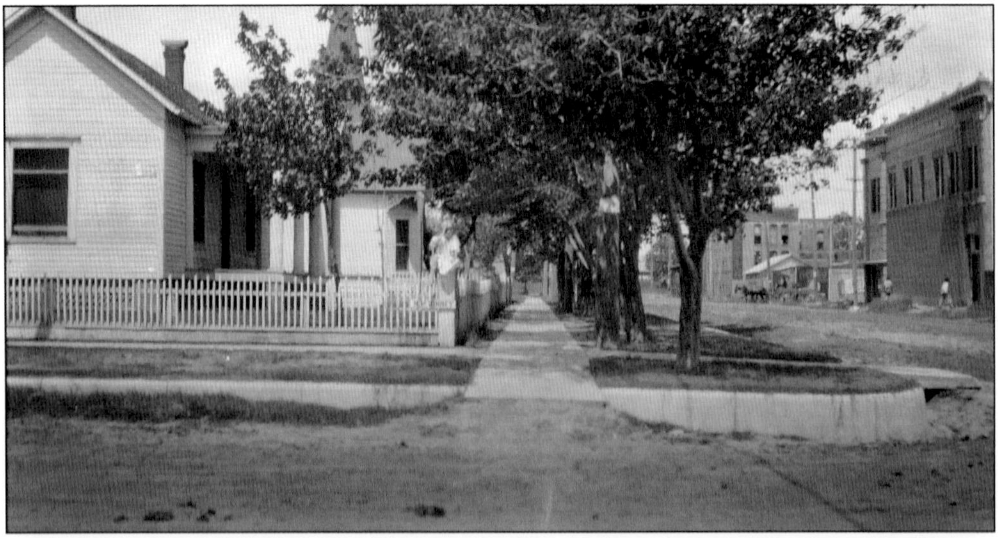

A young boy is pictured sitting on a fence post at the northeast corner of Baylor and McKinney Streets during the first decade of the 1900s. The streets have yet to be paved, and horses can be seen down the road on Baylor Street. (Courtesy of Ennis Public Library.)

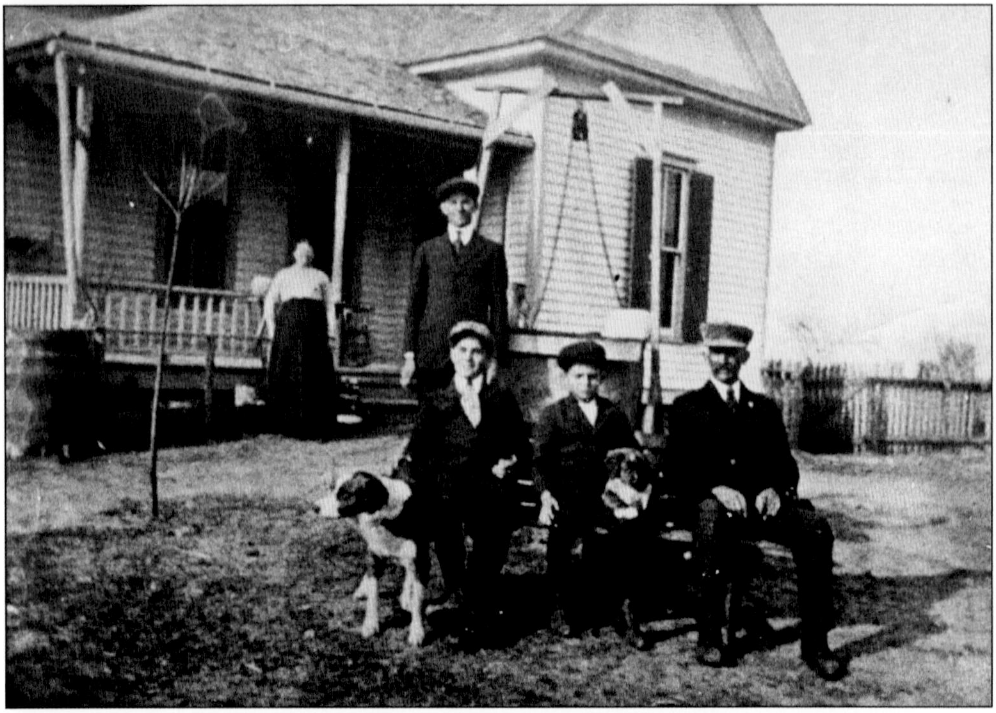

William Nesuda came to Ennis in 1886 from the village of Kocelovice in Bohemia. He met and married Anna Haskovec, and they raised a family at their farm just east of Ennis. The farm has been in the Nesuda family for over 100 years. Pictured from left to right are Anna, Edwin (standing), Milton, Alvin, and William Nesuda in front of their home. (Courtesy of Dorothy Kudrna.)

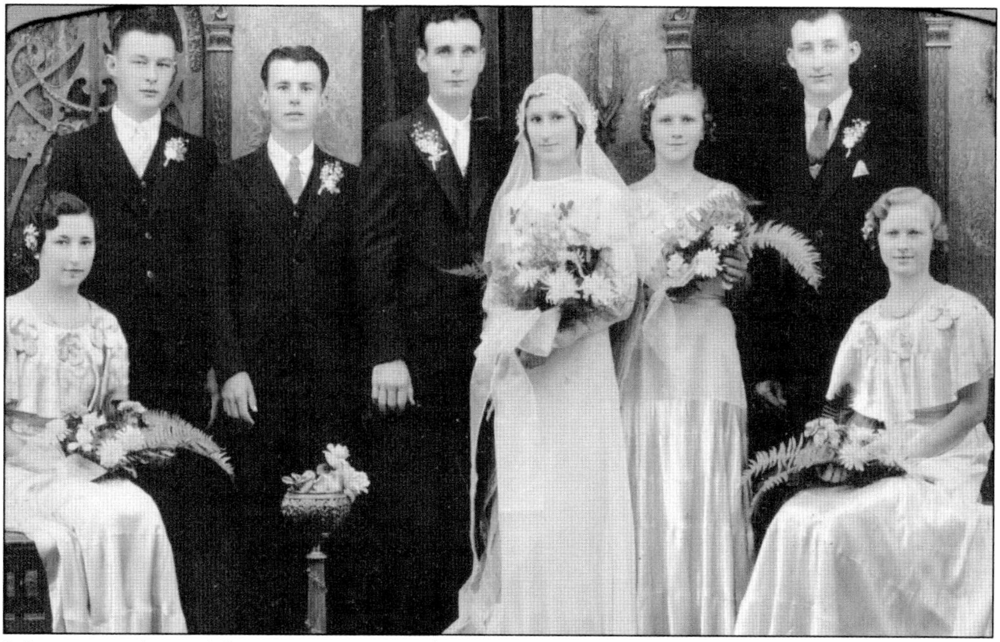

Like many others of their generation, Walter Zmolik and Wilma Bobalik, descendants of Czech immigrants, chose to make Ennis their home. Pictured with their wedding party are, from left to right, Agnes Vavra Pekar, Frank Mach, Frank Zmolik, Walter Zmolik, Wilma Bobalik, Anna Bobalik Zmolek, Frank Elleven, and Lydia Bobalik Kucera. (Courtesy of Mary Ann Zmolik Sibley.)

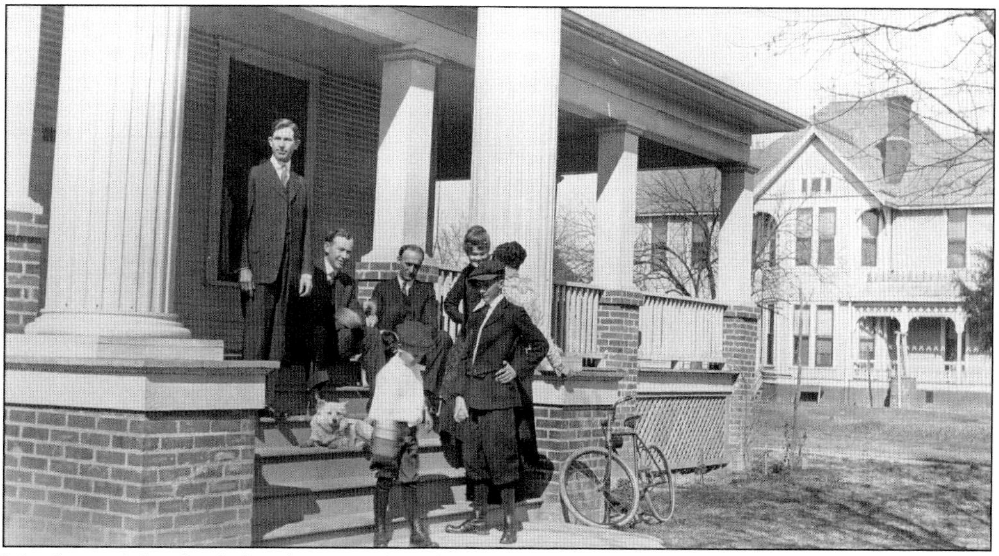

Members of the Cook family are gathered on the porch of their family home, a structure once located at 400 West Knox Street. Dr. Charles Cook practiced medicine in Ennis for decades, spending much of his time during the 1918 flu epidemic at the small hospital only blocks from his home. The Rowe home, at 308 West Knox Street, is seen in the background. (Courtesy of Ennis Public Library.)

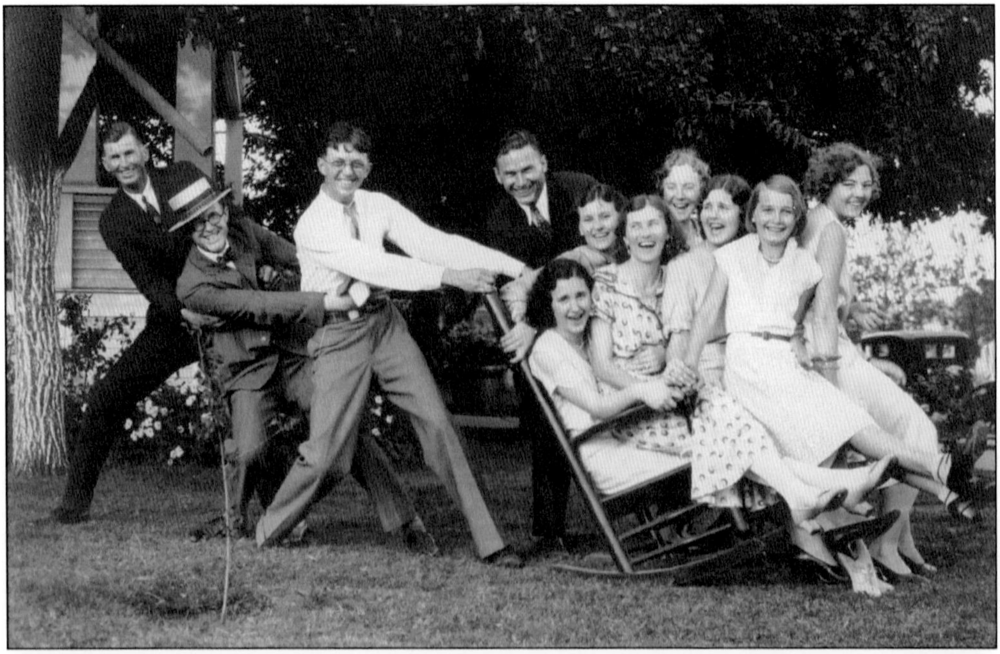

Members of the Maresh, Kubelka, and Matcek families are pictured outside the home of longtime Ennis photographer Henry Maresh, second from left, at 302 East Crockett Street in the 1930s. (Courtesy of Mary Ann Novy Lamkin.)

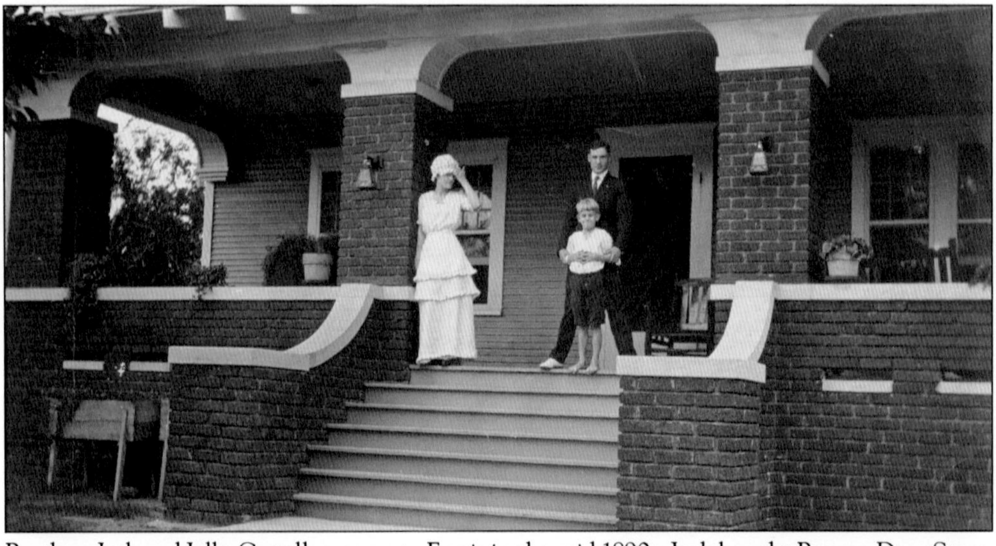

Brothers Jack and Jelks Castellaw came to Ennis in the mid-1890s. Jack bought Broxon Drug Store, which he later relocated to the northwest corner of Knox and Dallas Streets. Jelks owned Castellaw Department Store on West Knox Street. Both were active in civic organizations, including the chamber of commerce. Family members pictured here include Janie Castellaw (left), in front of her home. (Courtesy of Ennis Public Library.)

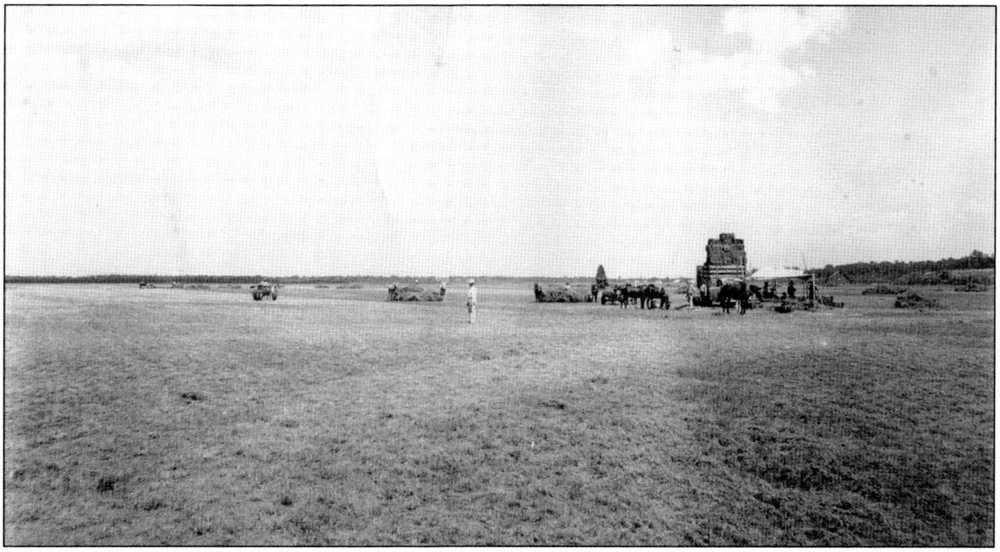

Many chose to live outside the city proper of Ennis. Frank Newton ("Newt") Wilson is pictured here standing in his field near Telico in the 1930s. To the right can be seen a wagon filled high with hay, a sign of the season. (Courtesy of Dorothy Betts.)

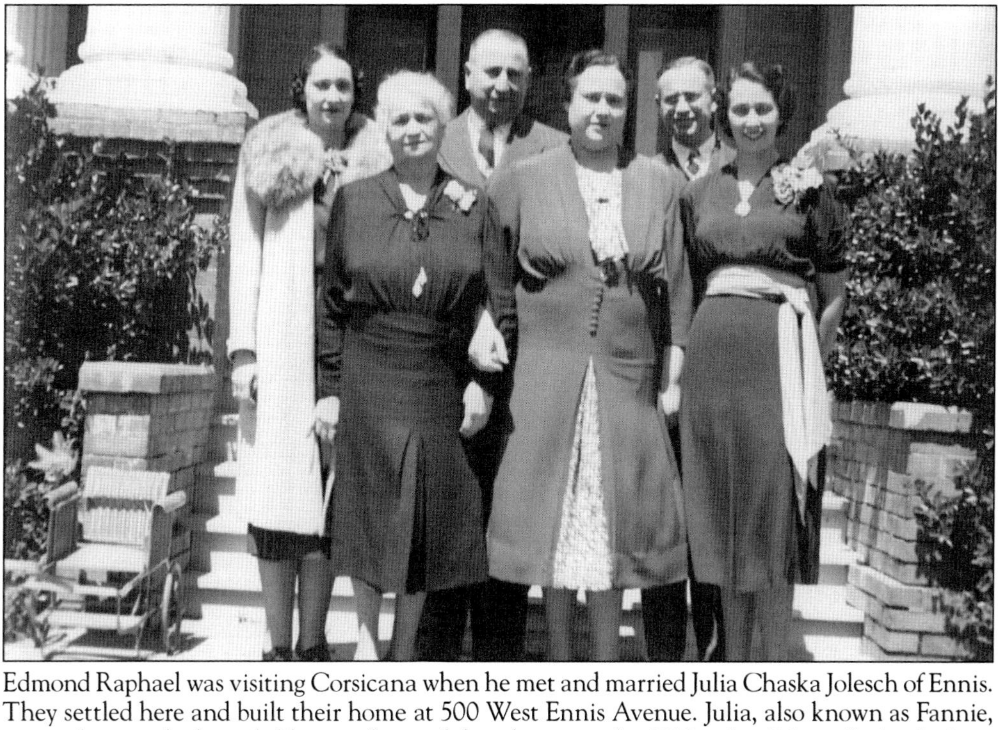

Edmond Raphael was visiting Corsicana when he met and married Julia Chaska Jolesch of Ennis. They settled here and built their home at 500 West Ennis Avenue. Julia, also known as Fannie, is seen here with their children in front of their home in the 1930s after Edmond's death; from left to right are (first row) Fannie, Wilhelmina, and Alleyne; (second row) Julia, Raymond, and Ernest. (Courtesy of Harriett Adams.)

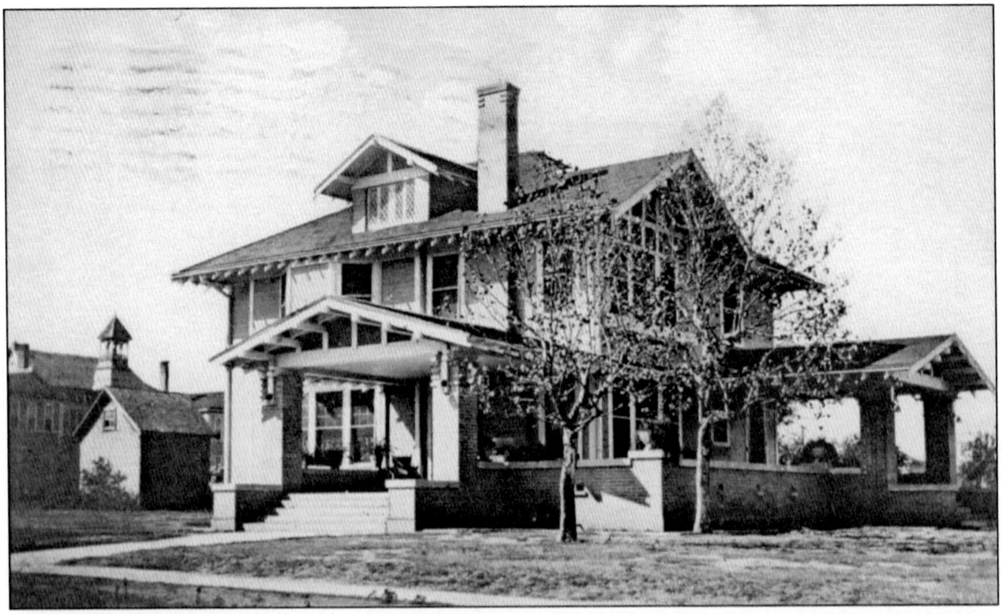

In 1909, Earl Fain, a cotton buyer, built his home in the 400 block of North Preston Street at a cost of approximately $18,000. The second Ennis High School, known as Old Faithful, can be seen in the background.

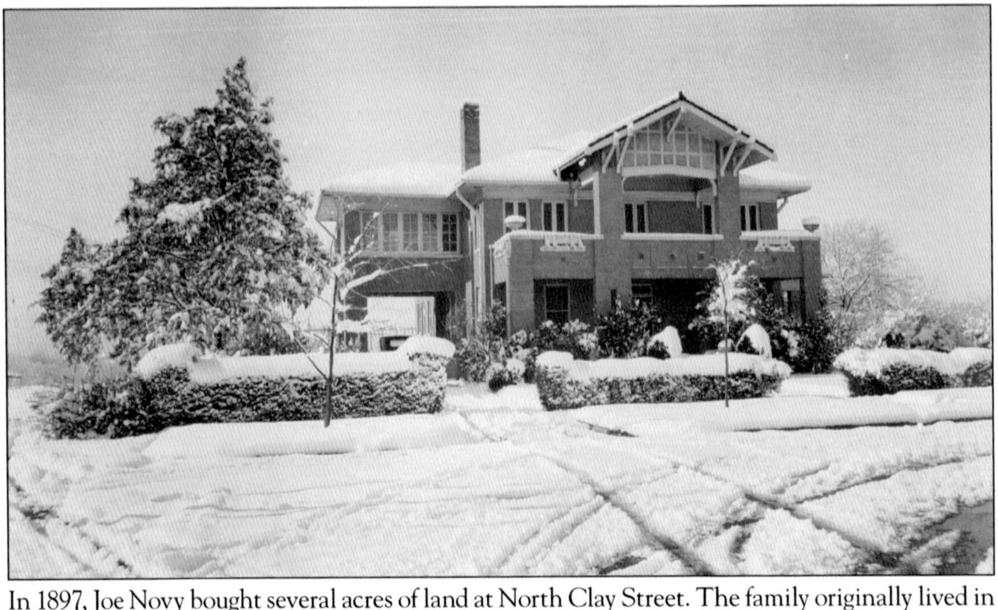

In 1897, Joe Novy bought several acres of land at North Clay Street. The family originally lived in a Victorian home on the property near the original barn. The "House Joe Built," pictured above at 401 North Clay Street, was completed in 1919. Everything was hand cut and milled on site and completed with a central coal heating system and 14-inch-thick exterior walls. (Courtesy of Mary Ann Novy Lamkin.)

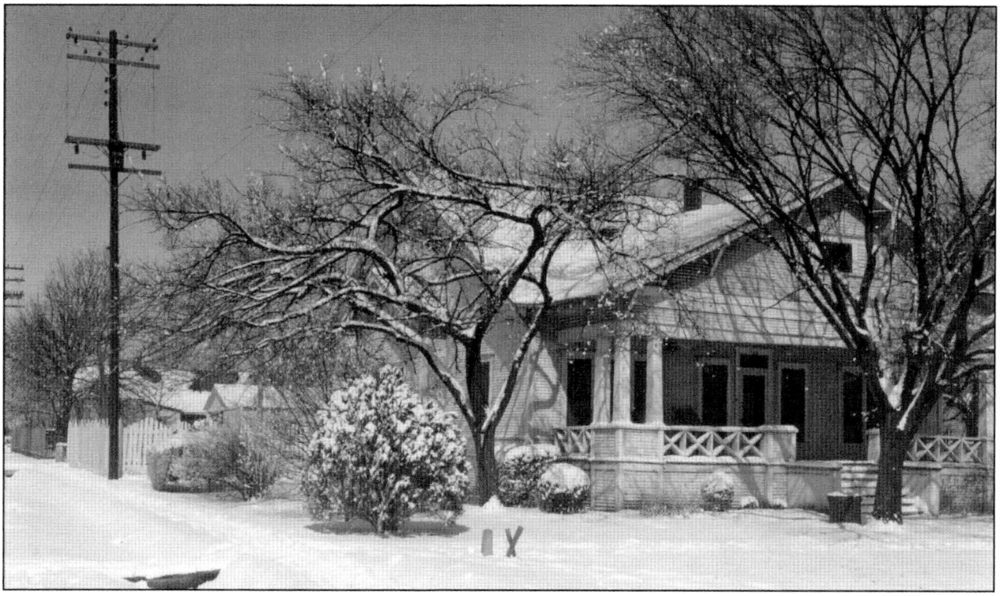

The Maresh home at 302 East Crockett Street and South Kaufman Avenue, pictured in the 1940s, still stands today. It was built in 1916. Long the home of Henry and Bessie Valek Maresh, it remains the property of their descendants. (Courtesy of Mary Ann Novy Lamkin.)

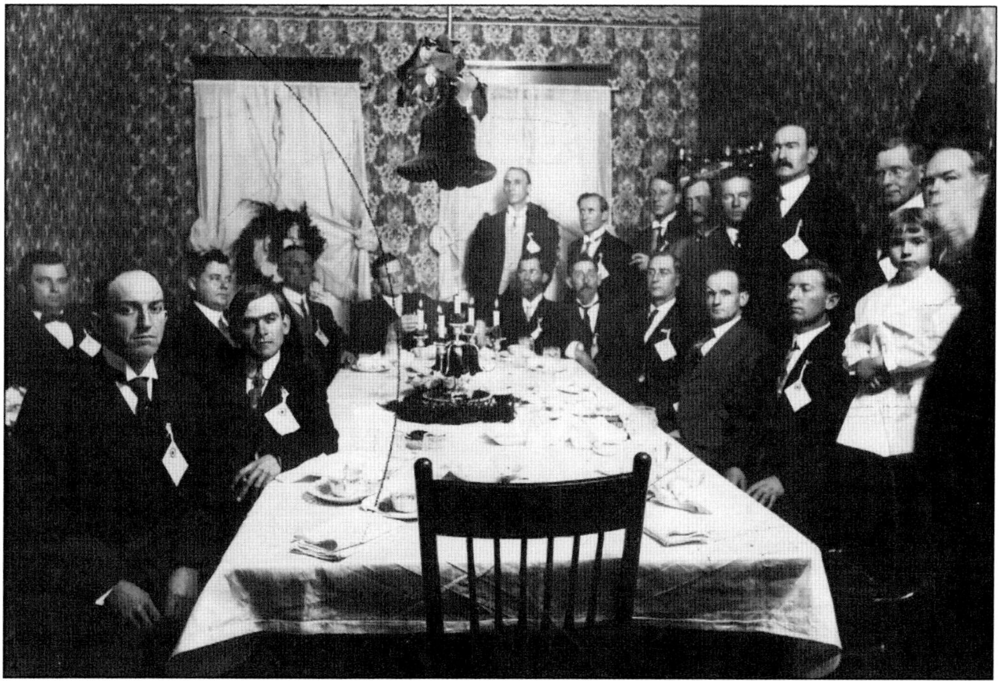

Many in the Ennis medical community gathered at the Ennis home of Dr. Tom White around 1912, including, from left to right, (seated) Dr. A. L. Thomas, Dr. W. C. Tenery, Dr. L. E. Clark, Dr. J. P. Clark, unidentified, Dr. ? Griffin, Dr. ? Parks, Dr. J. C. Loggins, unidentified, Jack Castellaw, and unidentified; (standing) Dr. Charles Cook, William Brittain, Dr. ? Watson, Dr. ? Timms, unidentified, Dr. Walter McCall Sr., Dr. ? Terry, Dr. Tom White, and unidentified. (Courtesy of Ennis Public Library.)

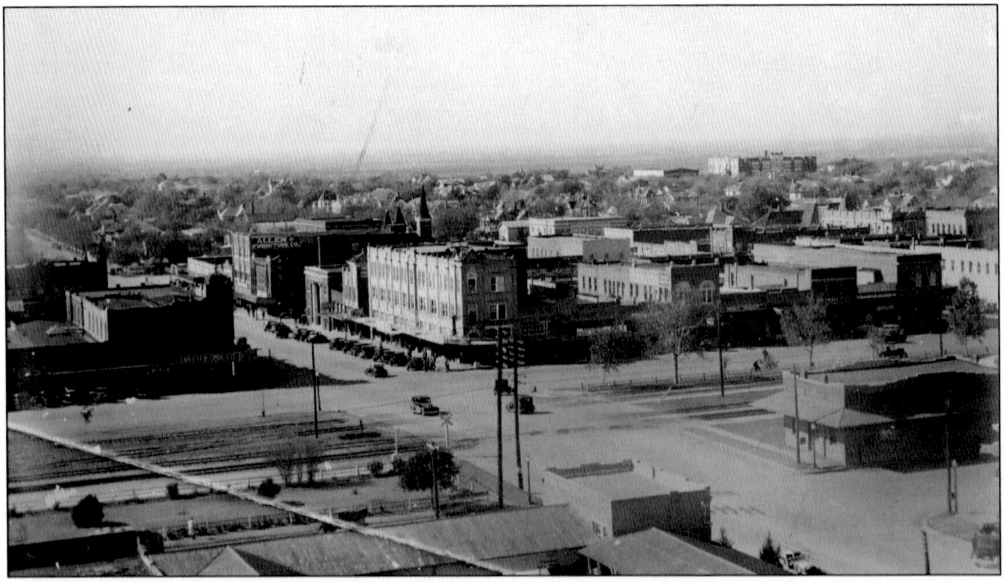

The city grew tremendously in the first decades of the 20th century. These northwest views show the vast expansion of the residential area. In the view above, believed to be taken from the grain silo at East Brown and Breckenridge Streets, the Ennis High School is visible in the background to the right, standing tall over the surrounding neighborhood. The downtown area and northern edge of the residential area are the focus of the photograph below. The railway can be seen at the lower left with West Main Street running alongside it. (Above, courtesy of Mary Ann Novy Lamkin; below, Ennis Public Library.)

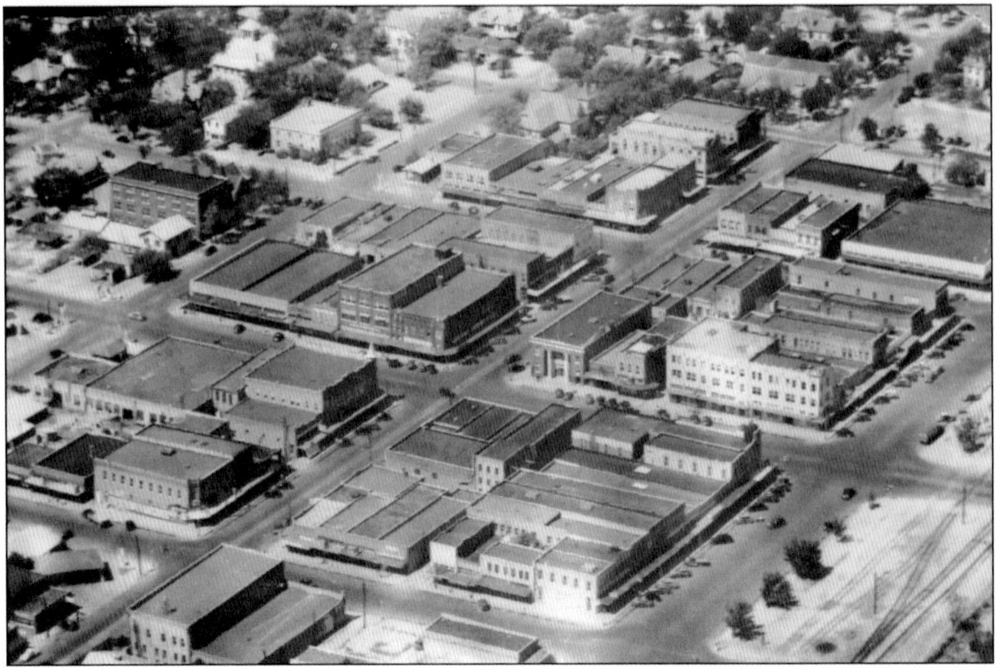

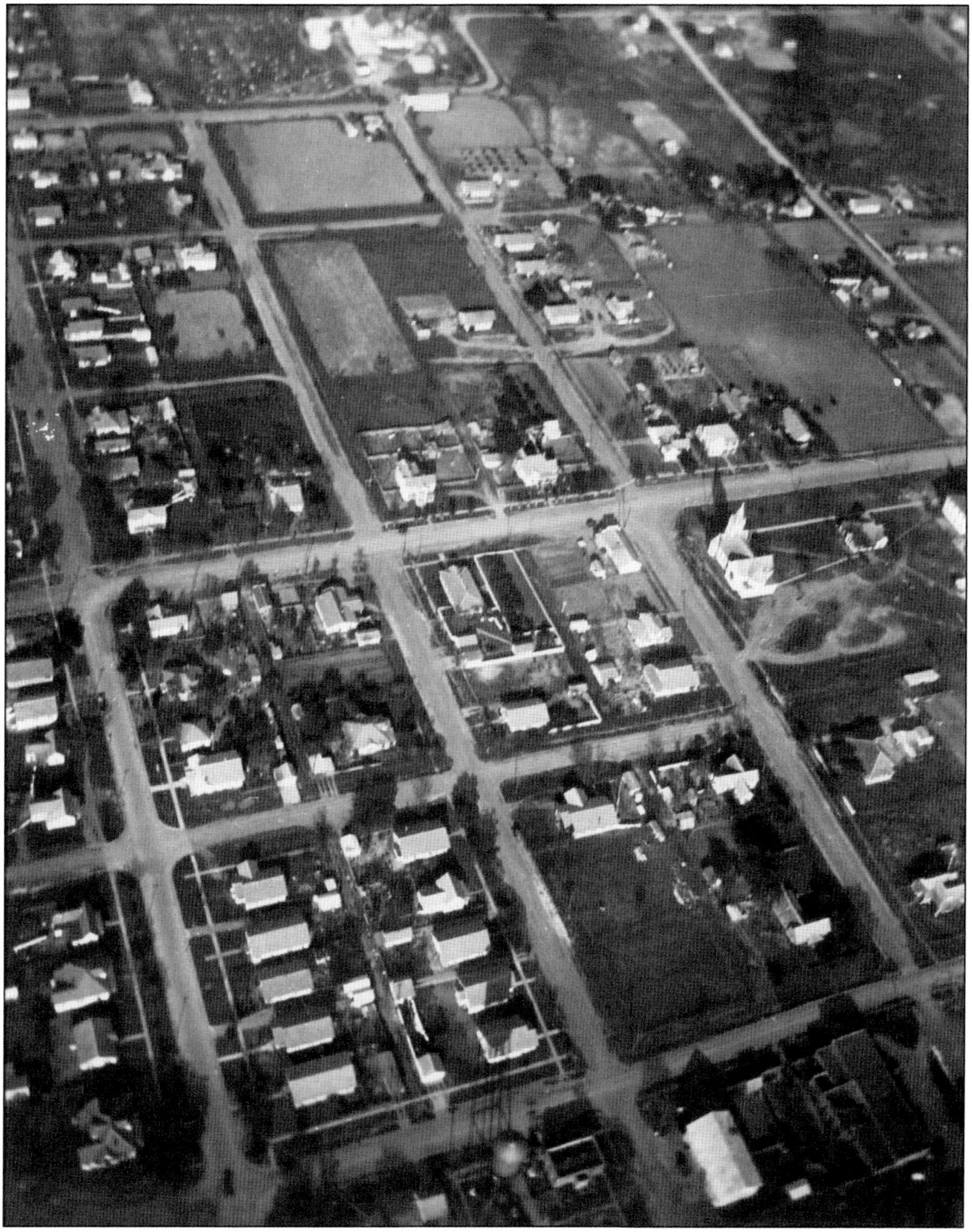

An aerial view of the neighborhood surrounding St. John Catholic Church is pictured in the 1930s. Running from left to right, from the lower edge of the photograph are South Kaufman, Shawnee, and Paris Streets. St. John Catholic Church can be seen at Paris and Lampasas Streets. Running the length of the map from left to right are Milam, Waco, and Lampasas Streets. (Courtesy of Mary Ann Novy Lamkin.)

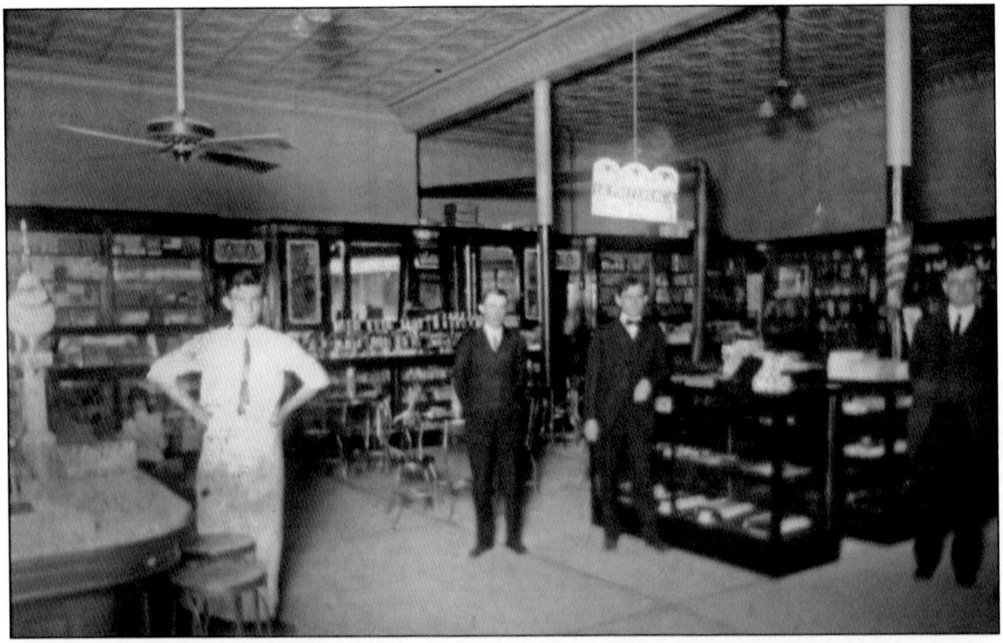

Glover and Guthrie Drug Store, pictured above, was established around 1901 by E. E. Glover. It was located at the northwest corner of Ennis Avenue and Dallas Street, pictured below. Early accounts from Glover show that H. P. Hilliard was the first customer in his new store. Dr. Harry Kent, a dentist in the early 1900s, had the corner office on the second floor of the building, and his profession is seen advertised on his windows. Next door to the right, Duff's advertises "the lowest prices since 1912." (Above, Courtesy of Ennis Heritage Society; below, Ennis Fire Department.)

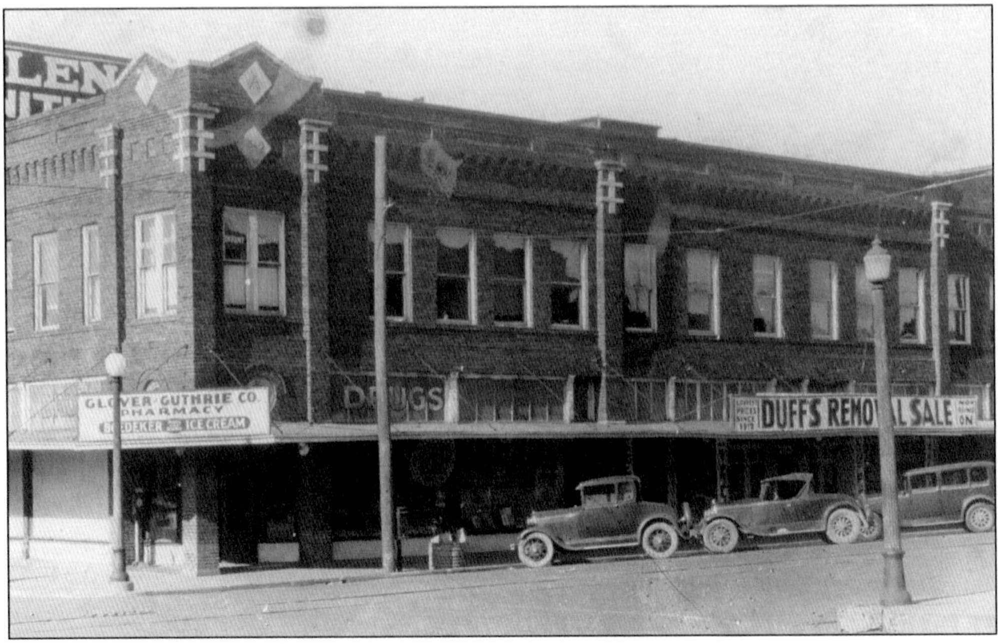

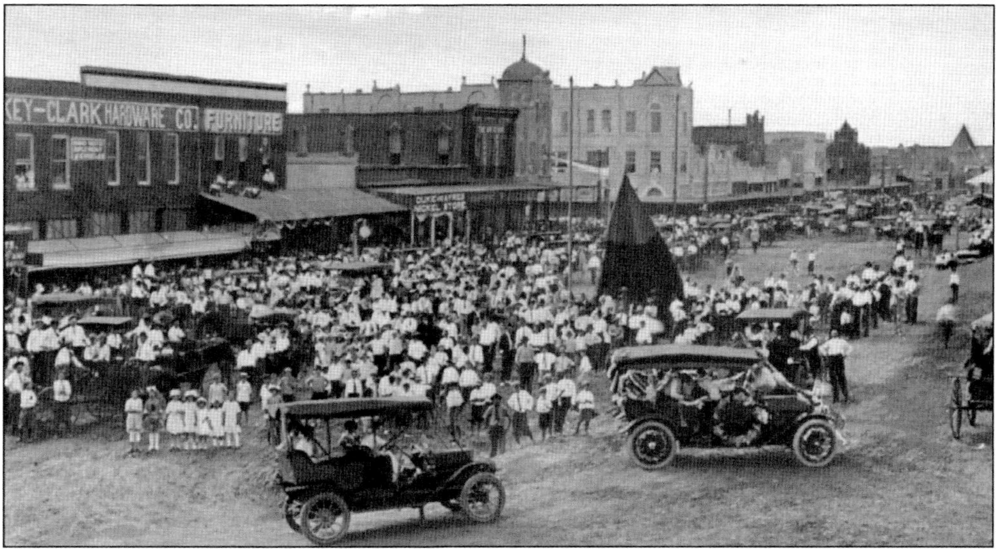

In the late 1800s and into the early 1900s, Ennis had a number of "nickel" or variety stores. Tyra's Nickel Store opened in the late 1890s along the 100 block of Southwest Main Street. Duke and Ayres Nickel Store, pictured above to the right of the furniture store, could be found at the same location in the early 1900s. Unidentified individuals are seen below outside Tyra's Nickel Store. (Both courtesy of Ennis Heritage Society.)

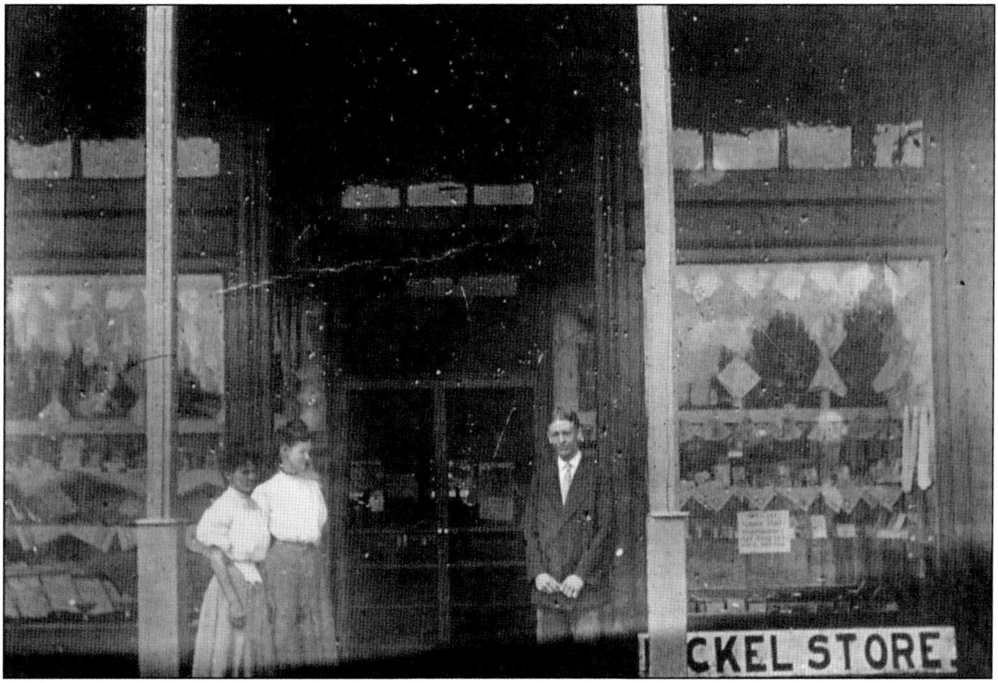

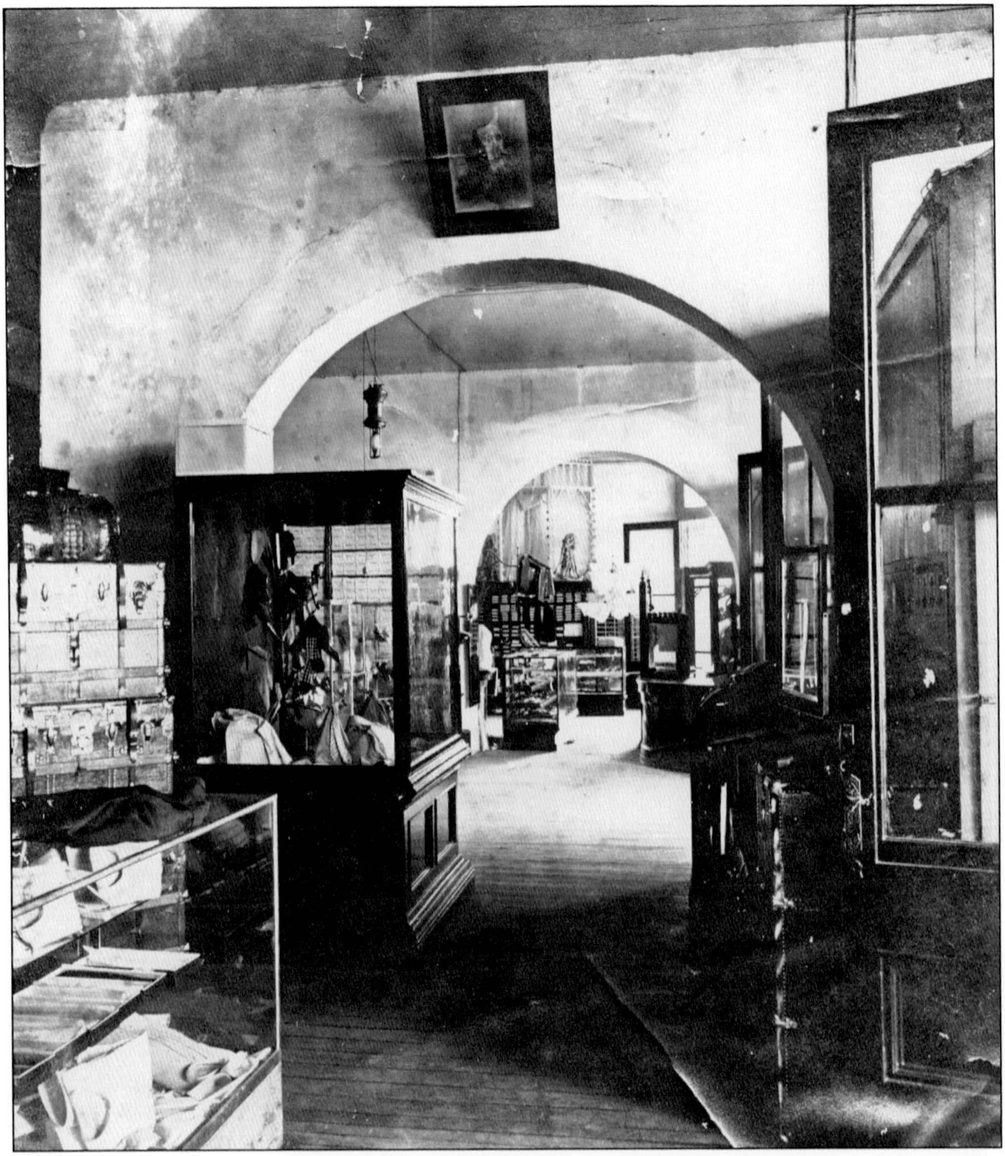

William Jolesch came to Ennis in 1875 and established the Jolesch Dry Goods Store at the corner of Ennis Avenue and Main Street. It came to be known as one of the most successful stores in Central Texas during its 44 years in business. Jolesch attributed this to the extensive line of dry goods carried in his store, as pictured here. Because of its success, he later opened other stores in the surrounding cities, including Italy and Ferris. Early newspaper accounts reported that it wasn't unusual for the store to have a large water cooler and tin cups outside for those in need of a cool drink on hot days. After William's death in 1901, his sons, Joe, Sam, and Ike, and son-in-law Edmond Raphael continued to run the business until 1919. (Courtesy of Harriett Adams.)

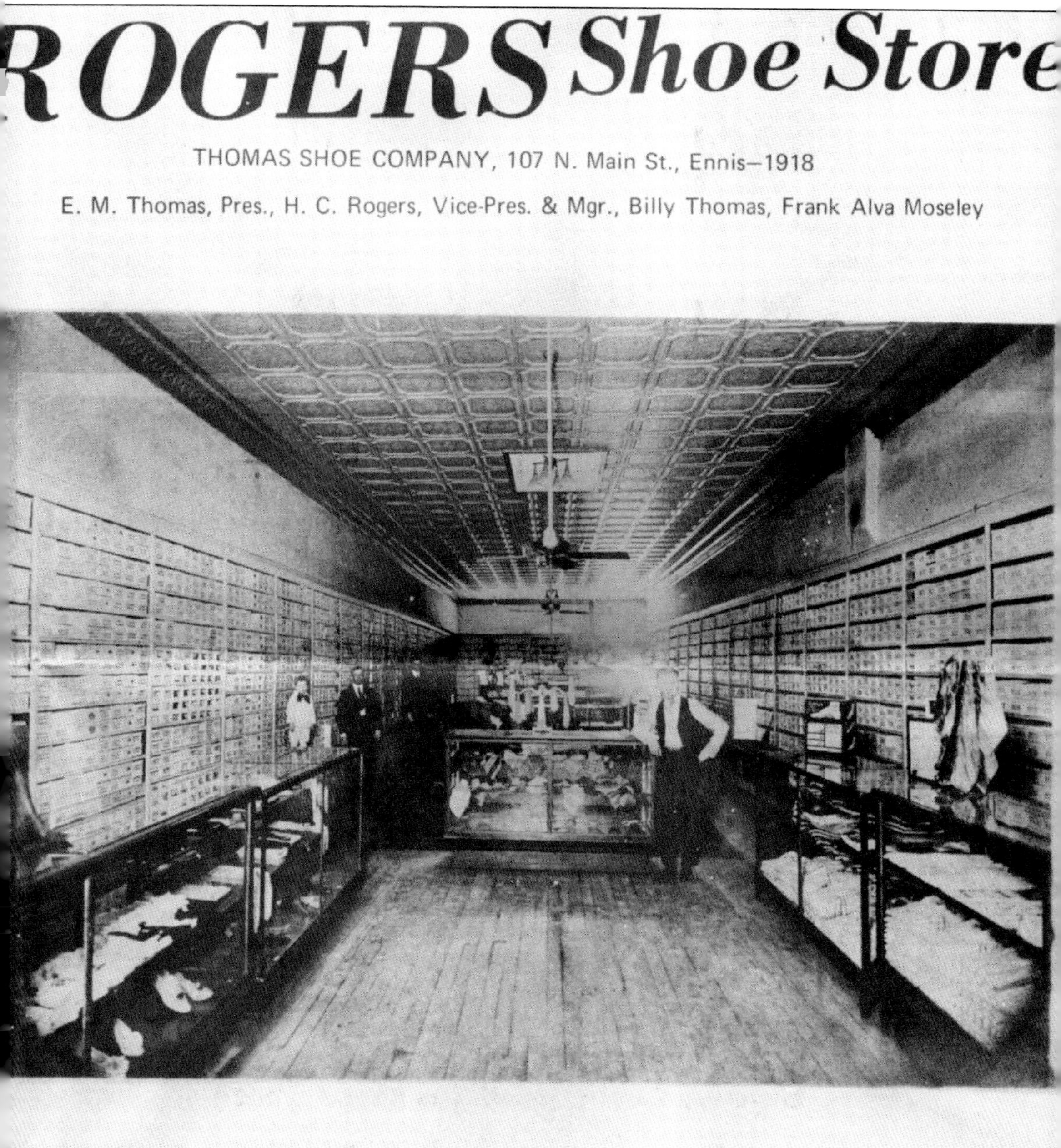

The Rogers Shoe Store first began as the Thomas Shoe Store, owned by E. M. (Enoch Marvin) Thomas in 1901. It was located at 107 North Main Street. In 1915, Thomas took on Carl Hill as a partner. In 1919, Hill sold his interest in the company to Hubert Rogers, who had worked in the store for years and had just returned from serving in World War I. In 1923, a partnership to sell shoes wholesale and retail was formed between the Thomas and Jolesch families. Hubert Rogers then became a director of that company and manager of the Ennis store. In the 1930s, it became the Rogers Shoe Store and remained at the same location for several decades. Pictured from left to right are Marvin Thomas, Hubert Rogers, and unidentified in the shoe store around 1918. (Courtesy of Ennis Public Library.)

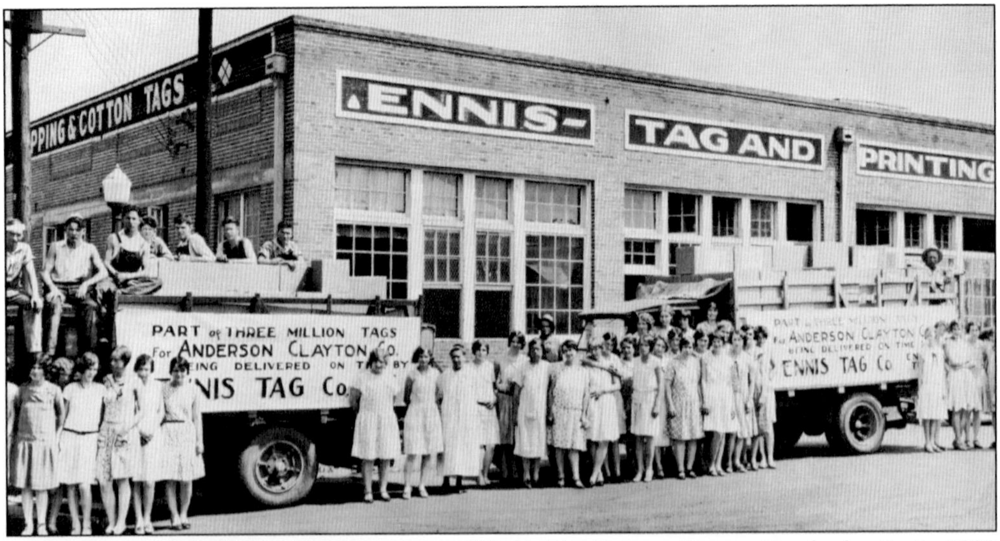

Ennis Tag and Salesbook Company was established by George Garner Dunkerley Sr. in 1909 and initially located on West Knox Street. Tags were printed for the cotton bales. Ennis Tag and Printing Company later located to North Main and East Baylor Streets as pictured. The company became Ennis Business Forms in 1959. (Courtesy of Ennis Public Library.)

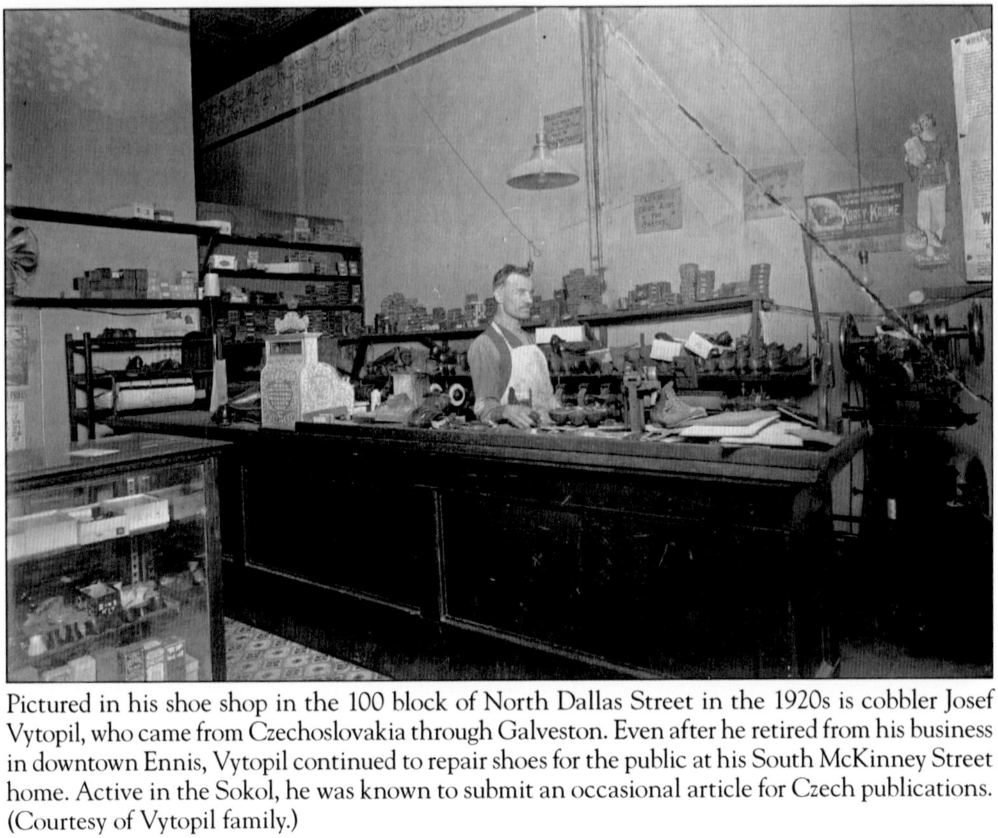

Pictured in his shoe shop in the 100 block of North Dallas Street in the 1920s is cobbler Josef Vytopil, who came from Czechoslovakia through Galveston. Even after he retired from his business in downtown Ennis, Vytopil continued to repair shoes for the public at his South McKinney Street home. Active in the Sokol, he was known to submit an occasional article for Czech publications. (Courtesy of Vytopil family.)

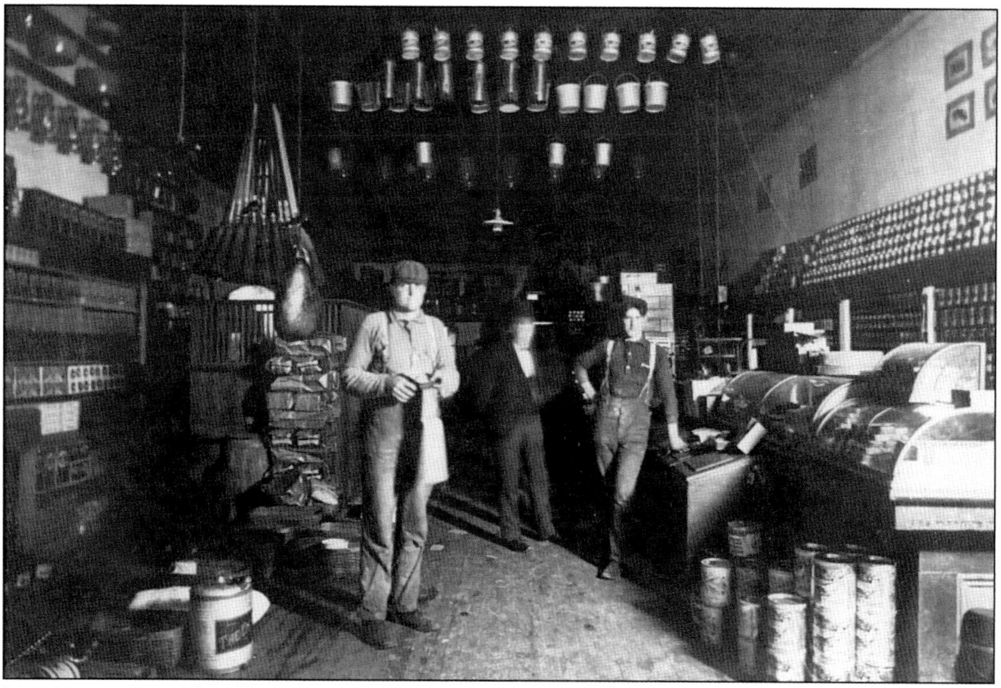

Joe Novy opened his Grocers Store at 205 Northwest Main Street in 1904 after learning the trade from his sister Annie Novy Egger of Waxahachie. Records show he often provided goods on credit for many Czech immigrants upon their arrival to the city. Pictured from left to right in the Novy Store around 1906 are Joe Novy, unidentified, and Novy's nephew Sam Egger. (Courtesy of Mary Ann Novy Lamkin.)

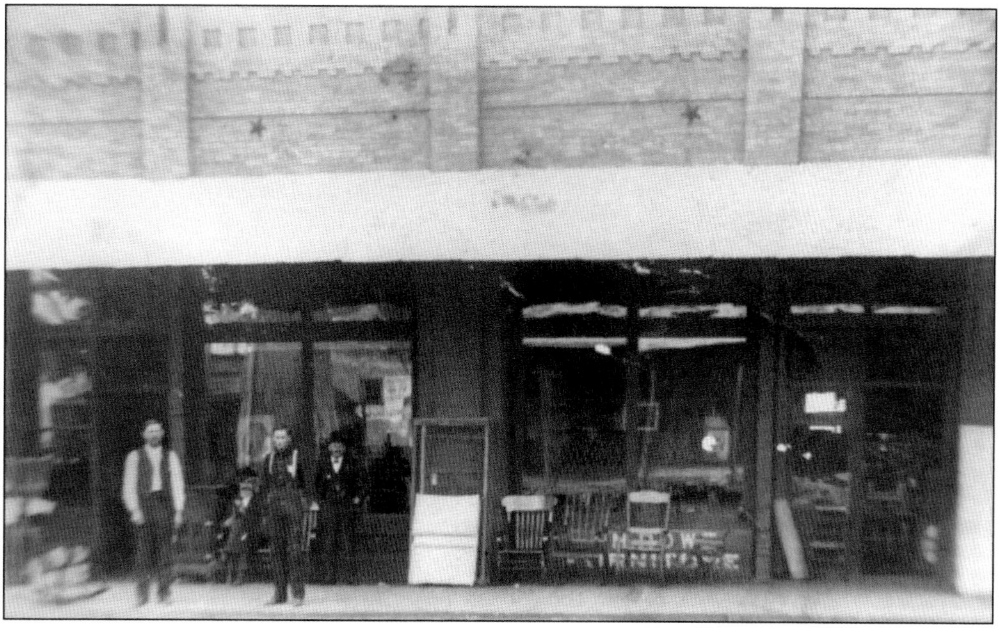

The Rowe Furniture Store was located on South Dallas Street near Brown Street, pictured here with several unidentified men gathered in front of the store. (Courtesy of Ennis Public Library.)

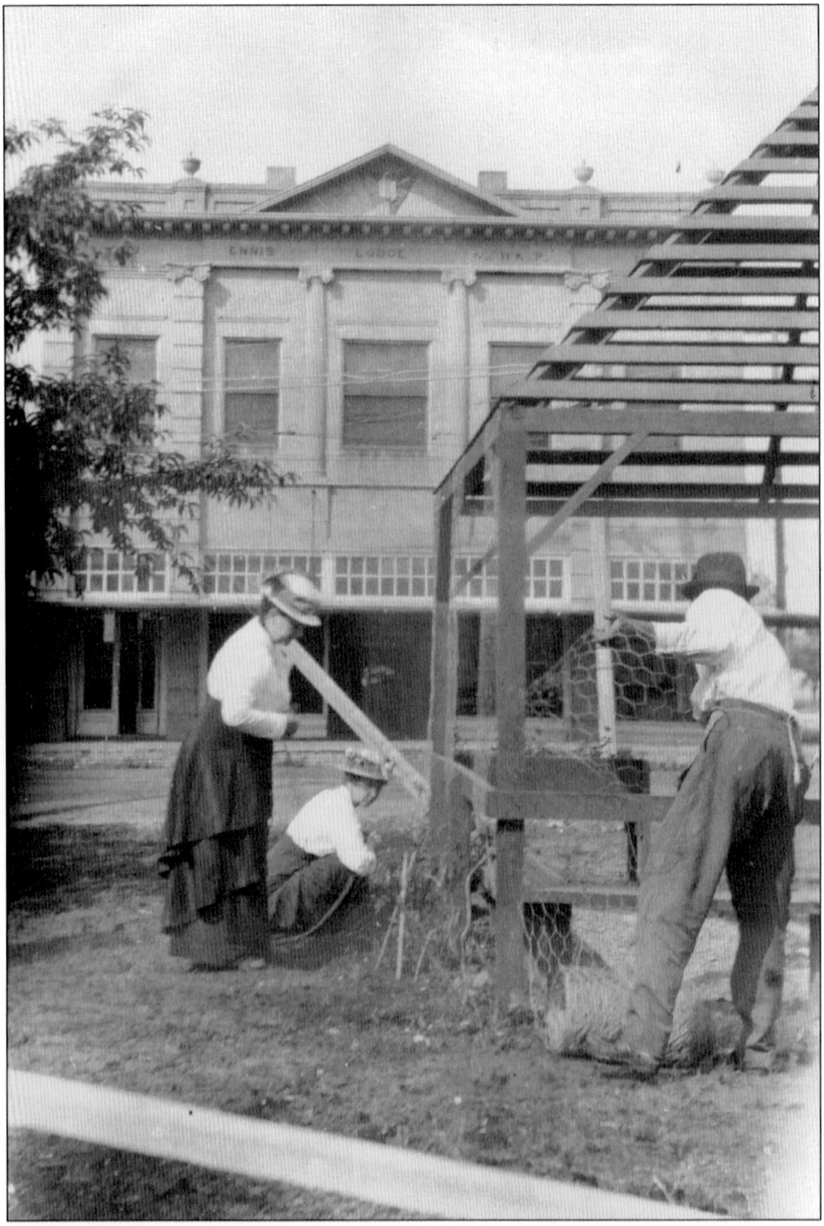

The lot at the southeast corner of Baylor and Dallas Streets remained vacant for many years until the interurban station located there around 1920. Earlier records show the area was possibly used as an amphitheater around 1910. Pictured is the construction of what may have been a gazebo or similar structure. Across the street is the Ennis Lodge, built in 1910 after fire destroyed the original structure. For years, its second floor was the home of the Knights of Pythias. J. W. Neal Undertakers occupied part of the first floor. The company was purchased in 1918 by J. E. Keever, who renamed it Keever Undertakers and Embalmers. Keevers remained in that location until 1963, when it relocated a block north on Dallas Street, where it is still found today. The *Ennis Daily News* today occupies the entire first floor of the Ennis Lodge building. Both companies continue to serve the Ennis community as they have for decades. (Courtesy of Mary Helen Nowlin Gentry.)

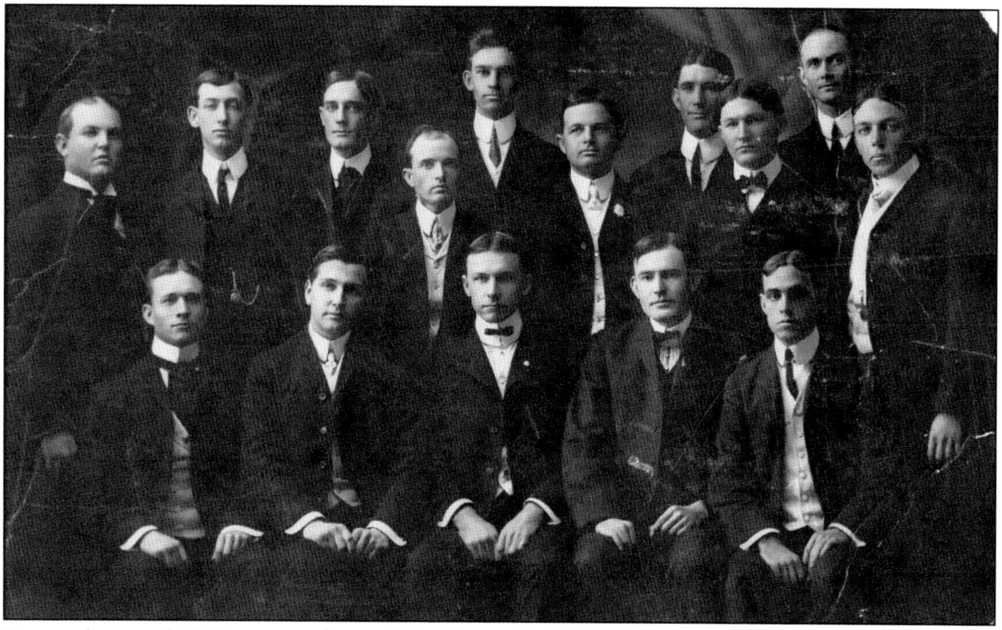

Pictured around 1905 are members of the Commercial Club. Founded prior to 1900, the group was the precursor to the Ennis Chamber of Commerce, incorporated in 1918. Members, who were primarily business leaders, included Jack Rowe, Hugh Gilpin, Pete Hemphill, Will Mann, Ed Crumley, and Val Morrison. (Courtesy of Ennis Public Library.)

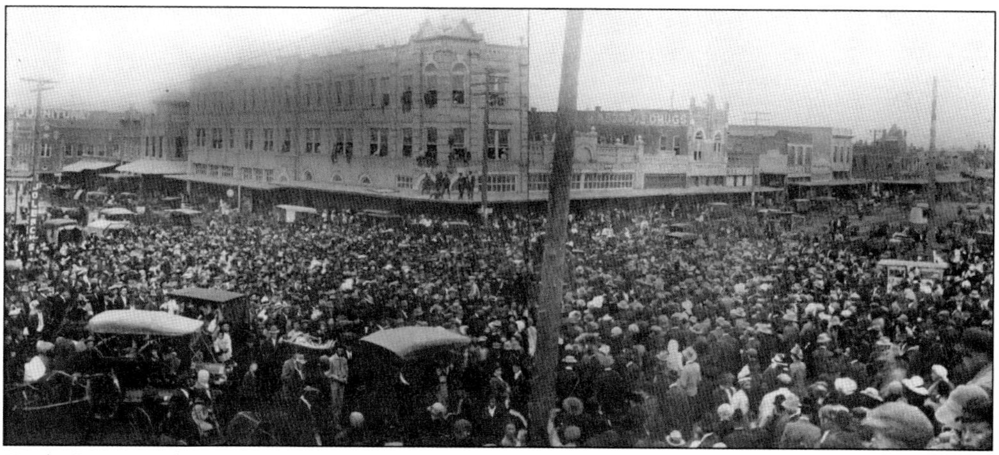

Trade Day crowds were a common scene in Ennis during the first decades of the 20th century. Thousands would gather to buy and sell one of the city's most valuable commodities—cotton. The streets would be packed with cars and people, up and down Main Street at the Ennis Avenue intersection as pictured on November 24, 1913. (Courtesy of Charlie and Betty Honza.)

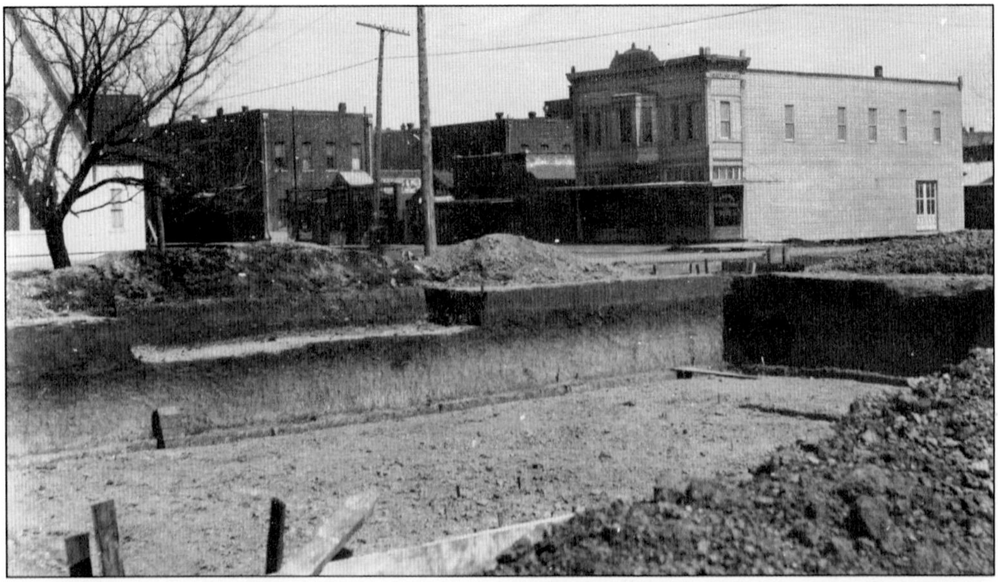

The earliest U.S. post office in Ennis was located along the east side of the railroad on North Main Street in Dixon's Dry Goods Store. John M. Dixon was the first U.S. postmaster in Ennis from 1872 to 1882. Once a week, on Fridays, outgoing mail was taken to Kaufman. Incoming mail arrived from Kaufman on Saturdays. The post office relocated to the 200 block of West Knox Street across from the "moving picture show" in the early 1900s. During these years, Abram Morrison served as postmaster from 1897 to 1910 and A. H. Culver from 1910 to 1914. In 1915, at the beginning of A. Buie's tenure as postmaster, ground was broken for a new permanent federal post office at 205 North McKinney Street. Pictured are early stages of the excavation in April 1915. (Both courtesy of Ennis Post Office.)

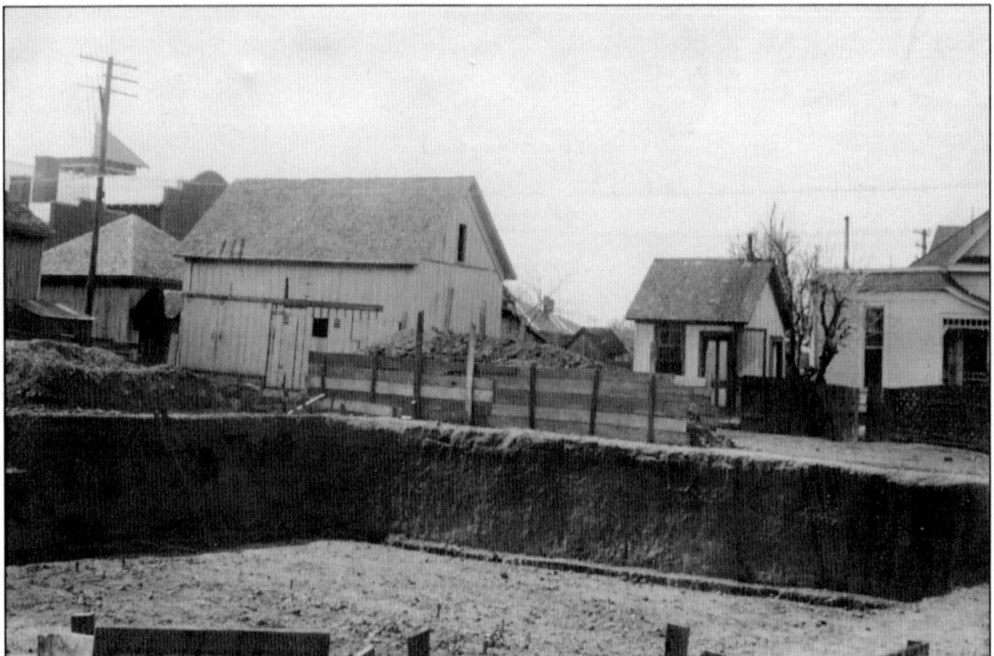

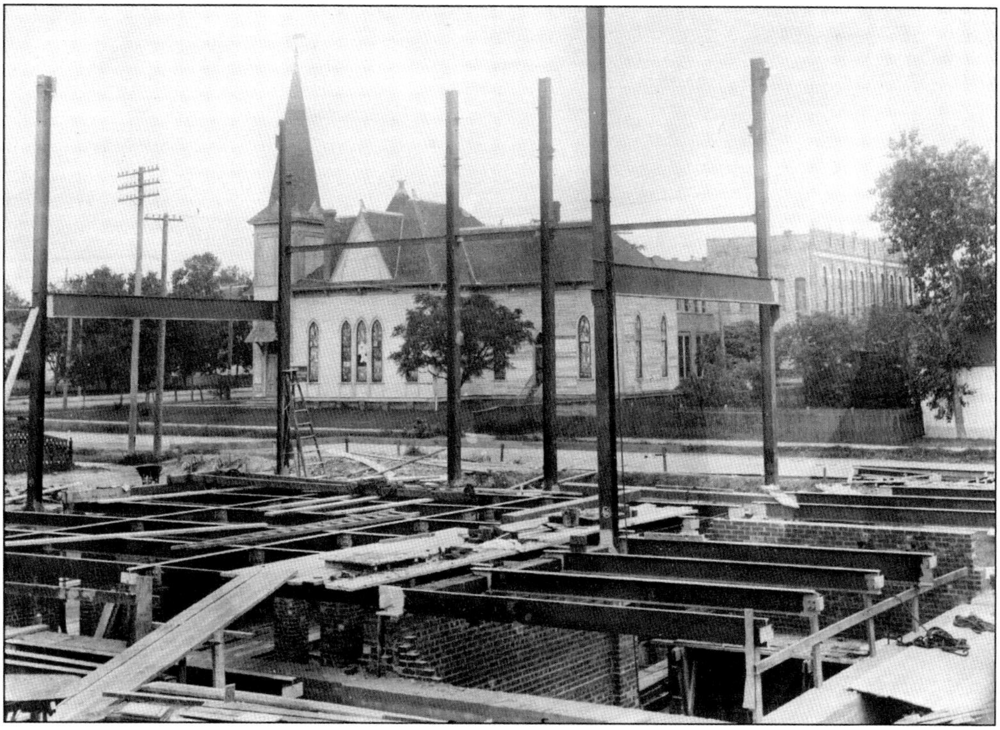

In the summer of 1915, progress on the federal post office was evident. The brick retaining walls and the first-floor construction is underway, as pictured above, with the First Presbyterian Church across the street at McKinney and Baylor Streets. Records show the precise details considered for the interior of the new post office, from the marble for the floors to the crown molding used along the walls and ceiling. In front of the new post office, pictured below, North McKinney Street is still a dirt road. It would be another decade before downtown streets were paved. (Both courtesy of Ennis Post Office.)

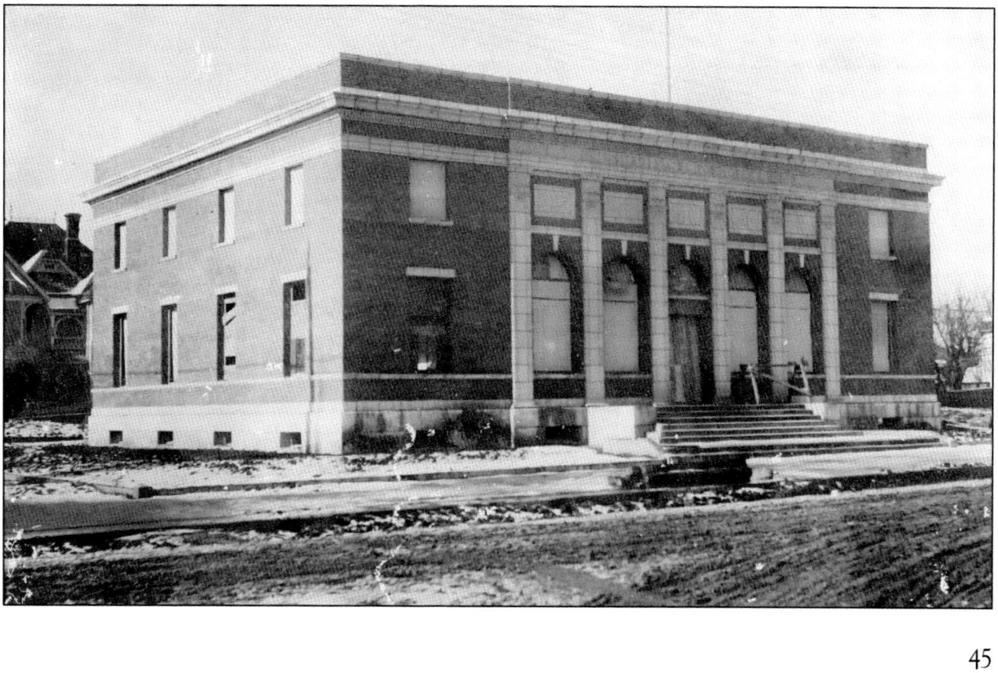

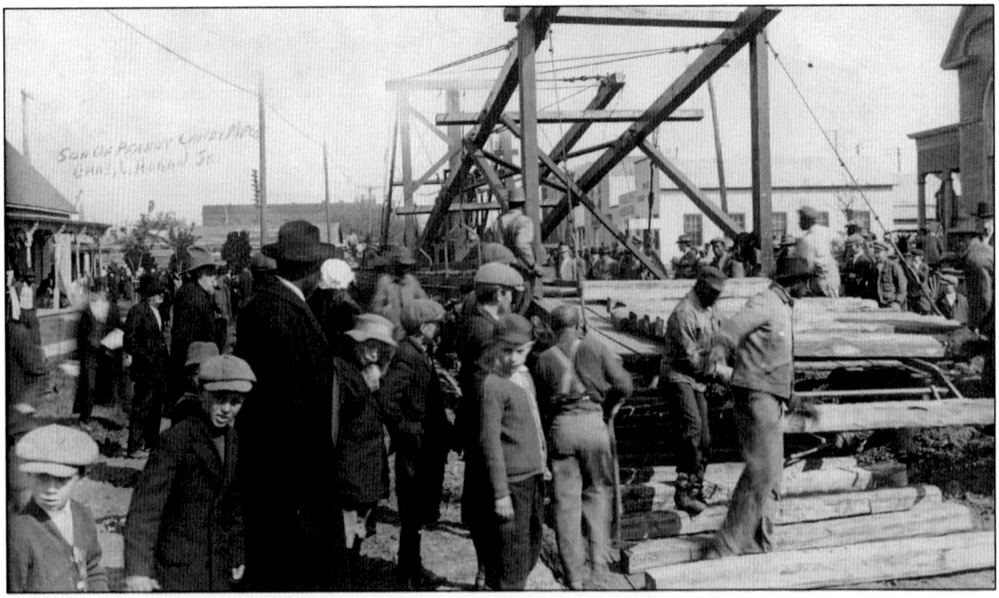

In 1913, the Texas Electric Railway Company provided Ennis residents with direct transportation to both Dallas and Corsicana. The Dallas-Corsicana line began service in October of that year. The effort to provide this direct route was a massive one. Pictured are the efforts to run the right-of-way for the rail through the city. Crowds gathered to watch as the way was cleared down Dallas Street, past the First United Methodist Church once located at South Dallas and Crockett Streets at the far right above. (Both courtesy of Ennis Fire Department.)

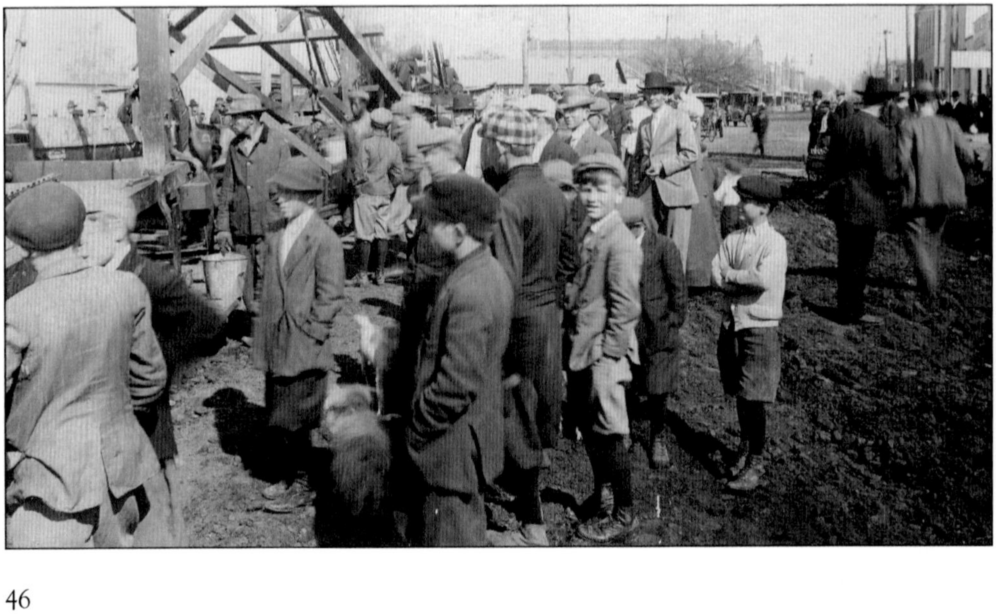

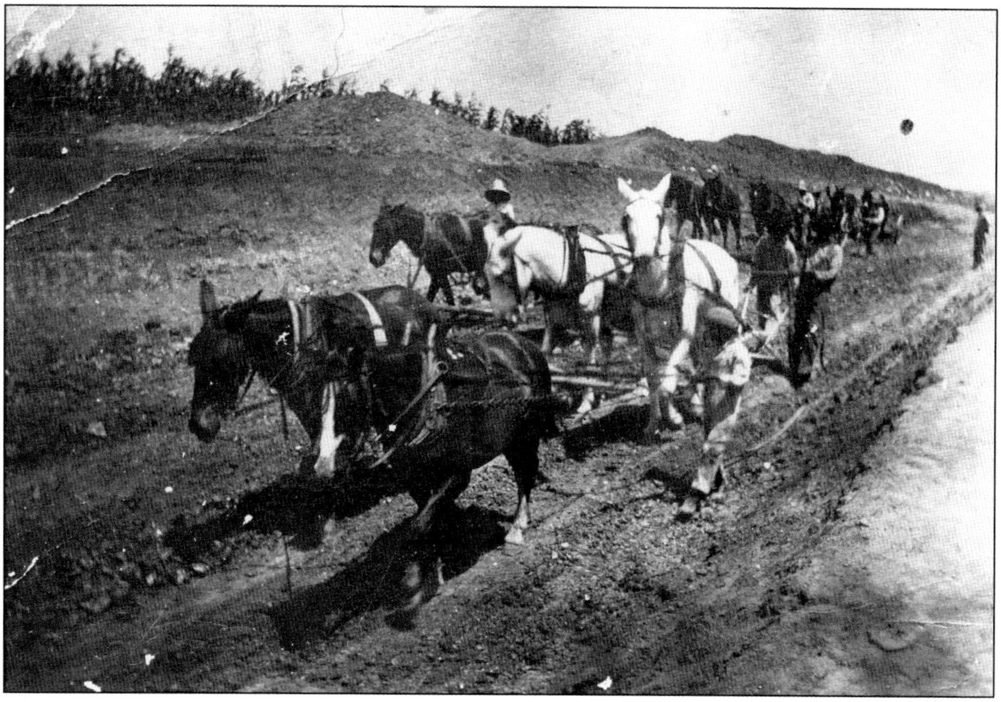

The work by teams of men and horses, with the necessary equipment of that time to clear the land as shown above, was a tremendous one. Upon completion, the line ran through Ennis along Dallas Street, providing daily service until the late 1940s, when the service was discontinued. Below are a number of Texas Electric Railway Company officials, city of Ennis officials, and other representatives gathered at Ennis Avenue and Dallas Street on October 13, 1913, to celebrate the inaugural trip of the "Interurban." (Both courtesy of Ennis Public Library.)

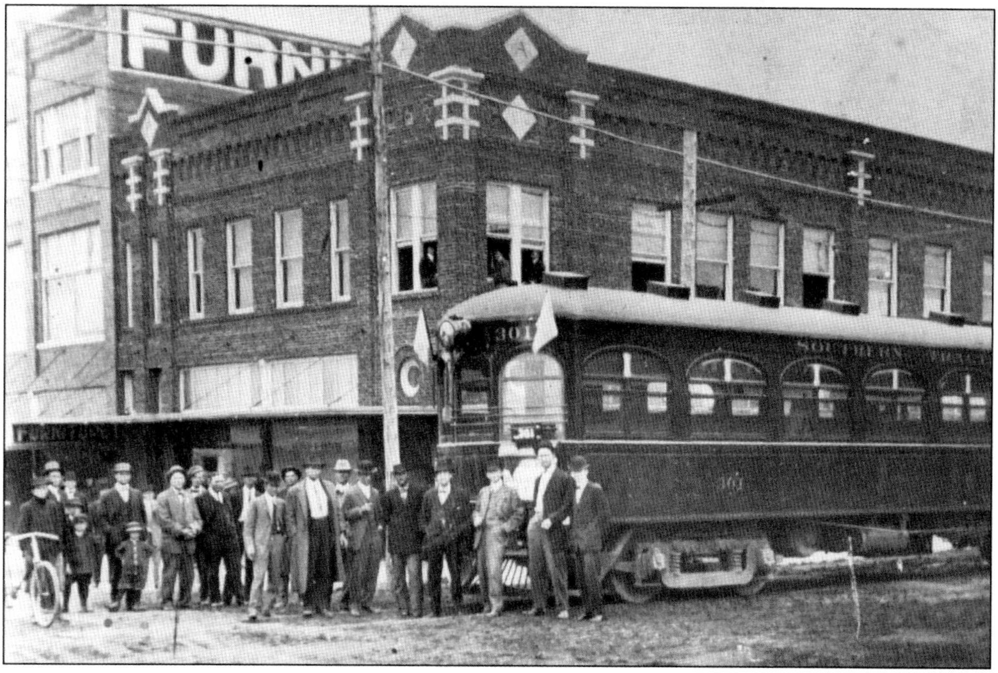

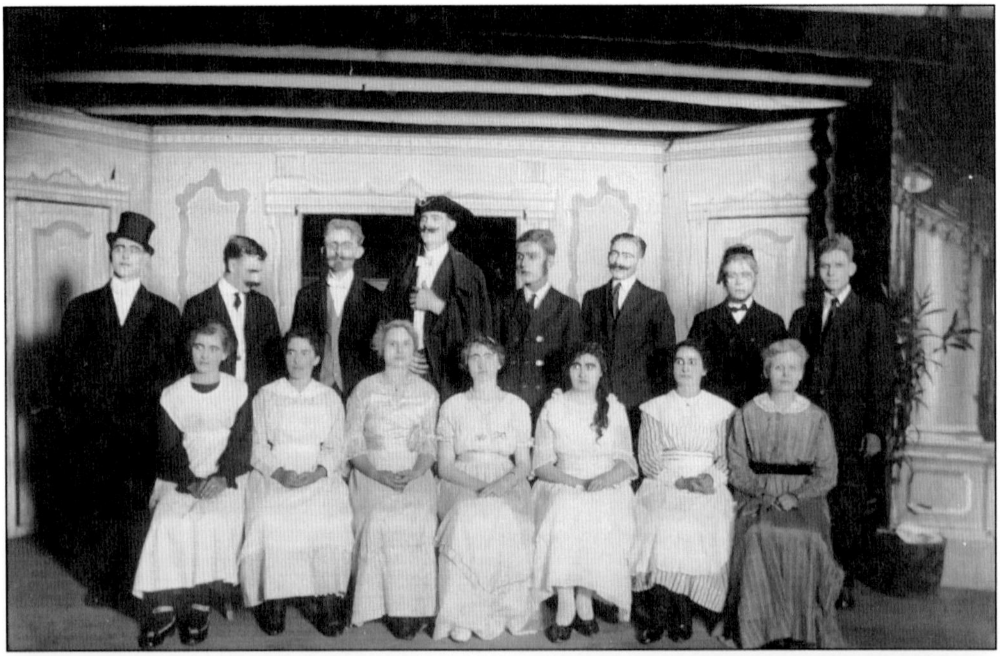

The cast, still in costume, of one of the many plays performed at the Slovanská Podporující Jednota Státu Texas (SPJST) Hall in the 1920s is pictured here. Many of the plays were Czech and often performed in their native language. (Courtesy of Mary Ann Novy Lamkin.)

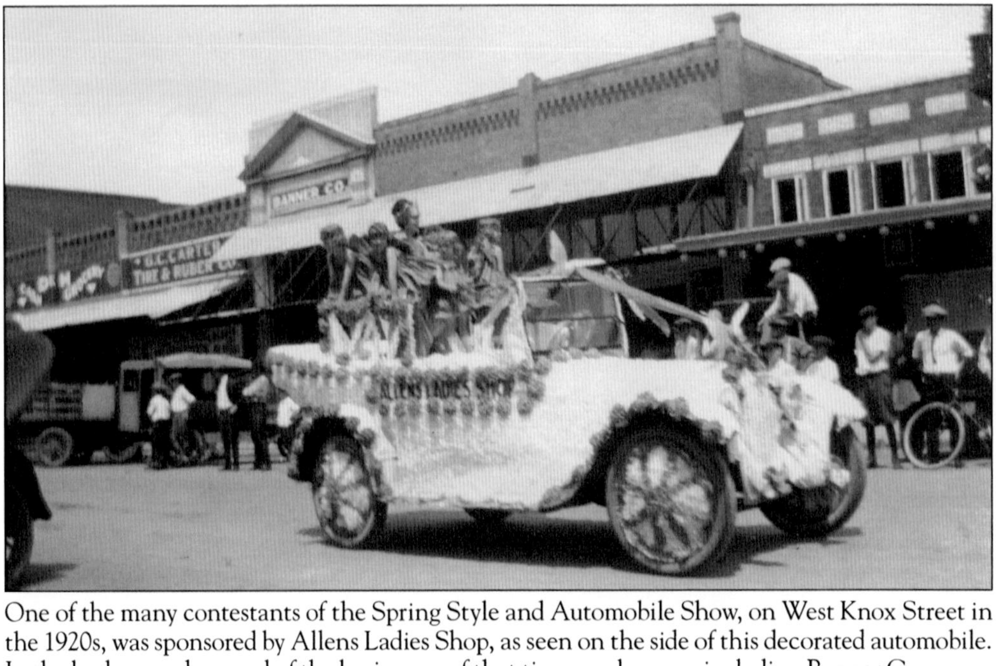

One of the many contestants of the Spring Style and Automobile Show, on West Knox Street in the 1920s, was sponsored by Allens Ladies Shop, as seen on the side of this decorated automobile. In the background, several of the businesses of that time can be seen, including Banner Company, G. C. Carter Tire and Rubber Company, and D&N Cash Grocery. (Courtesy of Mary Helen Nowlin Gentry.)

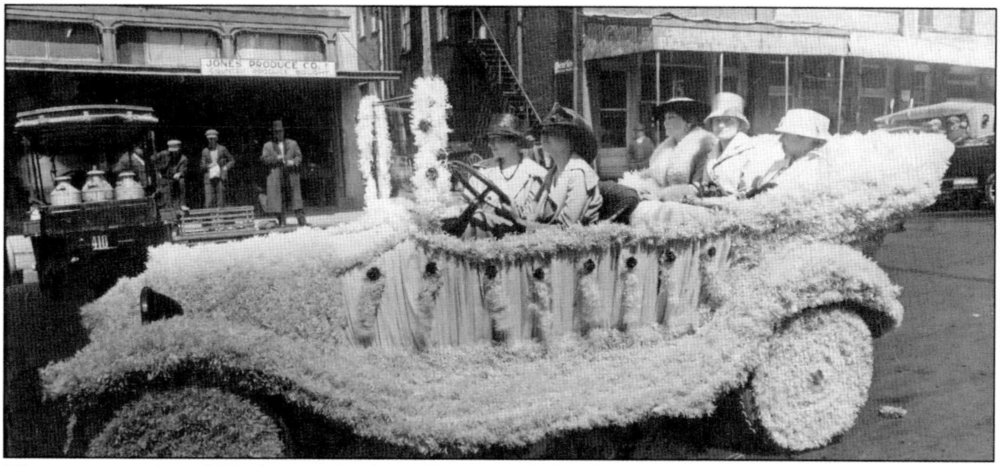

This winner of a 1920s Spring Style and Automobile Show has Kathleen Reagon behind the wheel and Alleyne Raphael in the front passenger seat. Those in the rear seat include Edna Lewis, Gertrude Mann Allen, and Henrietta Freeman Sellers. (Courtesy of Ennis Public Library.)

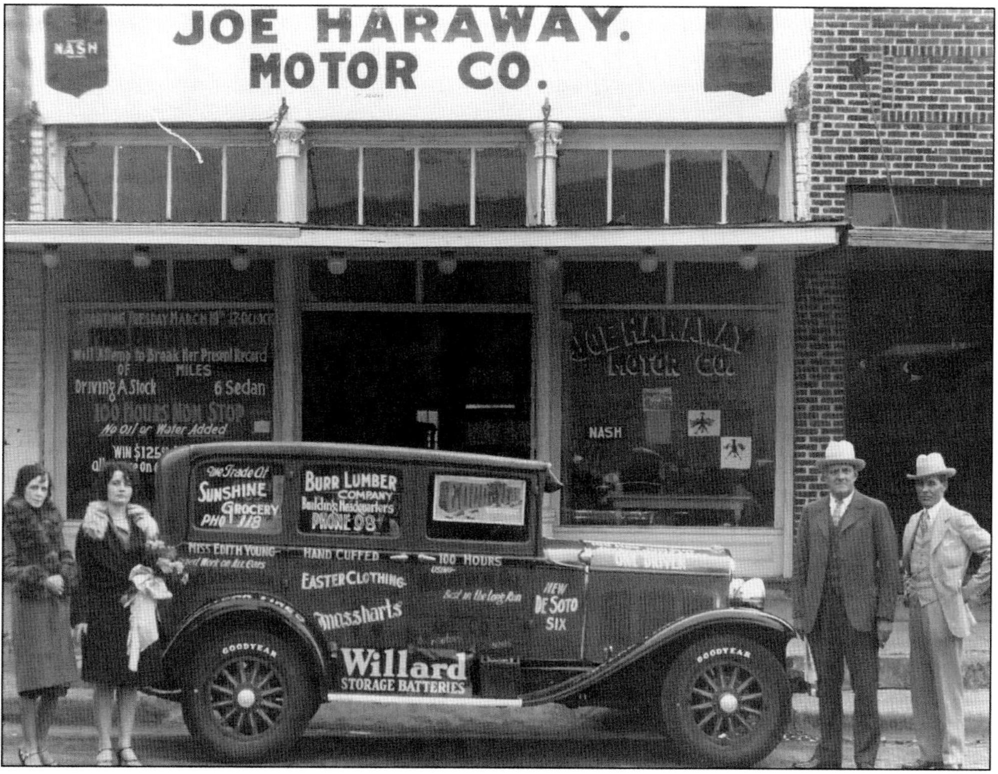

In 1928, Chrysler Automobiles introduced the DeSoto Six. Over the years, the car was publicized in many ways, including with cross-country drives to demonstrate their durability. In Ennis, auto dealer Joe Haraway wasn't to be outdone. Located at 107 South Main Street, Haraway displayed advertisements on the car itself to promote it, as pictured in front of Joe Haraway's storefront in early 1929. (Courtesy of Ennis Public Library.)

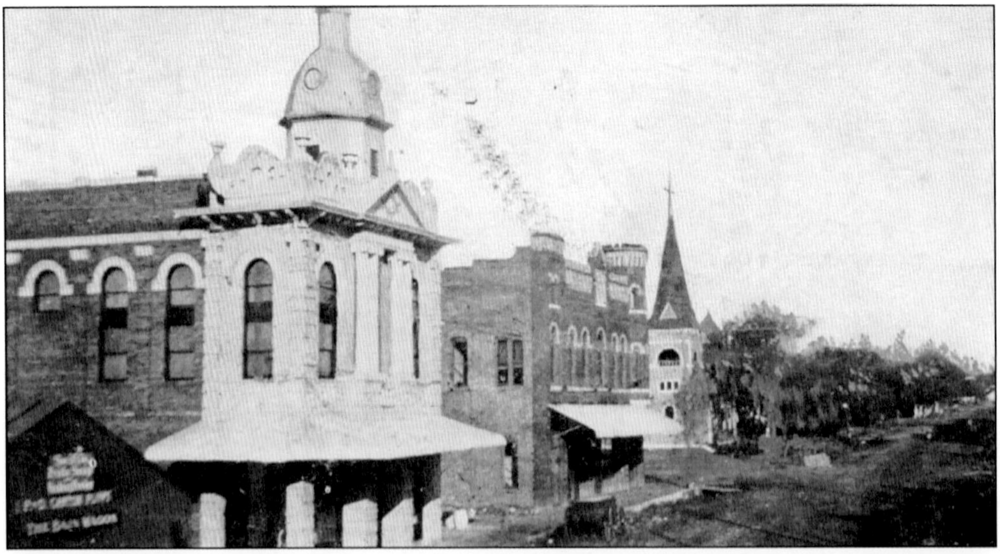

The northwest side of Dallas Street, pictured around 1908, was the location of an impressive row of buildings. From left to right are the Barn Wagon, the Masonic Temple, and the Ennis Lodge. Across Baylor Avenue, the First Baptist Church can be seen at the beginning of the residential area of the city.

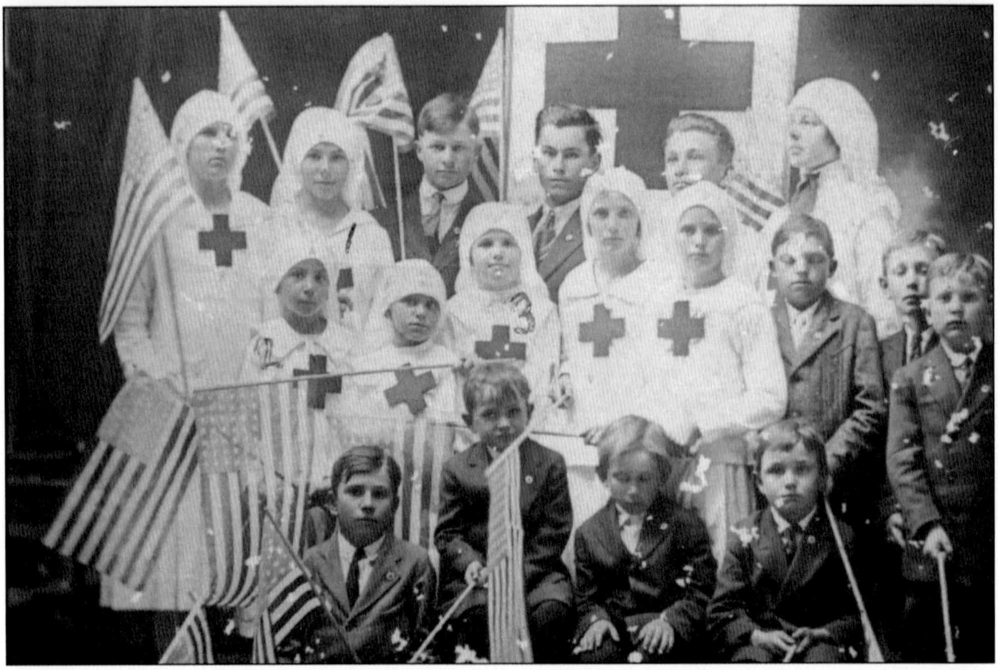

In 1916, the Cesko Narodni Sdruzeni was formed. The group organized at the Sokol during World War I and was one of the many Czech organizations in Texas formed to raise money to aid Czechoslovakia in gaining its independence. Pictured from left to right are (first row) an unidentified boy, Johnny Hrabina, and two unidentified boys; (second row) Mary Trojacek Laznovsky, Stacie Trojacek Hejny, Albie Trojacek Nesuda, Annie Haskovec Nekuza, Emilie Vitovsky Spaniel, Ed Honza, and two unidentified boys; (third row) Annie Honza Valek, Emma Trojacek Haskovec, Albert Petrash, George Vrla, Wesley Herzan, and Miss Lumpkin. (Courtesy of Dorothy Kudrna.)

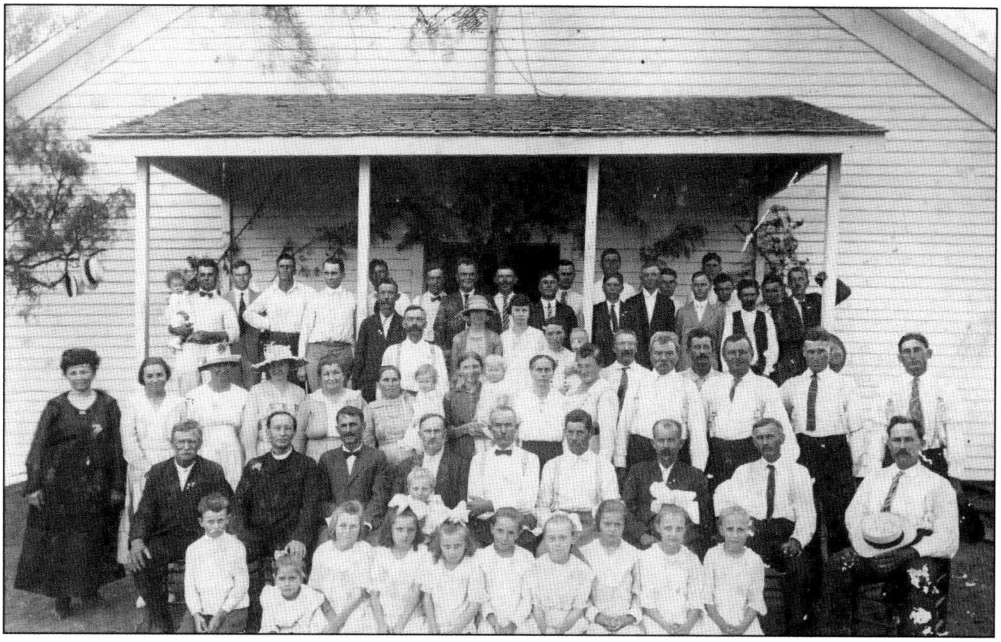

The first SPJST Hall, also known as the National Hall at that time, provided a place for its members to gather, such as those pictured here about 1915. It also opened its doors to other groups, such as Sokol, in those years before they had their own meeting place. (Courtesy of Ennis Sokol Museum.)

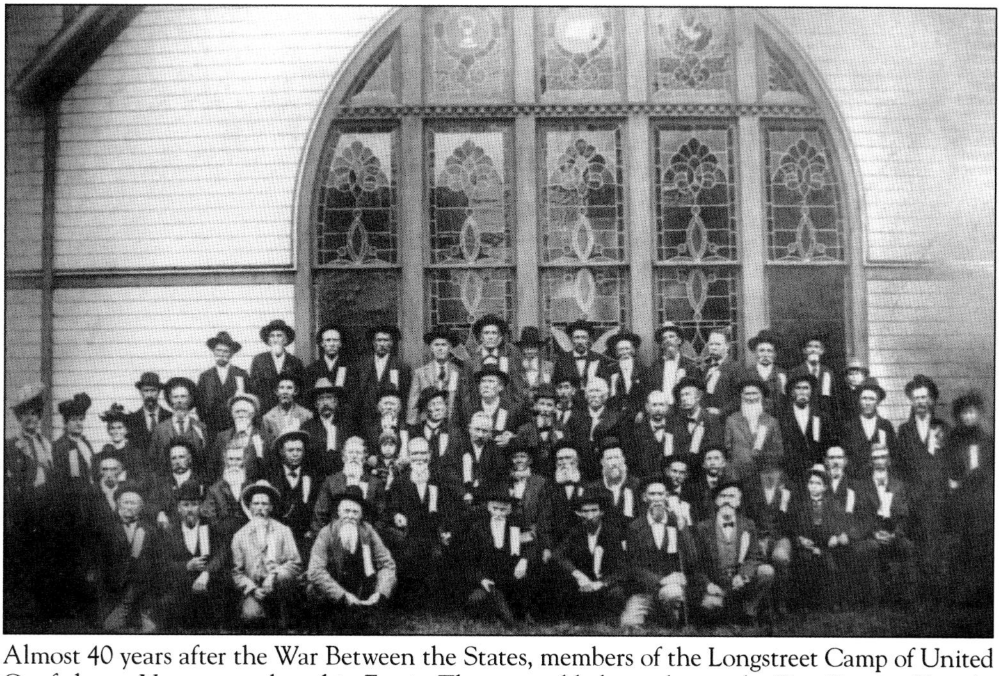

Almost 40 years after the War Between the States, members of the Longstreet Camp of United Confederate Veterans gathered in Ennis. They assembled together at the First Baptist Church, as pictured, and with them in the third row (far left), from left to right, are Katie Daffan, Mollie Daffan, and Caroline Spann Latimer. (Courtesy of family of Tina Beth Mulkey, given to Daffan-Latimer United Daughters of the Confederacy.)

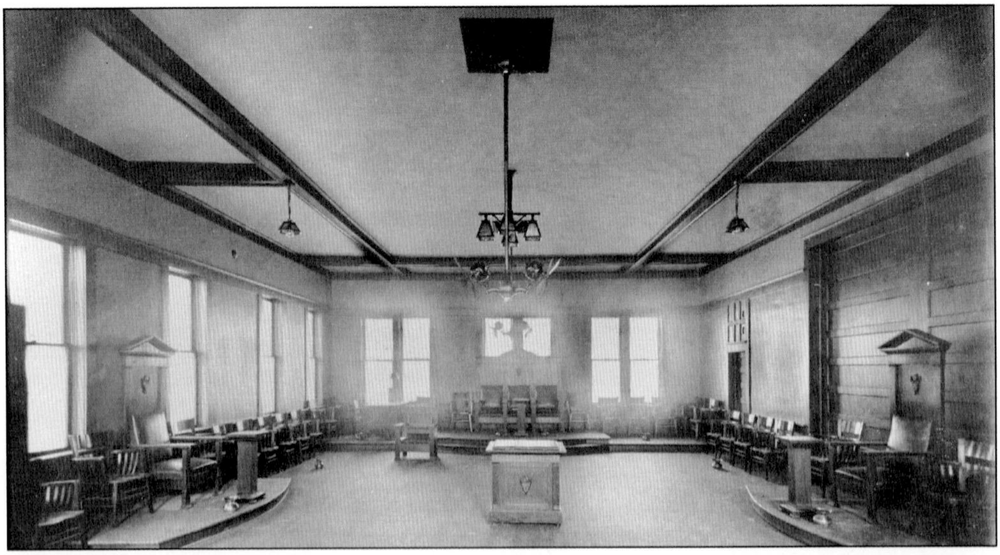

Members of the Order of Knights of Pythias met in Lodge Room No. 11, pictured above around 1911. They could also gather outside on a nearby rooftop, as seen below in a view that looks to the east. Among those pictured are S. Baldridge, W. D. Ferris, and Fred Abrams. Above them, intricately anchored from buildings on each side, appears to be the Knights of Pythias symbol. (Both courtesy of Ennis Public Library.)

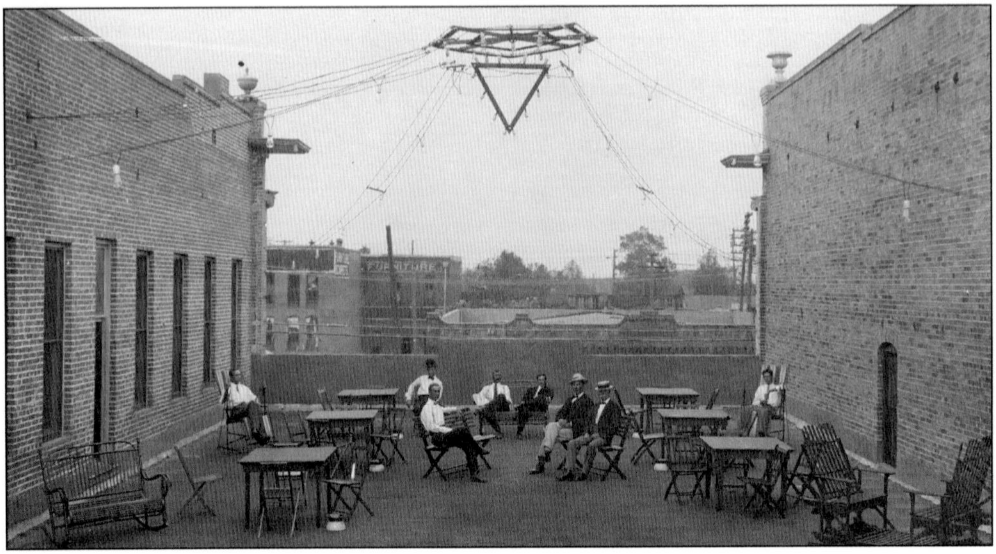

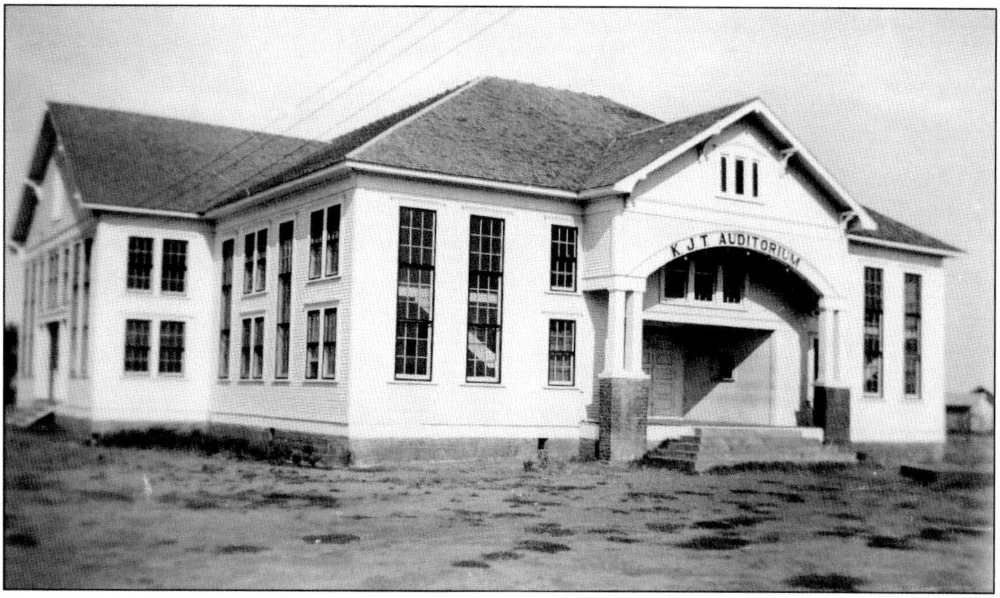

This KJT Auditorium was built around 1924. It was located at the same site where a newer KJT Hall stands today—at South Paris Street near Kaufman Avenue—and continues to serve as the meeting place for numerous community gatherings. (Courtesy of Mary Ann Novy Lamkin.)

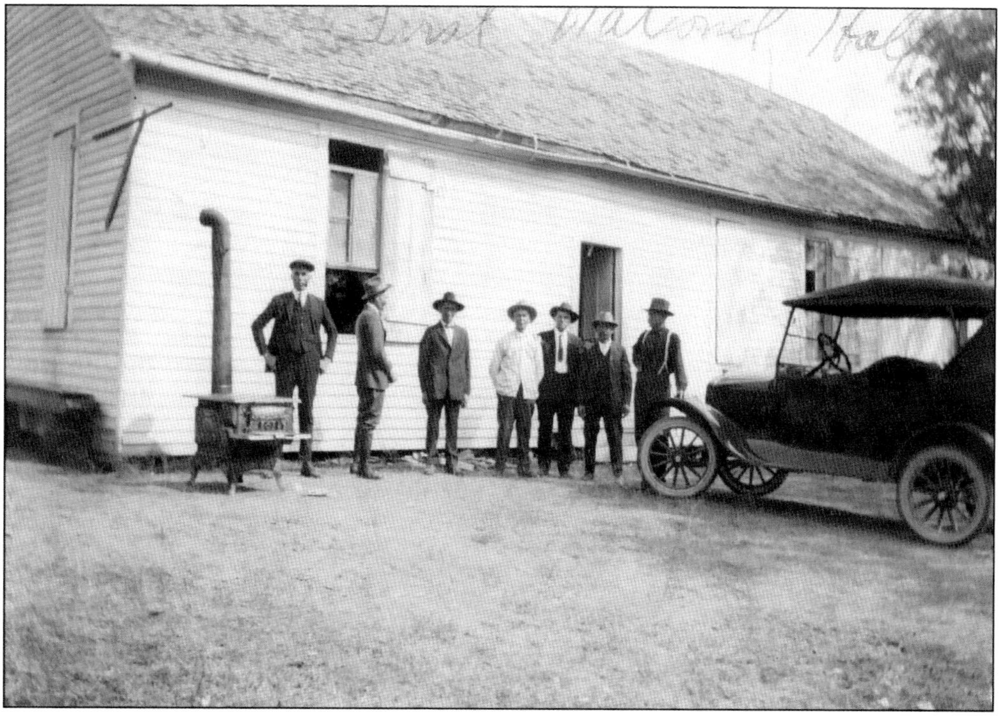

The first National Hall was built in 1901. Meetings were initially held at members' homes and businesses, including those of Josef Skroh and Vaclav Haskovec. The hall was built on land donated by Haskovec. Skroh loaned the funds needed for construction. Standing in front of the National Hall, from left to right, are Willie Trojacek, Will Haskovec, Joe Cvach, John Haskovec, unidentified, Frank Skrivanek, and Anton Trojacek. (Courtesy of Dorothy Kudrna.)

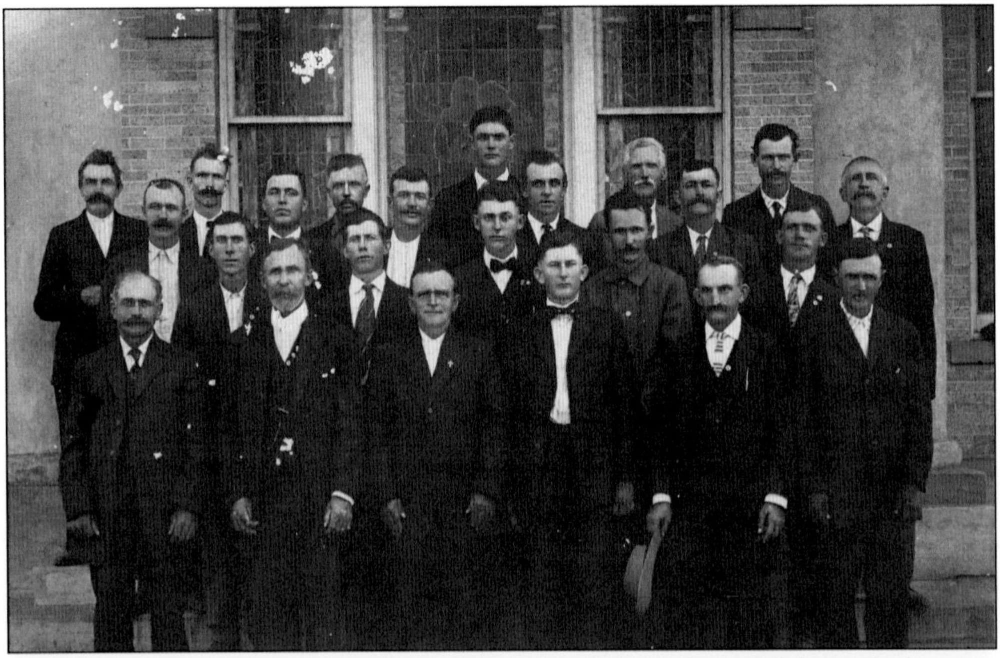

In 1908, several men gathered with the intention to form Sokol in Ennis. While they had a strong desire to be good Americans in their new country, they were just as determined to preserve their heritage. Pictured above, they included Anton Brozek, Robert Cech, Julius Chudej, Alois Dolezalik, L. O. Hosek, Joseph Houdek Sr., Frank Janicek, Karel Jares, John Jaresh, Thomas Jaresh, Alois Jurcik, Frank Moucka, Karel Moucka, Frank Novak, Frank Petr, Frank Petr Sr., Al Sedivy, Robert Skrivanek, Karel Sosolik, Joseph Toupal, Frank Toupal, Frank Trojacek, Frank Vrla, and Joseph Zazvorka. For many years, they met at the National Hall, now known as the SPJST No. 25. In 1913, Sokol members gathered below to rebuild after fire destroyed their first building within months of its completion. (Both courtesy of Ennis Sokol Museum.)

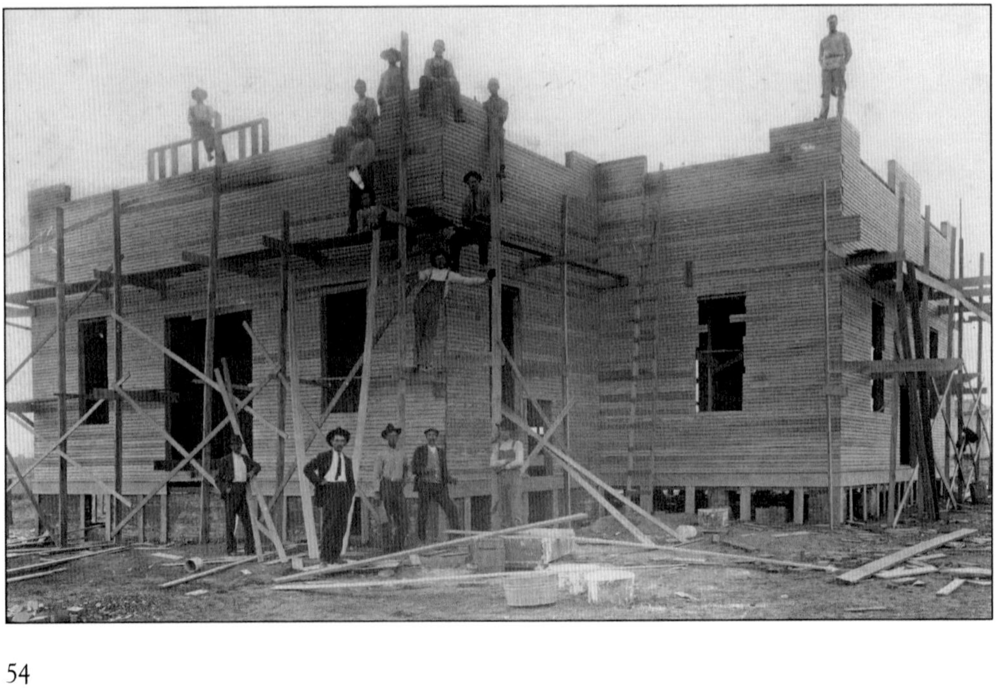

Three

THE WAY WE WERE

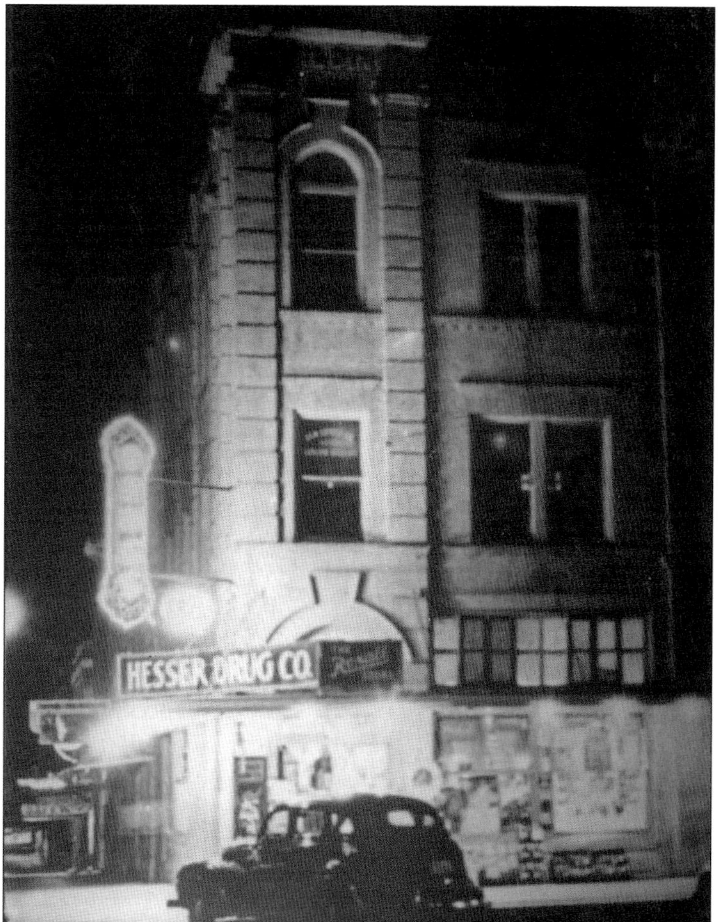

Hesser Drug Company, located at the northwest corner of Ennis Avenue and West Main Street, served as a focal point of the downtown area for many decades. Often referred to as the "Center of Town," it was a popular gathering place for young and old alike. (Courtesy of Ennis Public Library.)

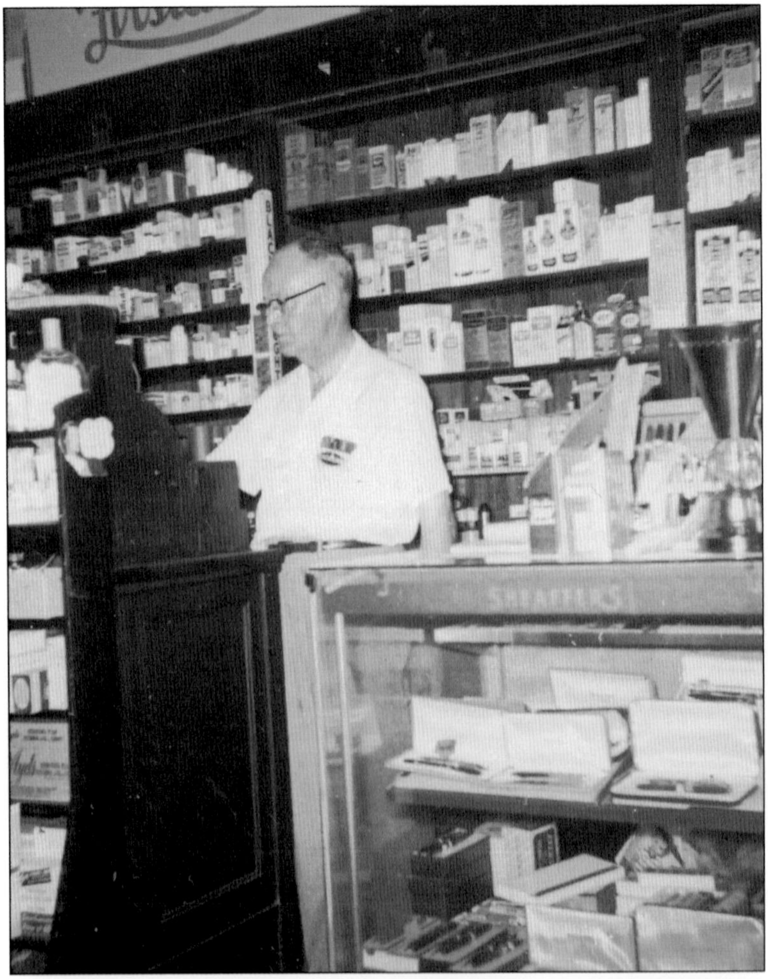

Bob Hesser opened the doors of his business in 1910. He is pictured with members of his pharmacy staff below at the Ennis Avenue and Main Street location in the 1950s; from left to right are Glen Felty, Bob Hesser, Vernon Tallent, and Thelma McDowell. At left is pharmacist Lee Roy Crow, who began working for Hesser Drugs in 1938. In the 1960s, the store was relocated a block west on Ennis Avenue. Hesser Drugs remained in business through 1996 when the building was destroyed by fire at which time the business closed. (Both courtesy of Lee Crow family.)

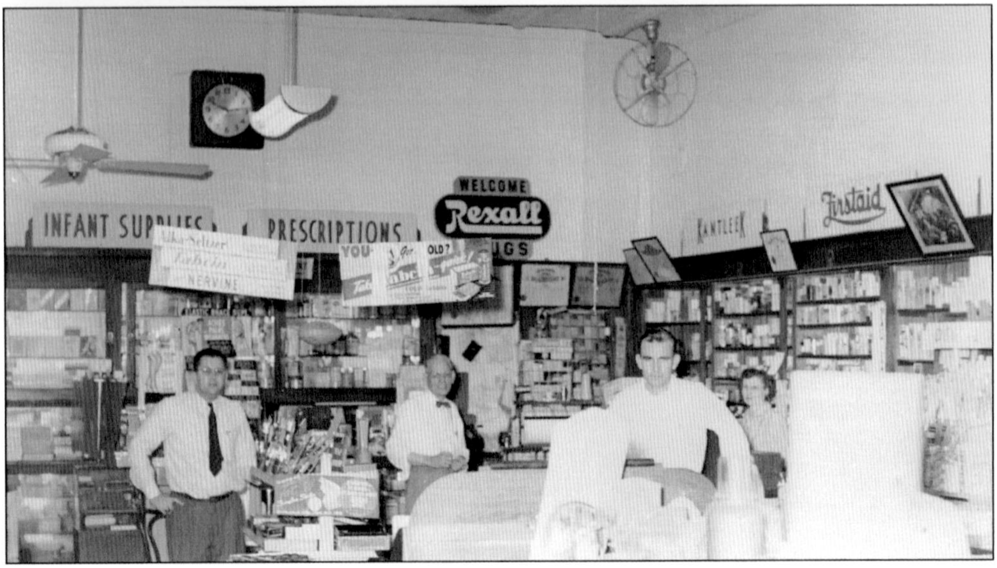

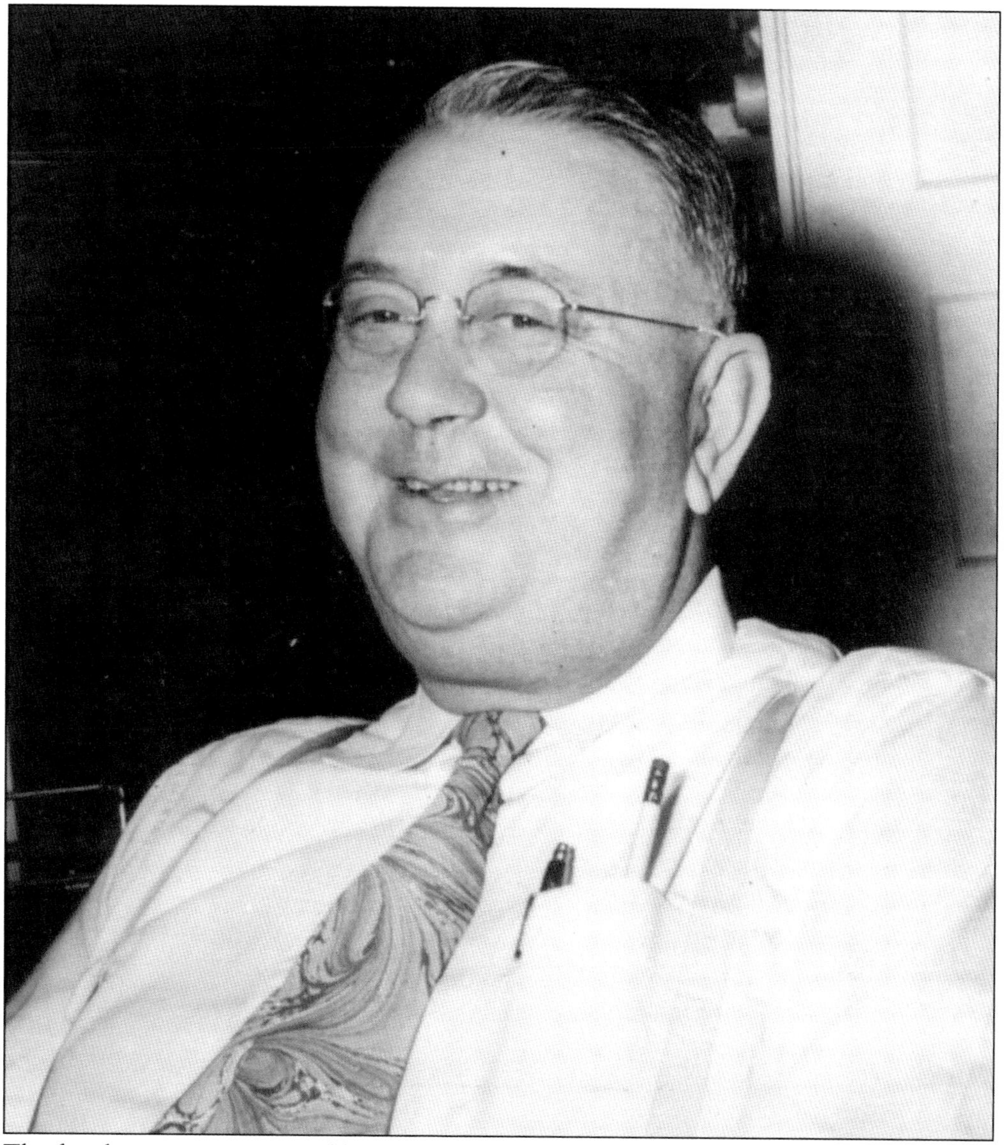

The first known newspaper publication in Ennis was the *Evening Argus*, founded by Col. Joe Rushing in 1873. Will C. Perry began the *Ennis Weekly Local*, renamed the *Ennis Evening Meteor* in 1891 and the *Ennis Daily News* in 1892. It was often the only source of information in those years, reporting local, national, and international news. The Nowlin family has been active with the *Ennis Daily News* for over 80 years, beginning in 1922. Chester A. Nowlin, pictured here, began with the newspaper as editor and later purchased controlling interest in 1939. After his death in 1947, his son Weldon took over until his early death in 1951. Chester's wife, Helen, and their son Gene then took over management of the paper along with son-in-law Charles Gentry. Charles continued in that role until 1997, when the paper was sold. Mary Helen Gentry, Chester's daughter, continues in the Nowlin tradition with her columns, "On the Avenue" and "Let's Talk Cooking," which still appear in the *Ennis Daily News* each week. (Courtesy of Mary Helen Nowlin Gentry.)

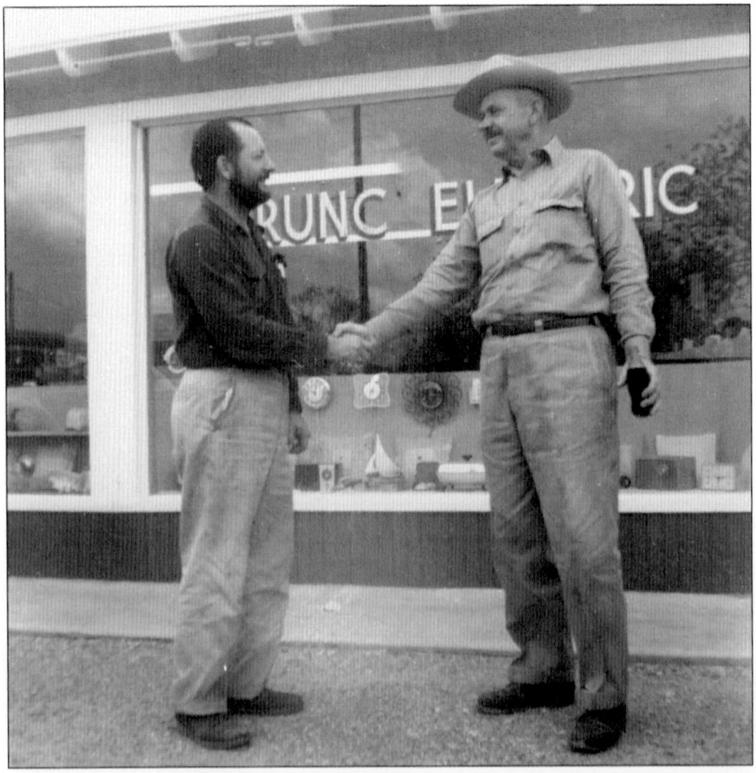

Family-owned businesses continued to be a way of life in Ennis onward into the 20th century. Strunc Electric was located at 409 East Ennis Avenue. George Strunc (left, shaking hands with an unidentified man in front of his store) was the son of a Czech immigrant. He trained as an electrician before establishing his own business in the mid-1950s. (Courtesy of Otile Strunc.)

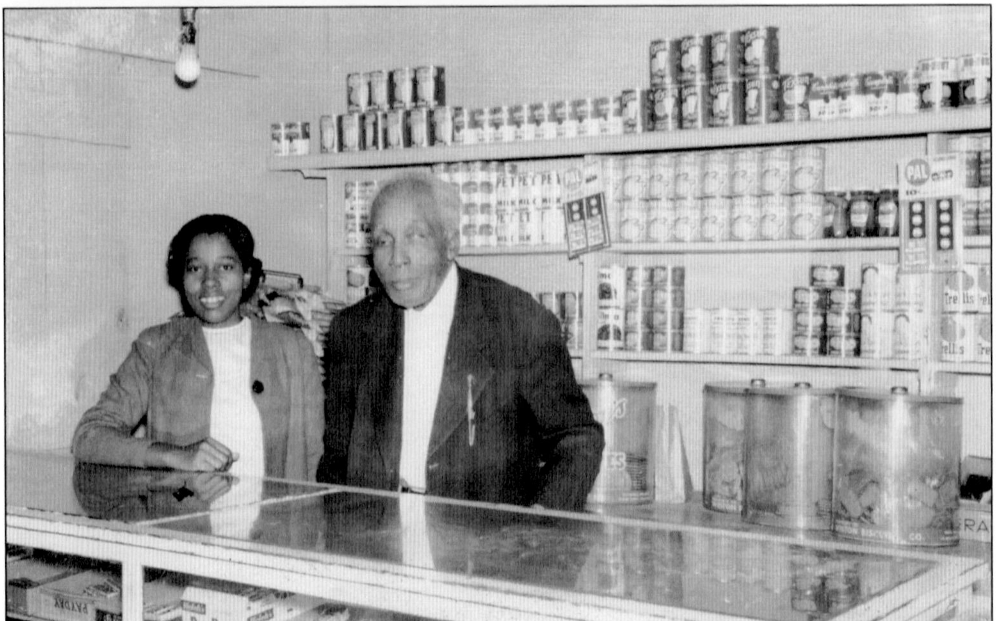

Jettie Laura Coleman and her father, John Coleman, pictured inside their store in the early 1950s, are another example of a family-owned and run business that served the Ennis community for several decades. Located at Tyler and Ripley Streets, the Coleman family grocery store was established around 1917. (Courtesy of Ennis Public Library.)

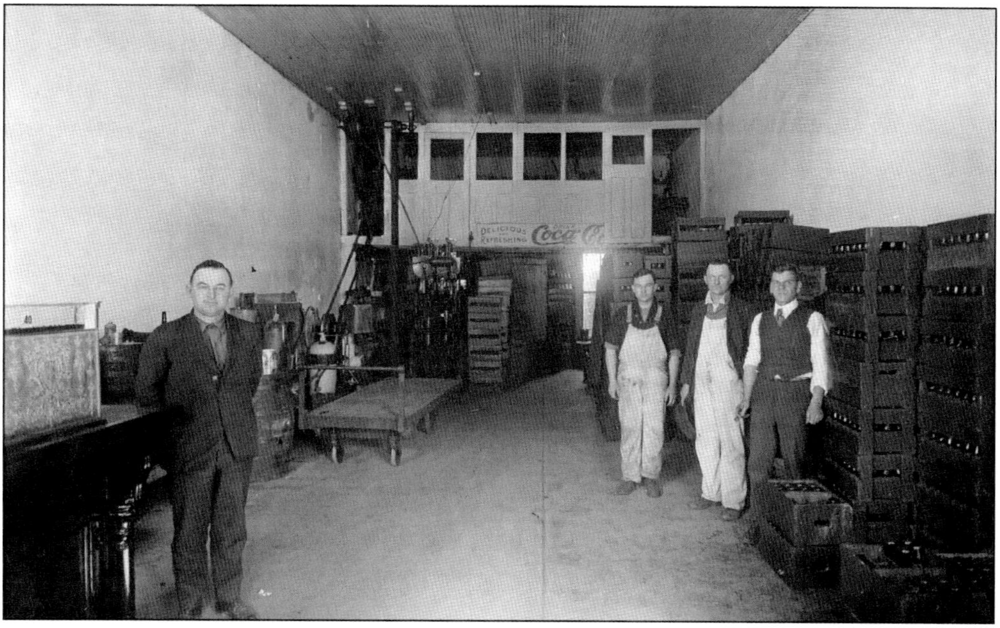

In 1928, Joseph Houdek (far left) sold his Coca-Cola bottling plant to his brother, Stanley Houdek Sr. (third from the left). Shortly after, it became a Nehi Bottling Plant at the same location in the 100 block of northeast Main Street, across from the railroad depot. Nehi Soda was a longtime favorite for many in the 1940s and 1950s. (Courtesy of Jeanette Houdek.)

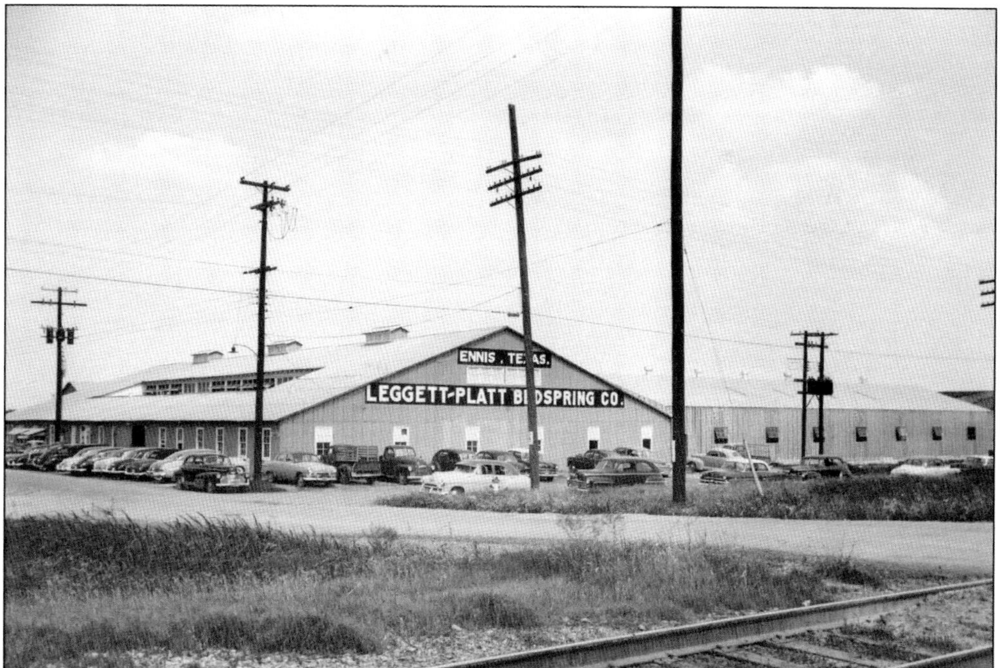

The Leggett and Platt Bedspring Company, established in Ennis in 1946, first opened operations in the facility pictured at Southeast Main and Lampasas Streets. Relocated along Highway 85 in 1996, it is one of the oldest continuing businesses in the city. (Courtesy of Ennis Public Library.)

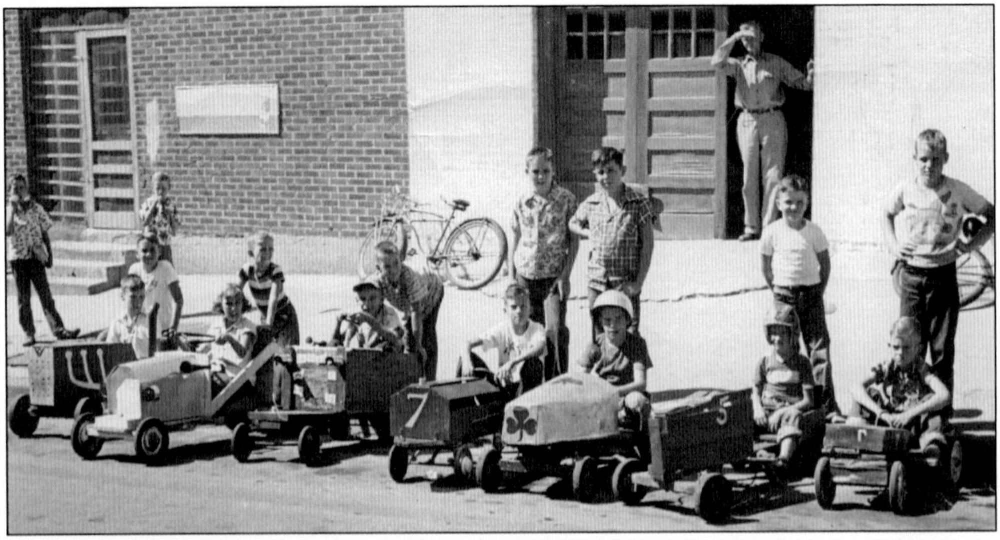

At a Derby Day in Ennis in the late 1940s, each child had his or her own, and often homemade, "go kart." They eagerly awaited the competition to begin. When it was over, Sharon Percival, second from the left, was the day's winner. (Courtesy of Telfair family.)

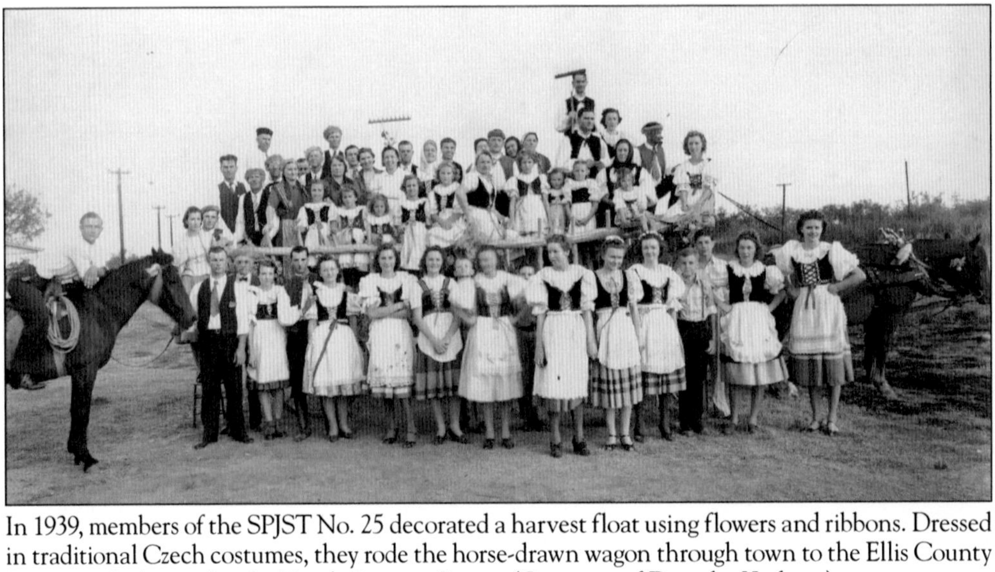

In 1939, members of the SPJST No. 25 decorated a harvest float using flowers and ribbons. Dressed in traditional Czech costumes, they rode the horse-drawn wagon through town to the Ellis County Fairgrounds, located at far North Preston Street. (Courtesy of Dorothy Kudrna.)

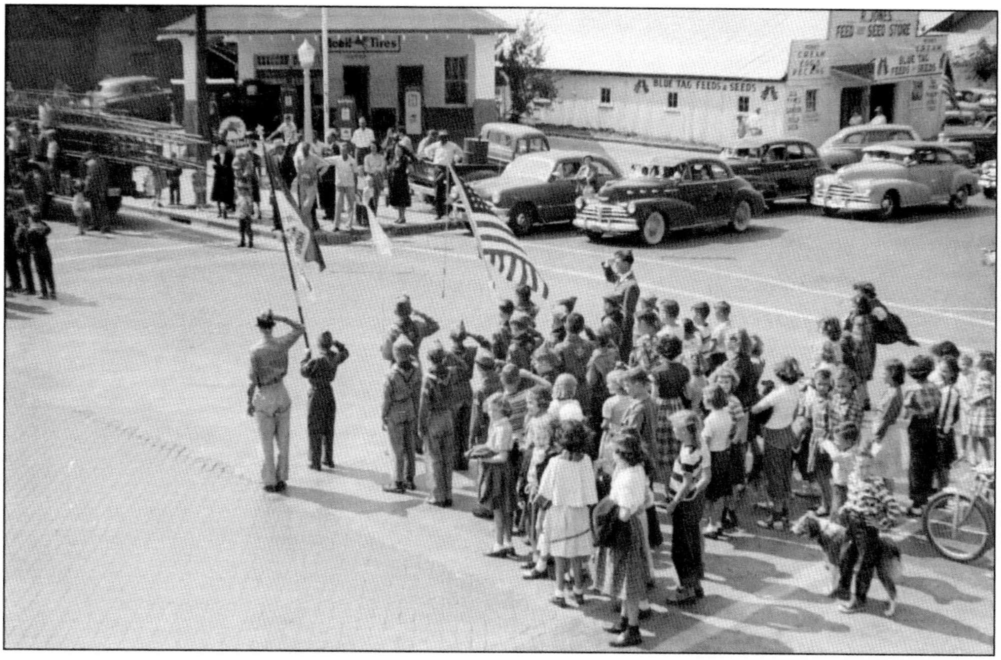

Ennis has always loved a good parade. The Kids Day parade in the late 1940s made its way down Dallas Street. At the corner of West Brown and South Dallas Streets (above) are a Mobil Station and R. Jones Feed and Seed Store along Brown Street. The old Burrs Department Store (below), is seen in the background as parade participants walk by. (Both courtesy of Telfair family.)

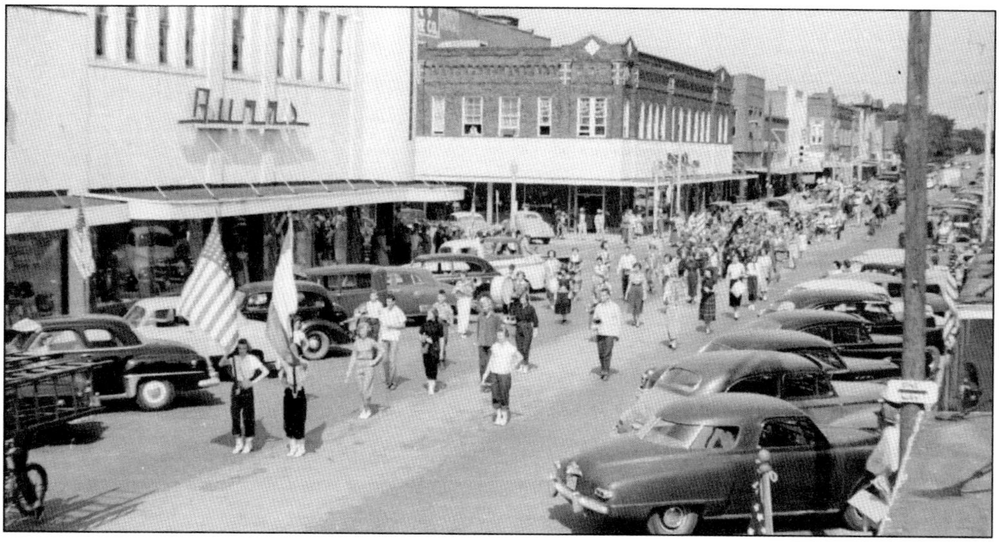

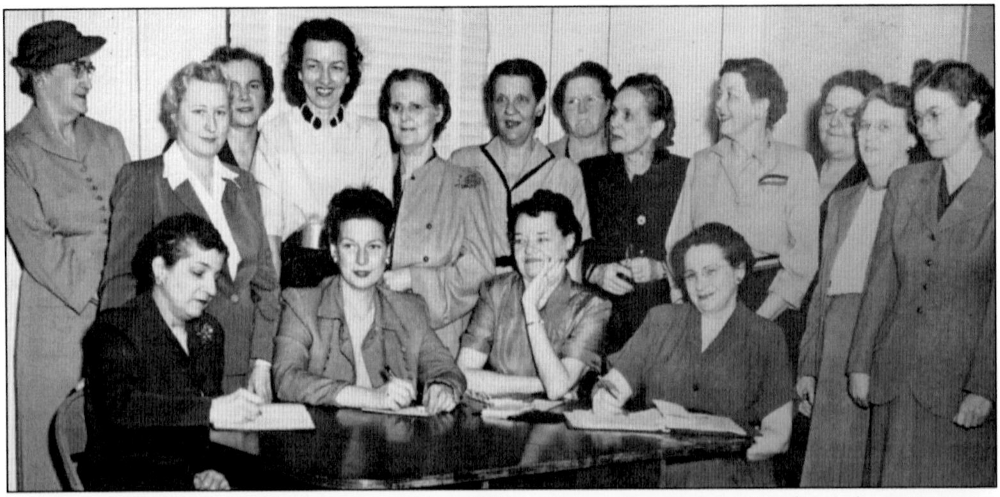

The Ennis Hospital Auxiliary organized in 1951 to serve the community through assisting its hospital. Among the first members were, from left to right, (first row) Lena McCall, Marian Gehrig, Muff Atwood, and Irma Hesser; (second row) Lillian Dunkerley, Frances Cerf, Gertrude Griffith, Addie Pinson, Nettie Andrews, Mary Rider, Ada Moser, Metka Templeton, Eugenia Todd, Sue Parker, Lillie Tolleson, and Linnie Morgan. (Courtesy of Sue Kirkpatrick Parker family.)

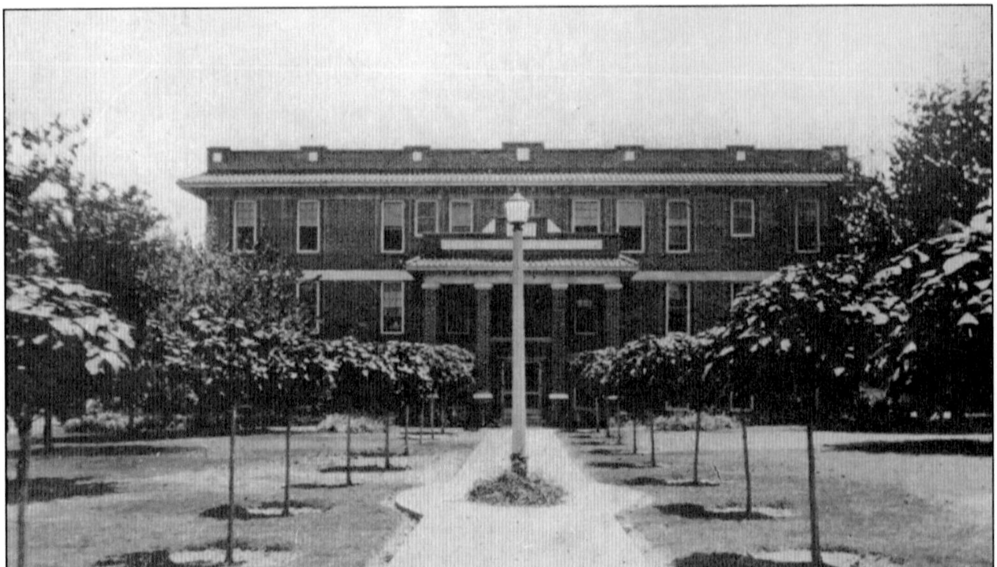

The Ennis Municipal Hospital opened in 1924. Some of the first doctors providing medical care through the hospital were Dr. W. E. Campbell, Dr. L. E. Clark, Dr. C. P. Cook, Dr. A. J. Cox, Dr. J. W. Germany, Dr. J. E. Gilcrest, Dr. C. E. Gray, Dr. R. A. McCall, Dr. Walter McCall, Dr. John Rains, Dr. F. L. Story, Dr. J. S. Terry, Dr. A. L. Thomas, and Dr. Tom White. (Courtesy of City of Ennis.)

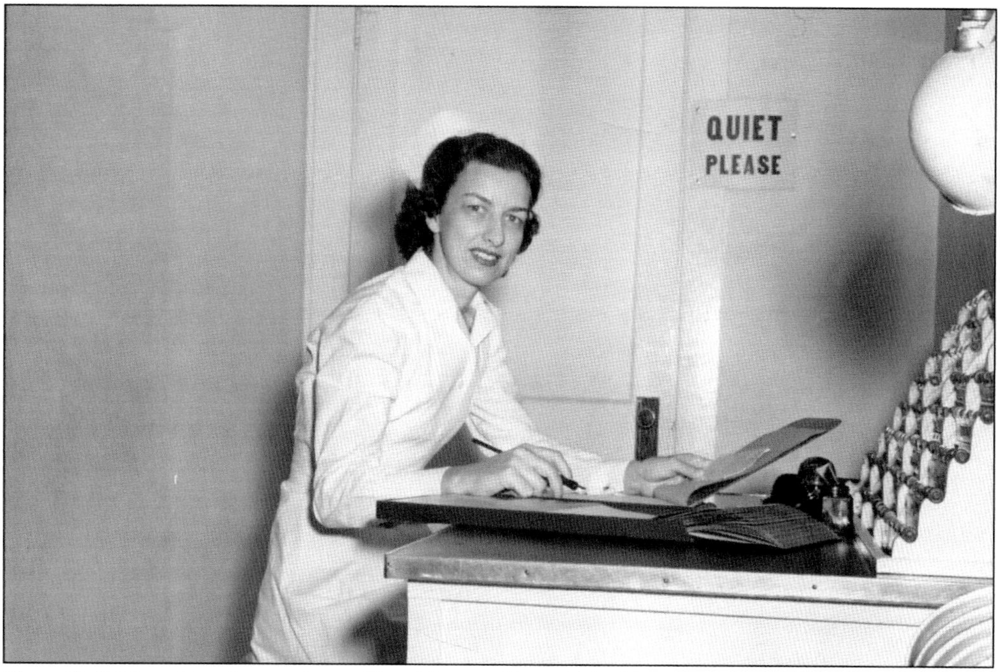

Nesta Bell, Flora Henderson, Lucy Worthley, and Lora Zaludek were among the first nursing staff to work at the new Ennis Municipal Hospital. Unlike today, home for many of these "resident" nurses were small sleeping rooms on the third floor of the hospital. In 1945, the city built a separate Nurses' Home with five bedrooms for them. It was built with bricks from an old building once used at the Ellis County Fairgrounds in Ennis. Some of the nursing staff of the early 1950s included Addie Pearl Pinson, pictured above, who worked at the hospital from 1949 to 1952. Seen below are Carolyn Lavada Wilson Griffin (left) and Zephr Collier, who worked at the hospital from 1926 to 1971. (Both courtesy of Ennis Public Library.)

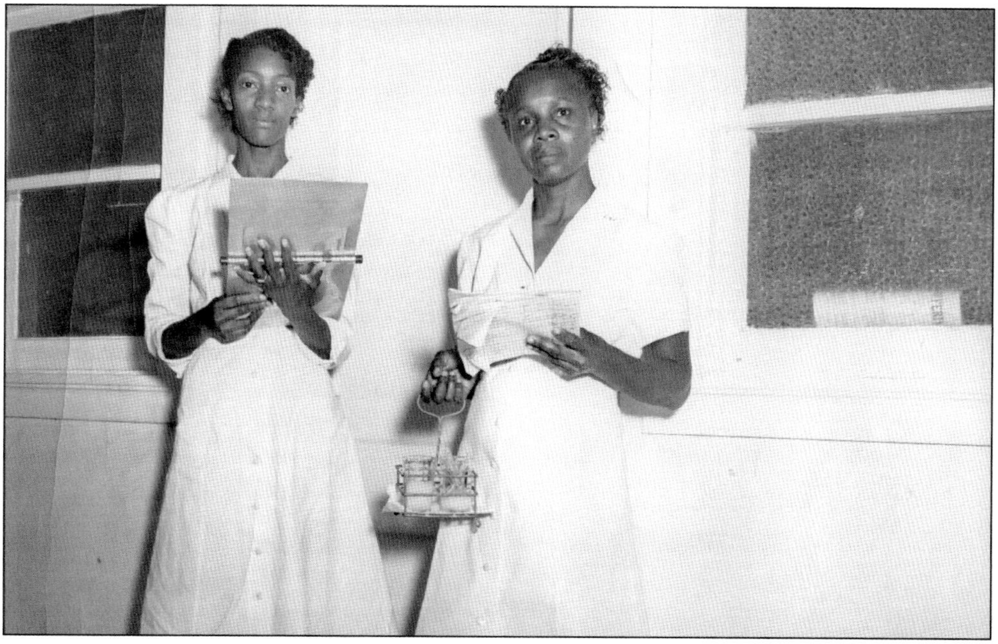

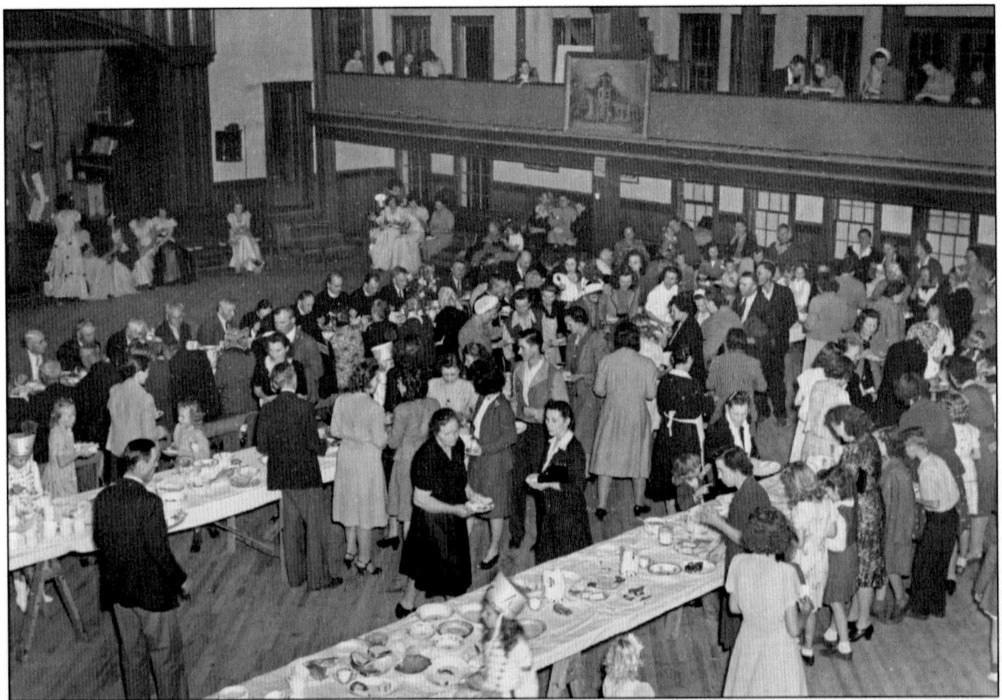

The KJT Hall, shown around 1940, was the site of many gatherings through the years, including wedding receptions, church celebrations, and family reunions. (Courtesy of Mary Ann Novy Lamkin.)

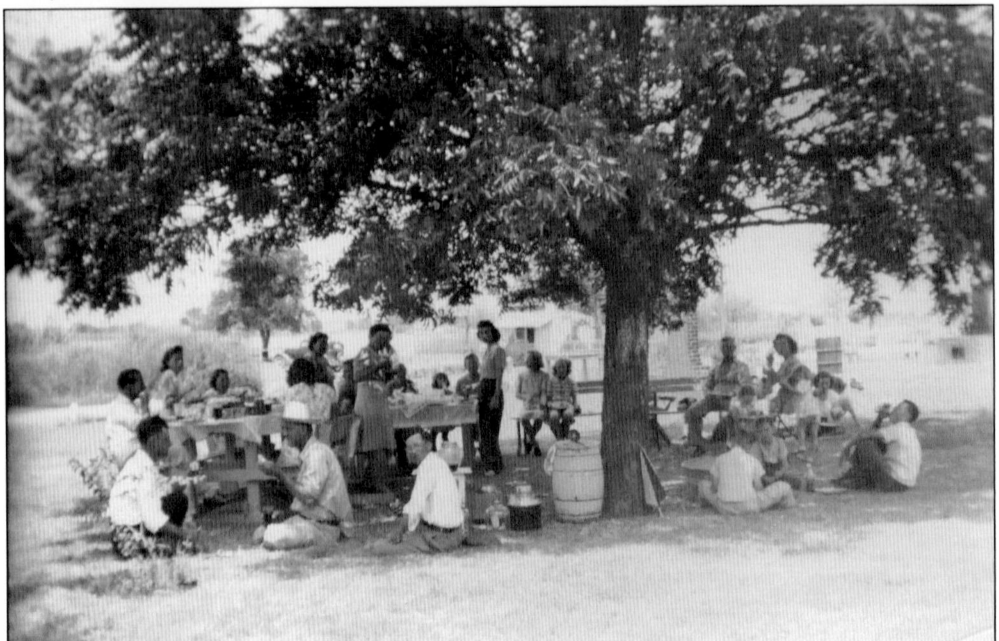

City Park was a popular spot for families through the years. Several families, including the Hejnys, Skrivaneks, Sebetkas, and Struncs, gather for a picnic at the park in 1945. (Courtesy of Frank Strunc family.)

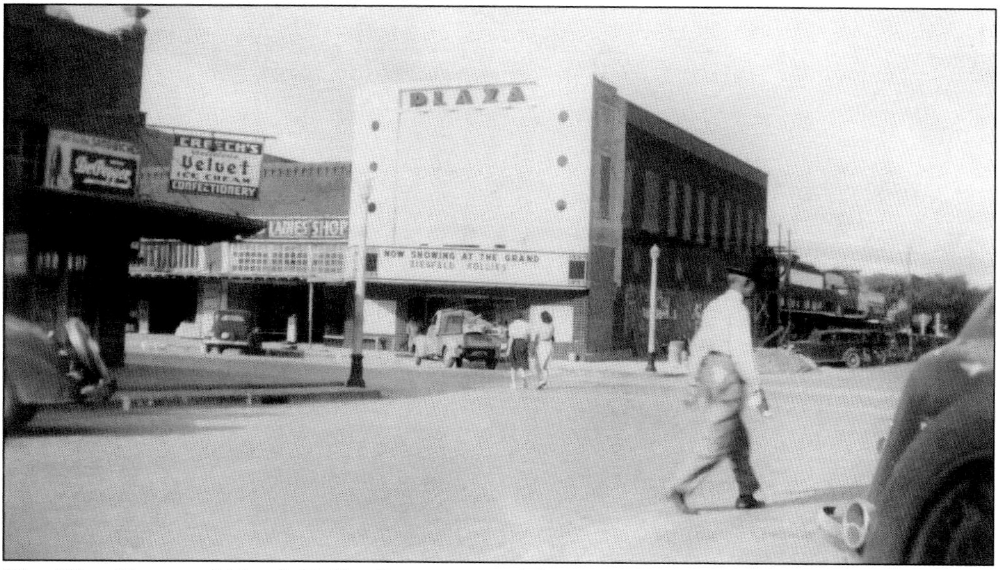

The West Knox and North Dallas Street area of downtown Ennis was a busy intersection in 1946 and never more so than after the reopening of the newly remodeled Plaza Theater. Vlasta Kubin and Mary Jurik, pictured above, are walking toward the theater, where the current feature is *Ziegfeld's Follies*. Creech's Confectionary, another popular downtown store, is seen across from the theater. (Courtesy of Frank Strunc family.)

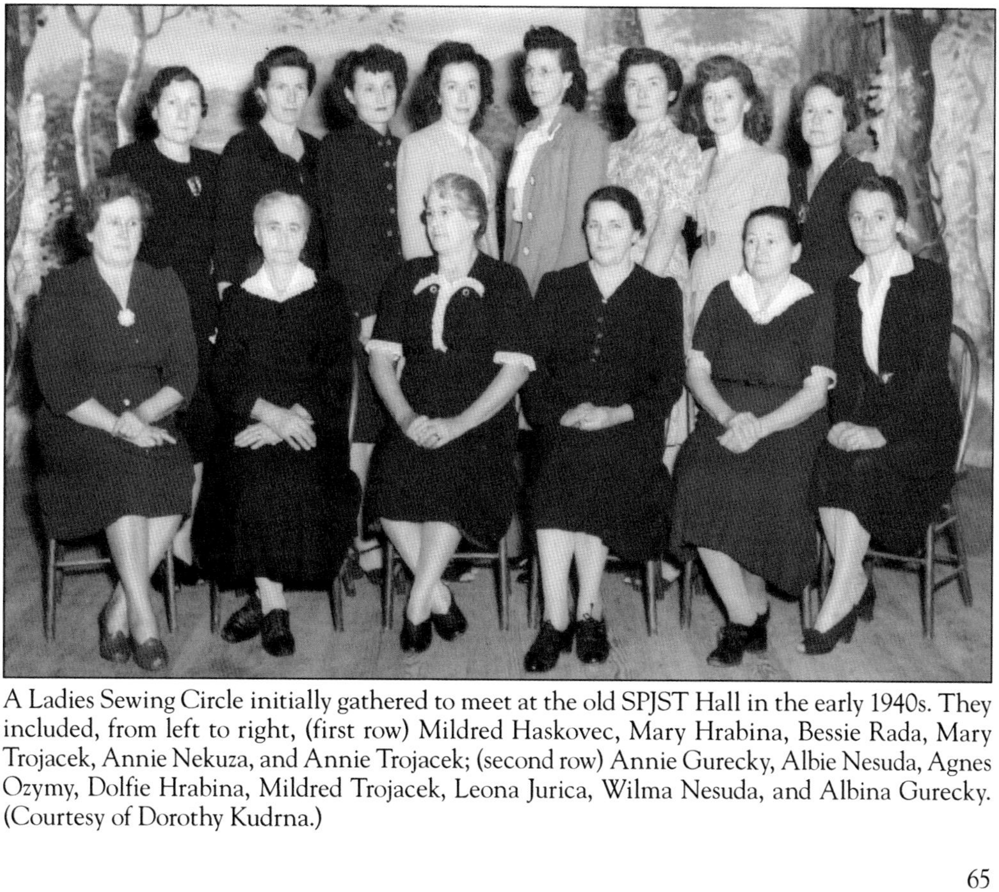

A Ladies Sewing Circle initially gathered to meet at the old SPJST Hall in the early 1940s. They included, from left to right, (first row) Mildred Haskovec, Mary Hrabina, Bessie Rada, Mary Trojacek, Annie Nekuza, and Annie Trojacek; (second row) Annie Gurecky, Albie Nesuda, Agnes Ozymy, Dolfie Hrabina, Mildred Trojacek, Leona Jurica, Wilma Nesuda, and Albina Gurecky. (Courtesy of Dorothy Kudrna.)

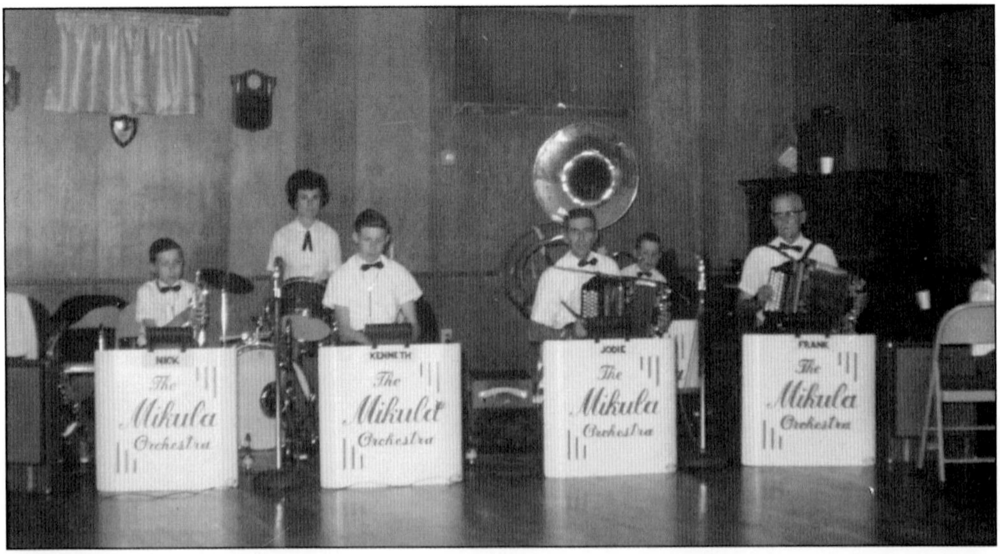

The Mikula Orchestra began as a family band in the 1960s. Jodie Mikula began the band with his wife, his three sons, and his uncle Frank Mikula. Pictured above from left to right are (first row) Nick, Ken, Jodie, and Frank; (second row) Rose and Andy. Jodie's sons Andy, Ken, and Nick continue their father's legacy, performing yearly at the National Polka Festival in Ennis. The Jodie Mikula Orchestra, still very much a family band, continues into the new century. Below from left to right are (first row) Pat Zapletal; (second row) Andy Mikula, Nick Mikula, Charlie Patak, and Ken Mikula; (third row) Mike Marek. (Both courtesy of Mikula family.)

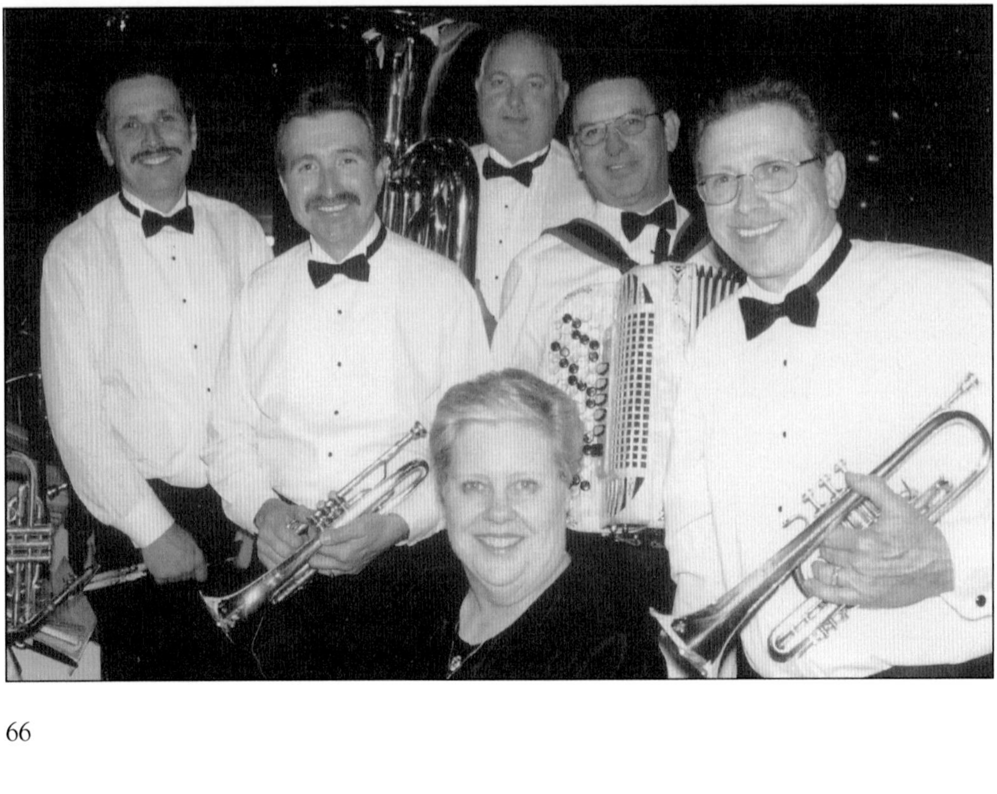

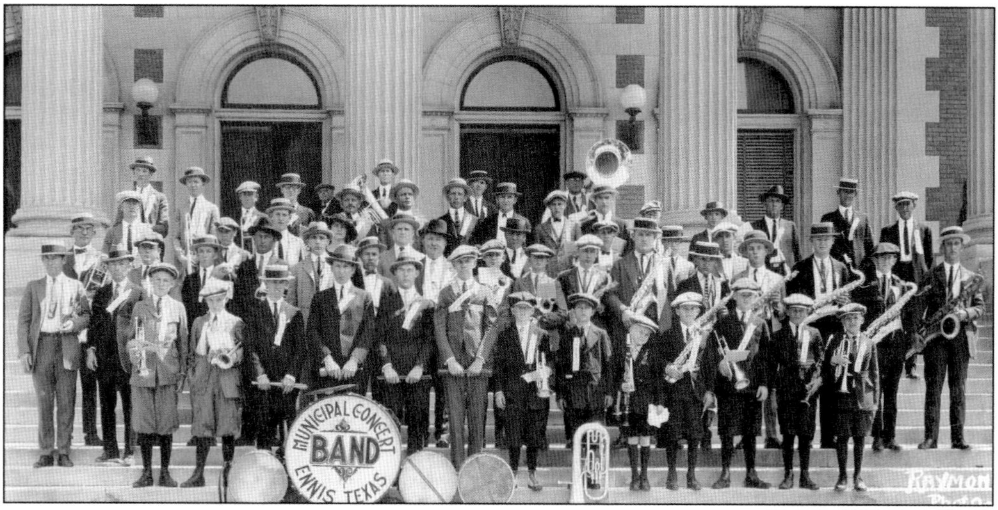

The Municipal Concert Band of Ennis included members of all ages and is pictured above at a Dallas location where they were performing. Early news accounts state that in the 1920s the band was sponsored by the Lions Club. (Courtesy of Olin Brown.)

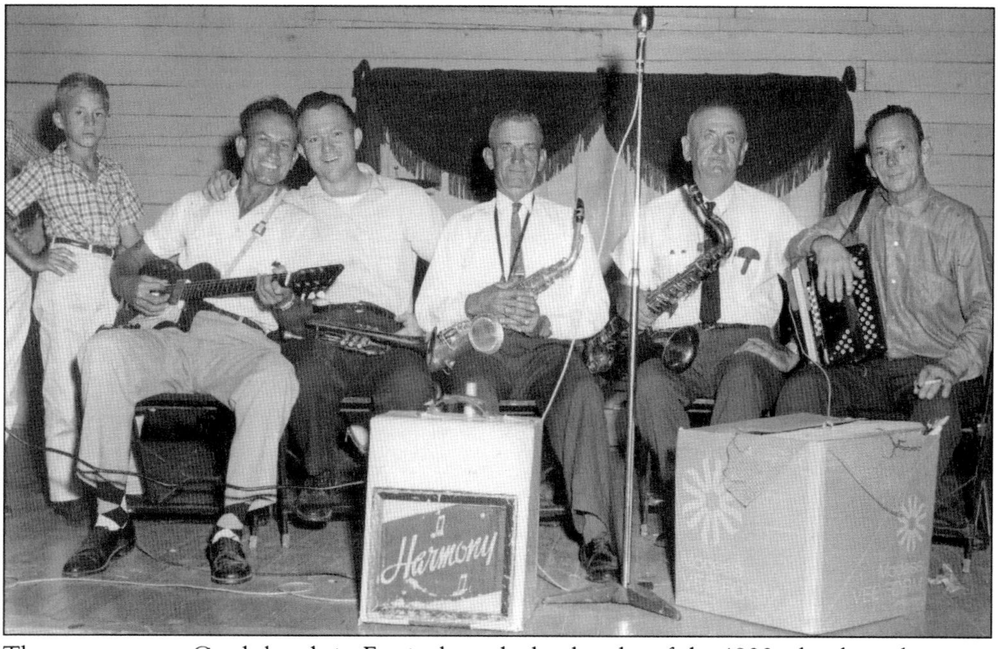

There were many Czech bands in Ennis through the decades of the 1900s that kept the music playing over the generations, including the Frank Kubin Band and the Eric Honza Band. Another was the John Dlabaj Band, pictured here in the 1950s; from left to right, they are John Dlabaj, Charlie Melin, Stanley Vrla, Louis Macalik, Wesley F. Laznovsky, and John Dlabaj. (Courtesy of Ennis Sokol Museum.)

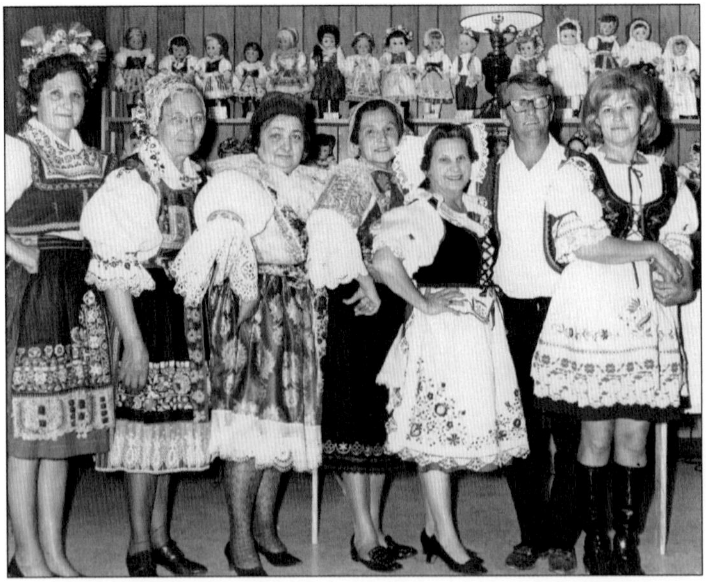

The beauty of Czechoslovakian embroidery is still found in traditional Czech Kroj worn during the National Polka Festival and other events in Ennis. Gathered in front of a collection of dolls in traditional Czech costume owned by Agnes Houdek are, from left to right, an unidentified woman, Vojteska Janicek, Agnes Houdek, two unidentified women, Jack Henning, and Joyce Henning. (Courtesy of Ennis Public Library.)

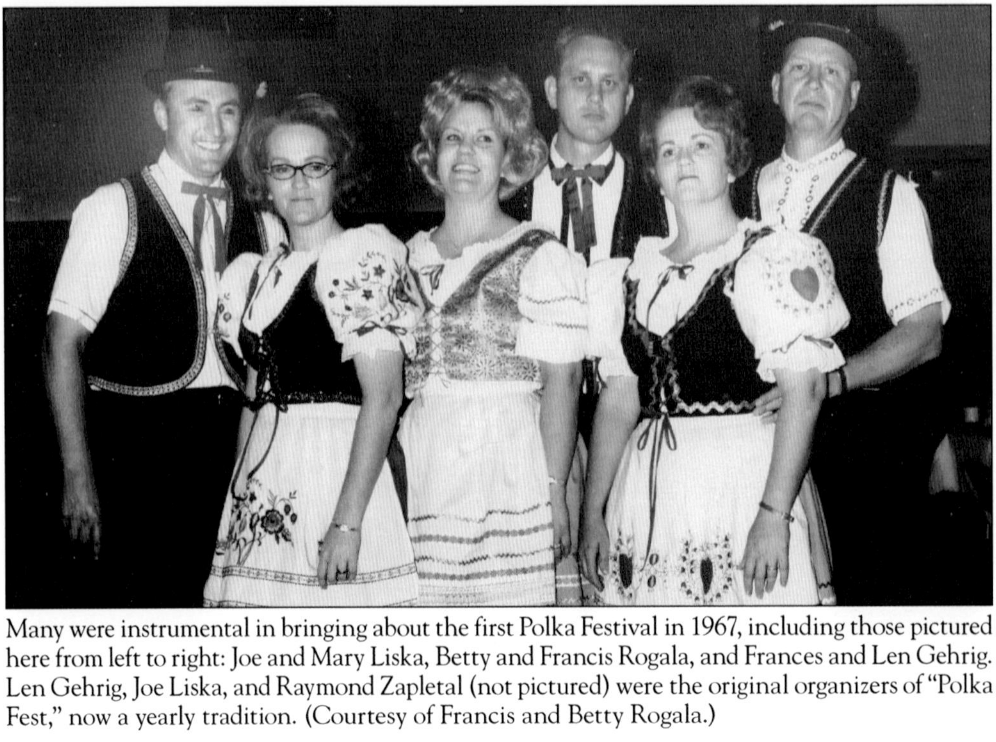

Many were instrumental in bringing about the first Polka Festival in 1967, including those pictured here from left to right: Joe and Mary Liska, Betty and Francis Rogala, and Frances and Len Gehrig. Len Gehrig, Joe Liska, and Raymond Zapletal (not pictured) were the original organizers of "Polka Fest," now a yearly tradition. (Courtesy of Francis and Betty Rogala.)

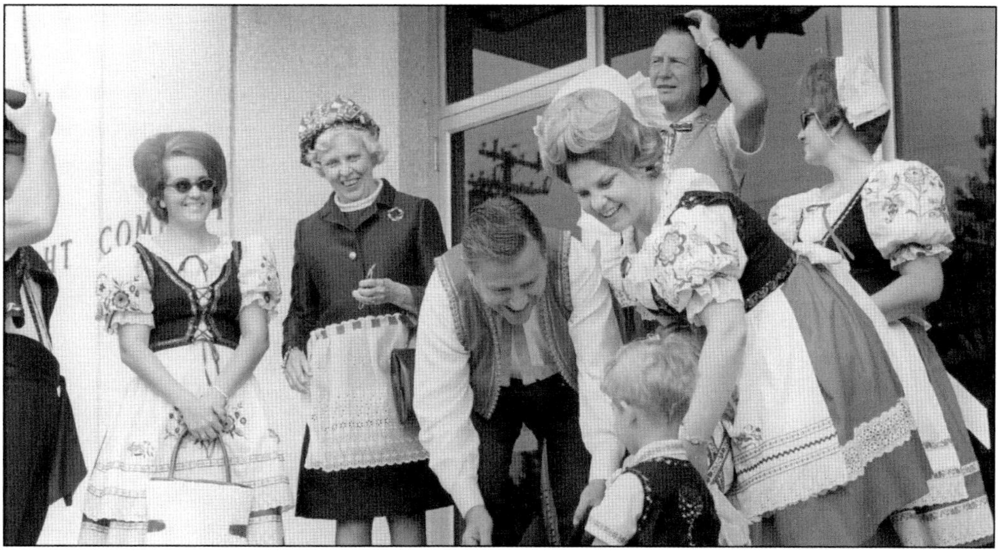

In the 1960s, "A Little Bit of Czechoslovakia" came to Ennis with the arrival of the National Polka Festival. The late Sen. Ralph Yarborough served as grand marshal in an early Polka Festival parade and, like thousands since, enjoyed the festivities. Pictured from left to right are (first row) Mary Liska, ? Yarborough, Sen. Ralph Yarborough, Betty Rogala, and David Lekar; (second row) Len Gehrig and Frances Gehrig. (Courtesy of Ennis Public Library.)

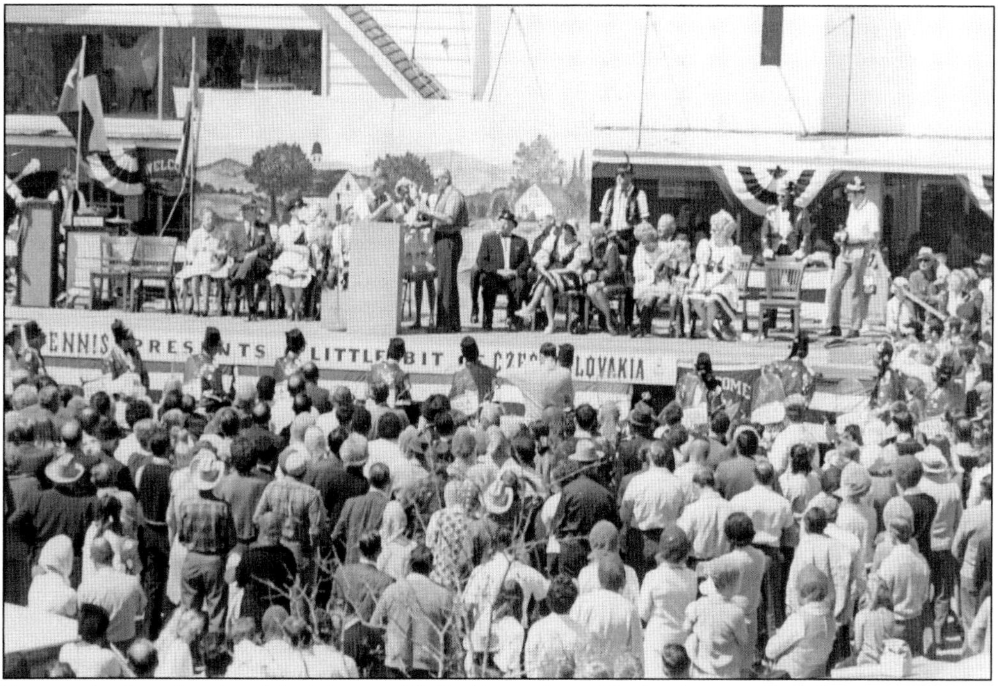

During the first decade of the National Polka Festival, an 18-wheeler provided the stage on Main and Knox Streets for "A Little Bit of Czechoslovakia." (Courtesy of Francis and Betty Rogala.)

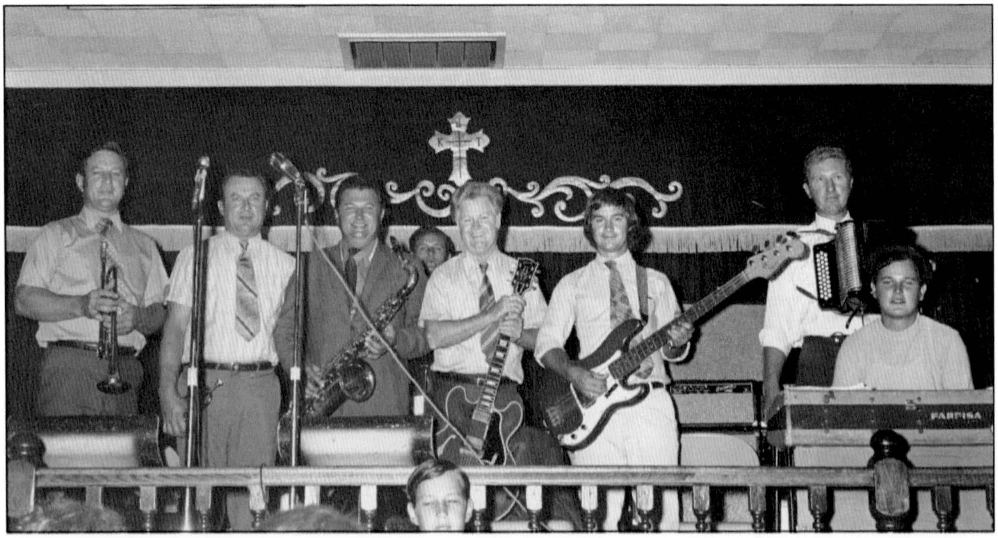

One of the highlights of National Polka Festival is the music played at each of the several participating halls, which keeps the dancers on the floor. A number of Czech and family bands have been the standard at Polka Fest, including the Johnny Mensik Band. The members, pictured above from left to right, are Joe Valek, Louis Valek, Johnny Mensik, David Dlabaj, Torchey McCluney, Randy McCluney, Andrew Potiska, and Tony Vitovsky. (Both courtesy of Francis and Betty Rogala.)

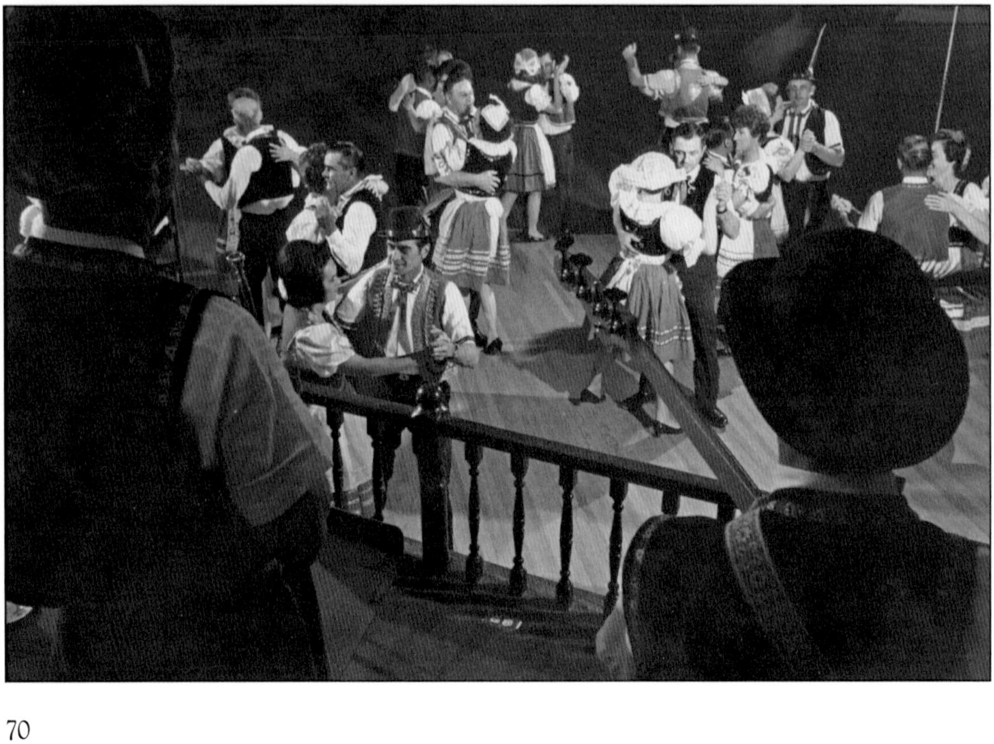

Four

Where the Rail and Cotton Met

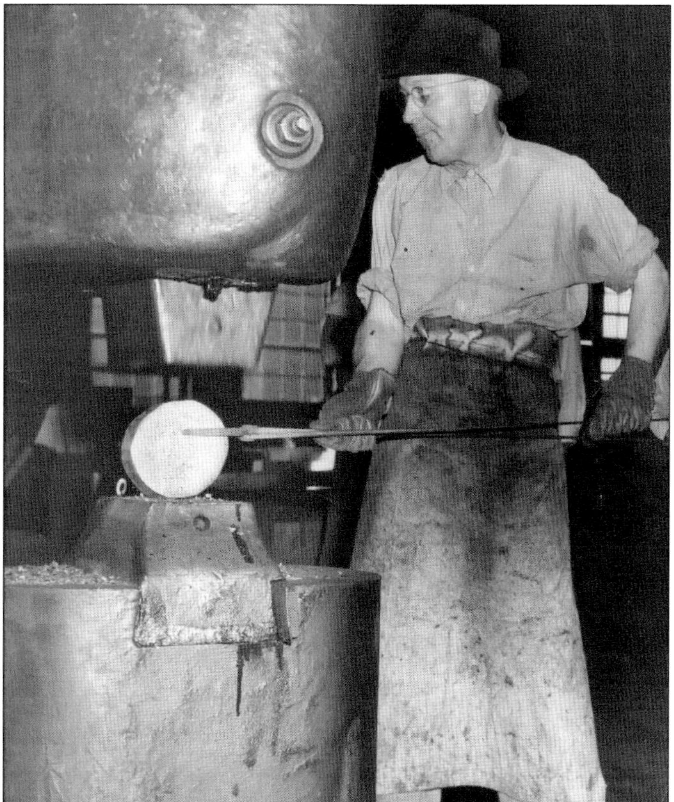

When the city won the contract for the roundhouse, machine shops, and division headquarters, many job opportunities were created. Ronald C. Percival, pictured here around 1941, was a Hammersmith at the Southern Pacific Blacksmith Shop in Ennis. He began with the Houston and Texas Central Railroad in 1911. The "great" steam hammer, at left, weighed around 3,500 pounds. (Courtesy of Ennis Public Library.)

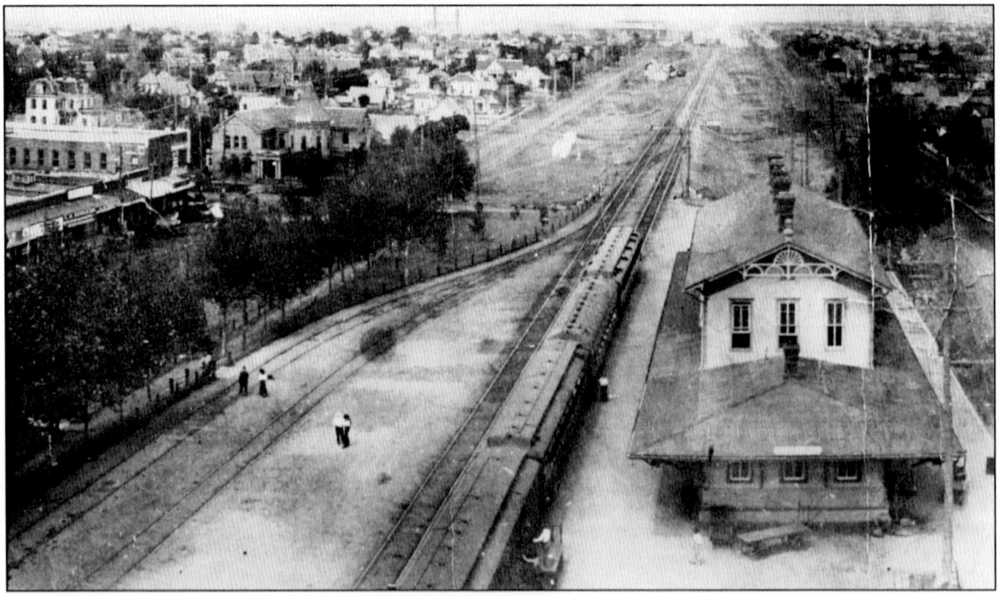

The original passenger depot was built in 1872 by pioneer carpenter John H. Stacey. A new depot, pictured above, was built to replace it in 1892. The first floor served as the passenger depot and had a lunch counter, two waiting rooms, and a dispatch office. Division headquarters were located on the second floor, along with the offices of the division superintendant. In the mid-1920s, an average of 10 trains a day came through Ennis. In the early 1930s, fire damaged much of the depot interior. The building was then torn down, except for the baggage area to the south side. The railroad restaurant, pictured below to the right of the old depot, then became the new passenger depot. It was built in 1915 primarily as a restaurant for railroad employees and travelers. (Below, courtesy of City of Ennis.)

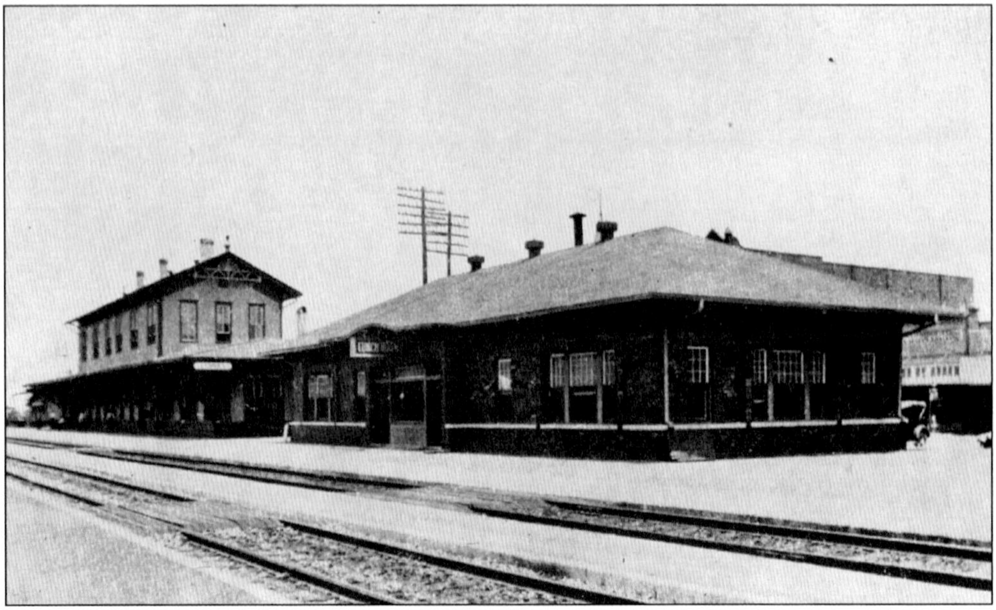

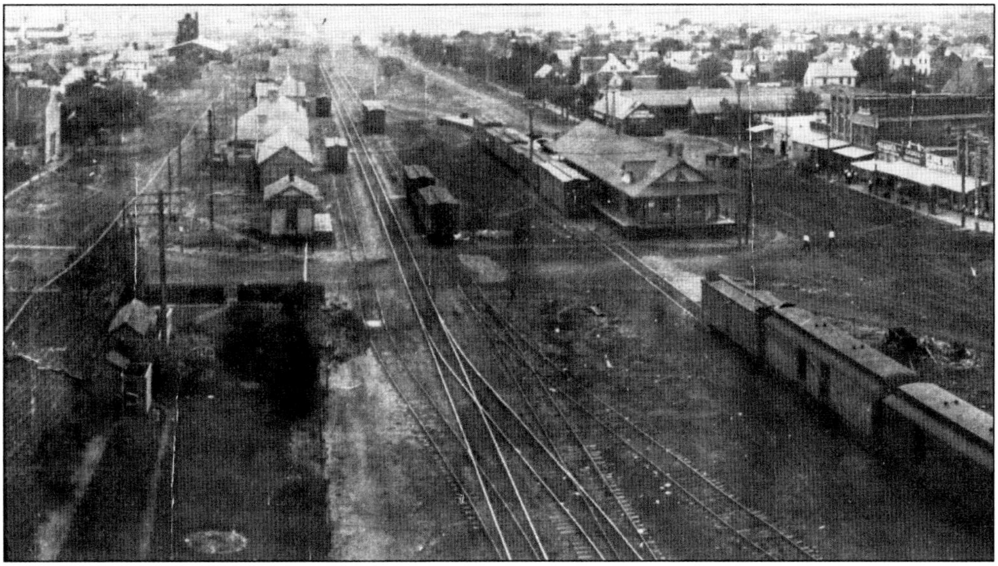

The freight depot (above) was located to the south of Ennis Avenue. It was the site of continuous activity as freight was loaded and unloaded literally in the middle of town. When it was closed in the 1970s, part of the building was moved, and it is now a barn in Seven Points, Texas (below). (Below, courtesy of City of Ennis.)

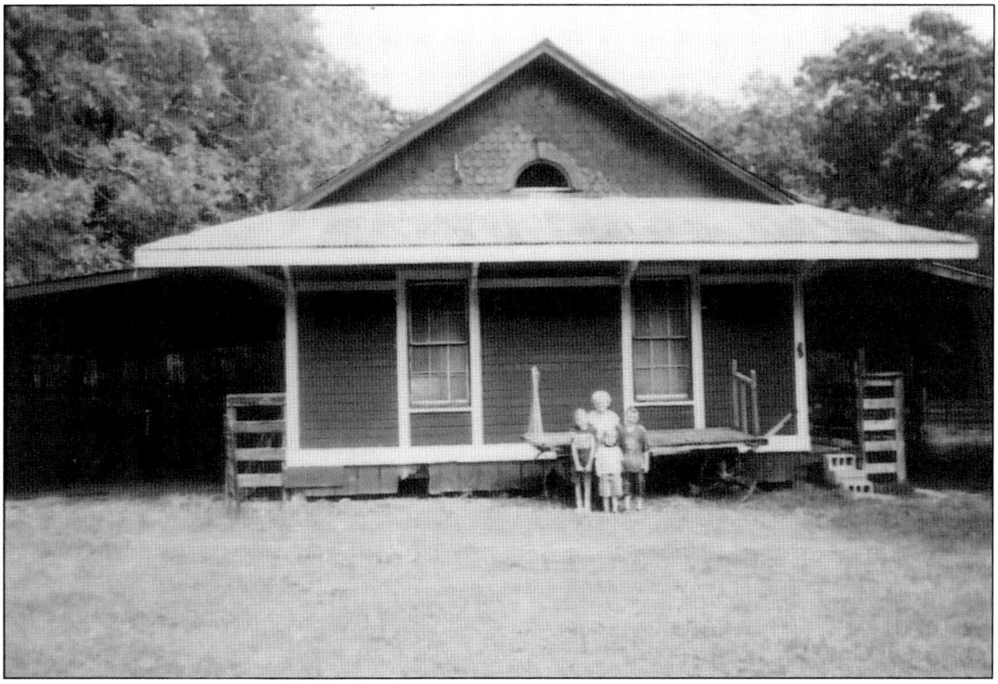

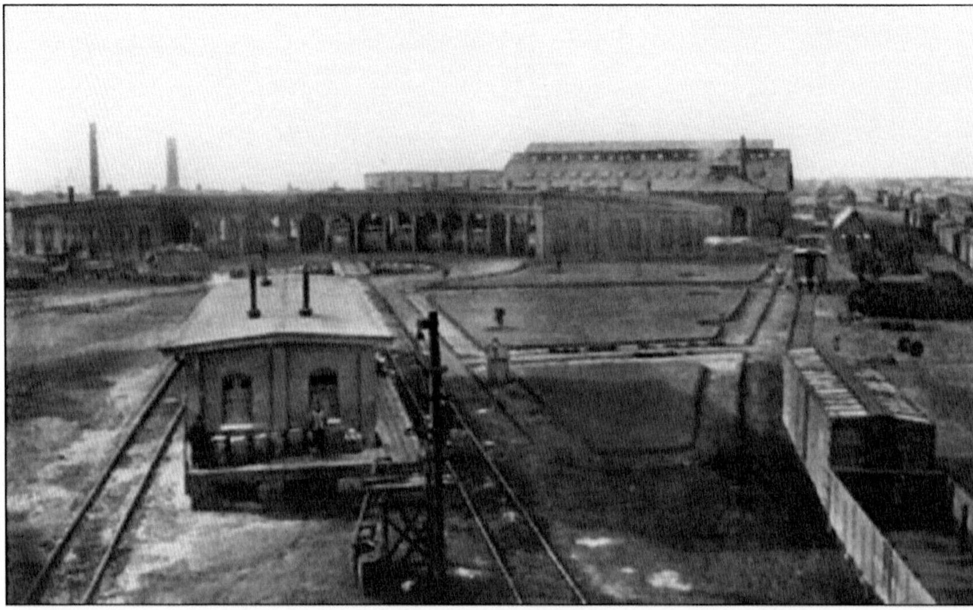

In 1891, when Ennis became a division point of the Houston and Texas Central Railroad, a roundhouse facility and machine shop (pictured) was built just to the north of the city. Several community leaders, including Joe Baldridge, Capt. Mark Latimer, Pete Freeman, Dr. J. C. Loggins, Louis Cerf, and J. Blakey, were instrumental in obtaining the contract with the railroad that brought the roundhouse to Ennis. (Both courtesy of City of Ennis.)

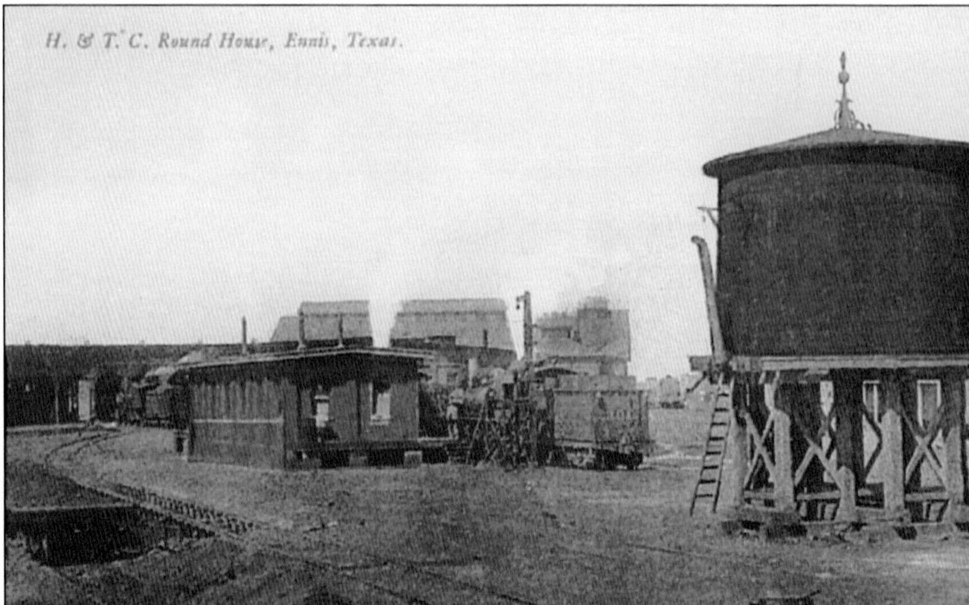

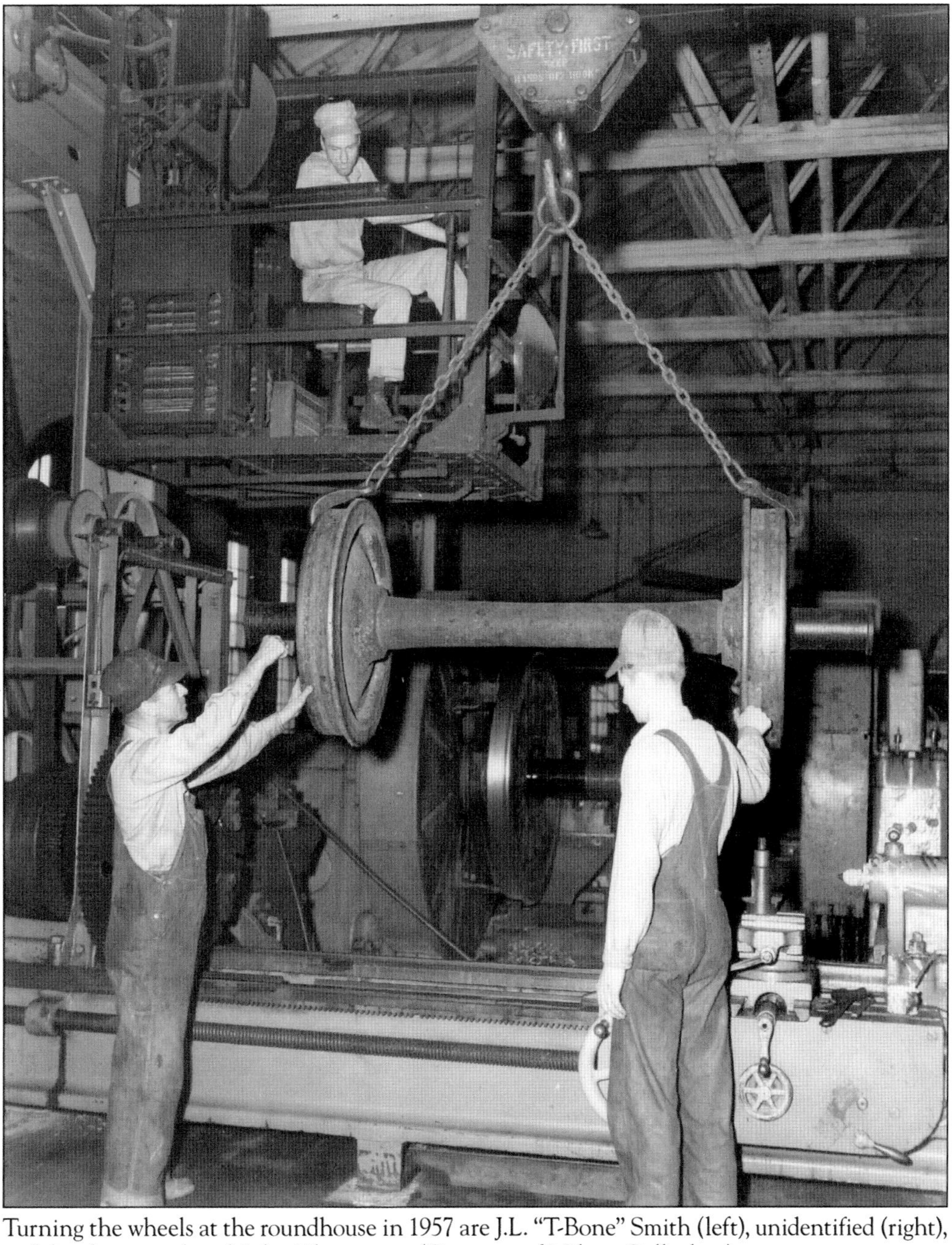

Turning the wheels at the roundhouse in 1957 are J.L. "T-Bone" Smith (left), unidentified (right), and (in the cage above) John Thompson. (Courtesy of Milton Gallagher.)

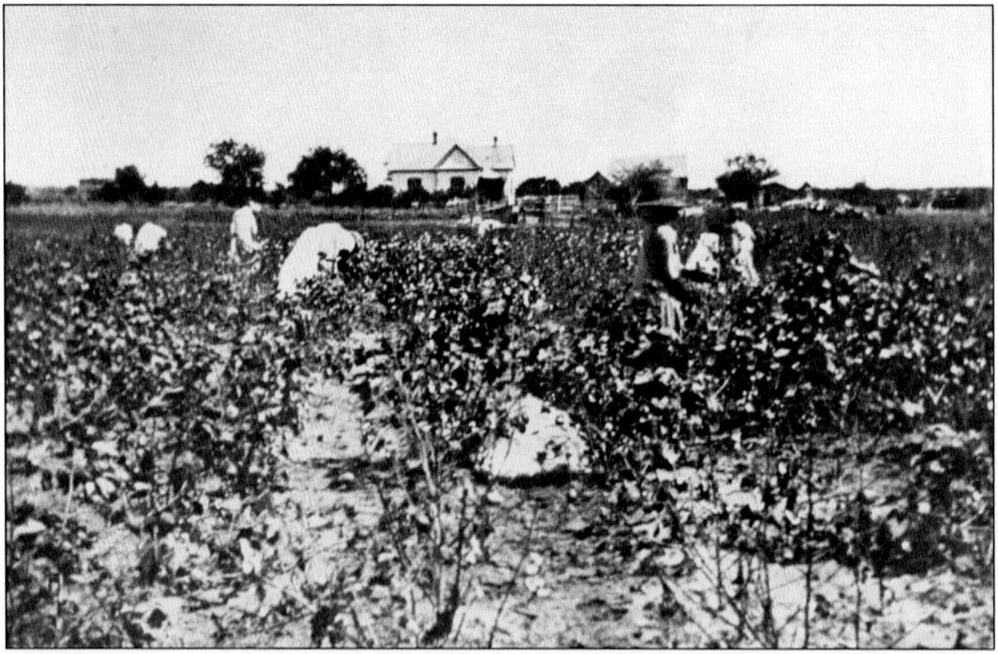

Cotton was a mainstay crop for many Ennis farms from almost the beginning. Picking the cotton was often a family venture, as seen in these pictures. (Above, courtesy of Dorothy Kudrna; below, Ennis Heritage Society.)

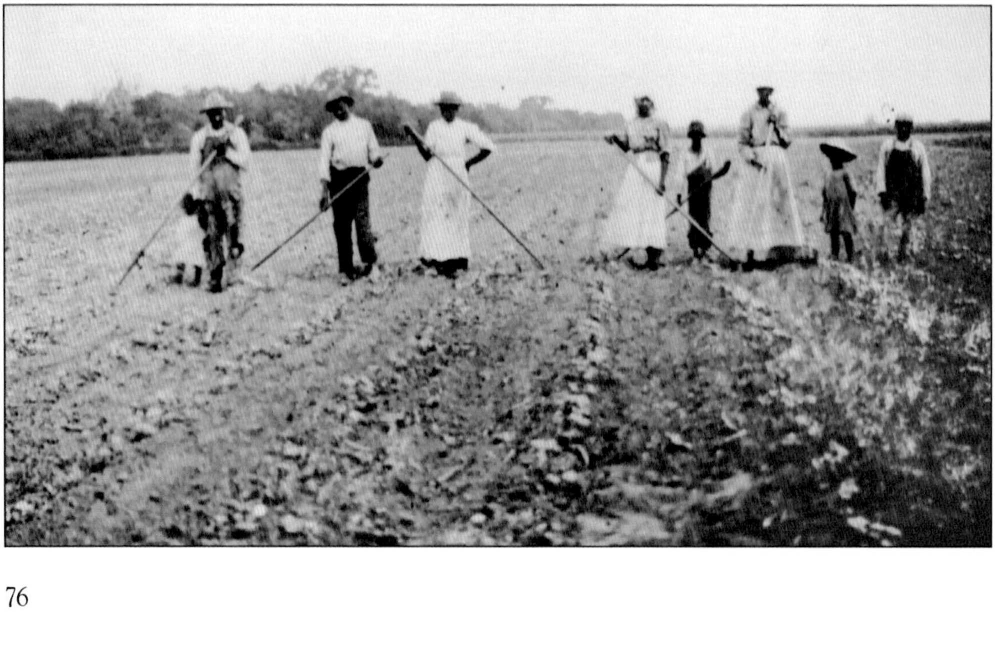

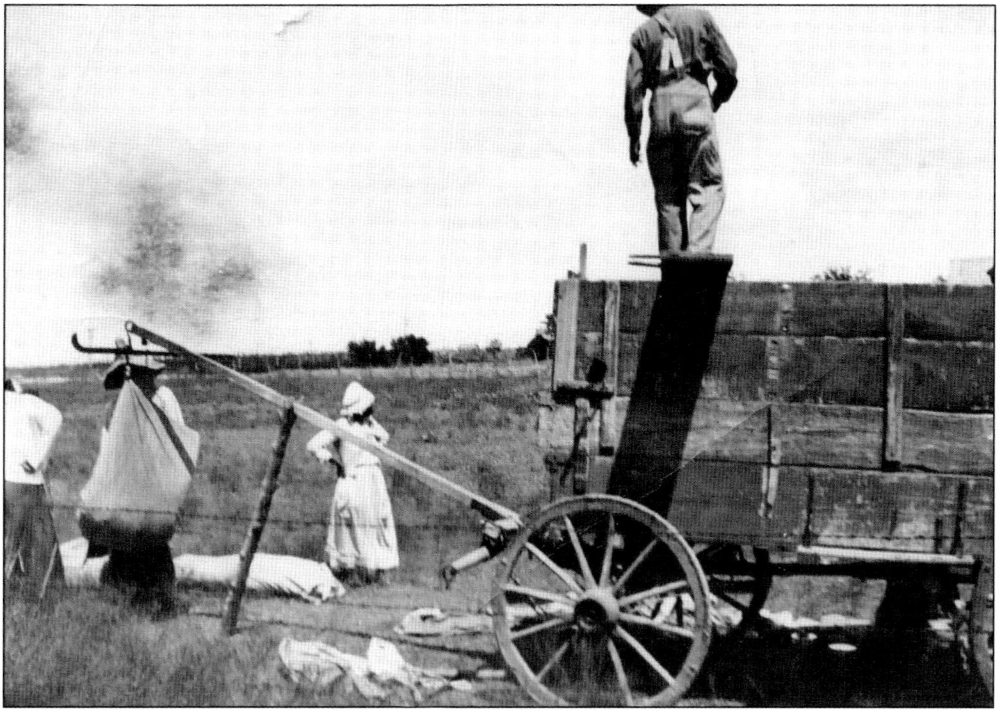

Farming involved hard and often backbreaking work. During cotton harvest time, canvas bags carried over the shoulder were used to gather the cotton. Once a bag was full, it was weighed and then emptied into a large trailer out in the field. Pictured above in the 1920s, William Nesuda is standing on a trailer while a cotton picker waits for the return of her bag. Pictured below in 1942 is a similar scene at the Sonka farm in Garrett. From left to right are (standing) Mary Cato, Milton Vitovsky, Carl Cato, and Mary Sonka (recording weight of the bag); (in the wagon) John Sonka and Adell Sonka. (Above, courtesy of Dorothy Kudrna; below, Adell Valek.)

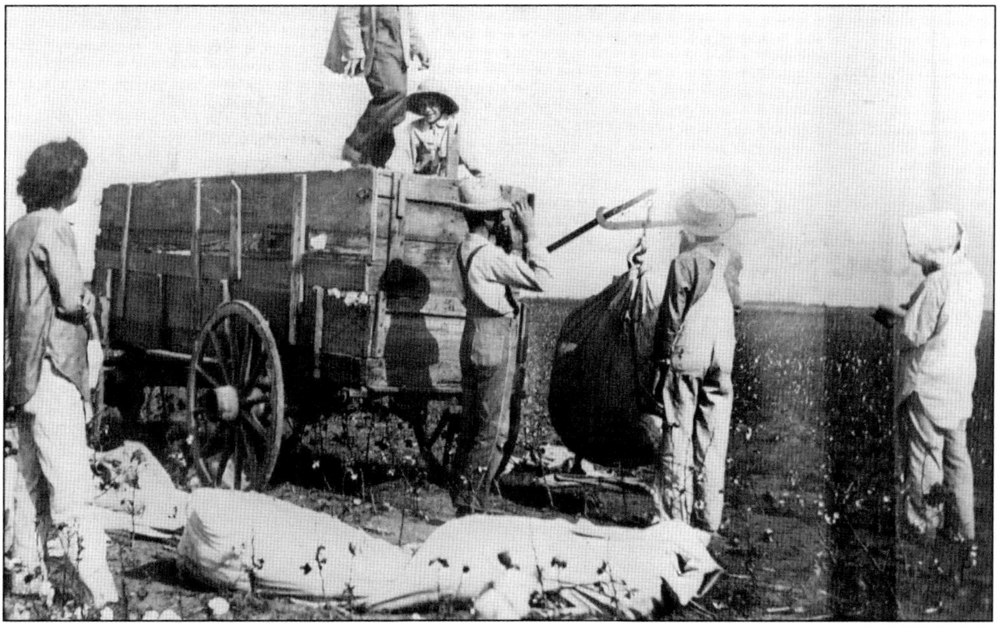

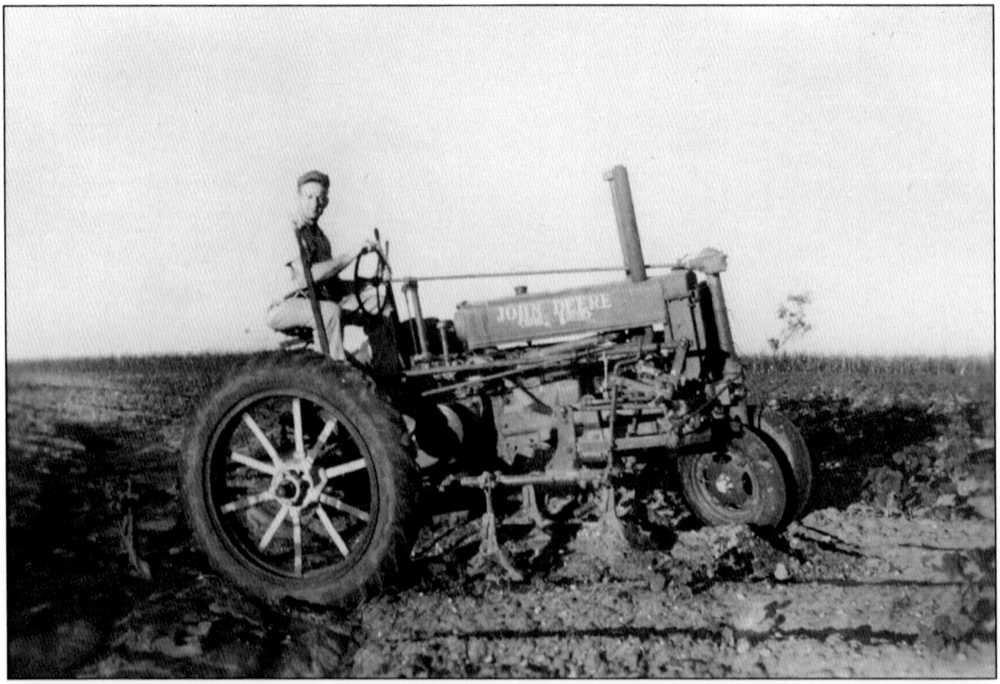

Machinery made a big difference during the harvest, but it was still a time when family and friends were often counted on to help out. Pictured working the field during harvest time in June 1946 is Frank J. Strunc. He is driving a John Deere tractor that belongs to his cousin Willie Haskovec. (Courtesy of Frank Strunc family.)

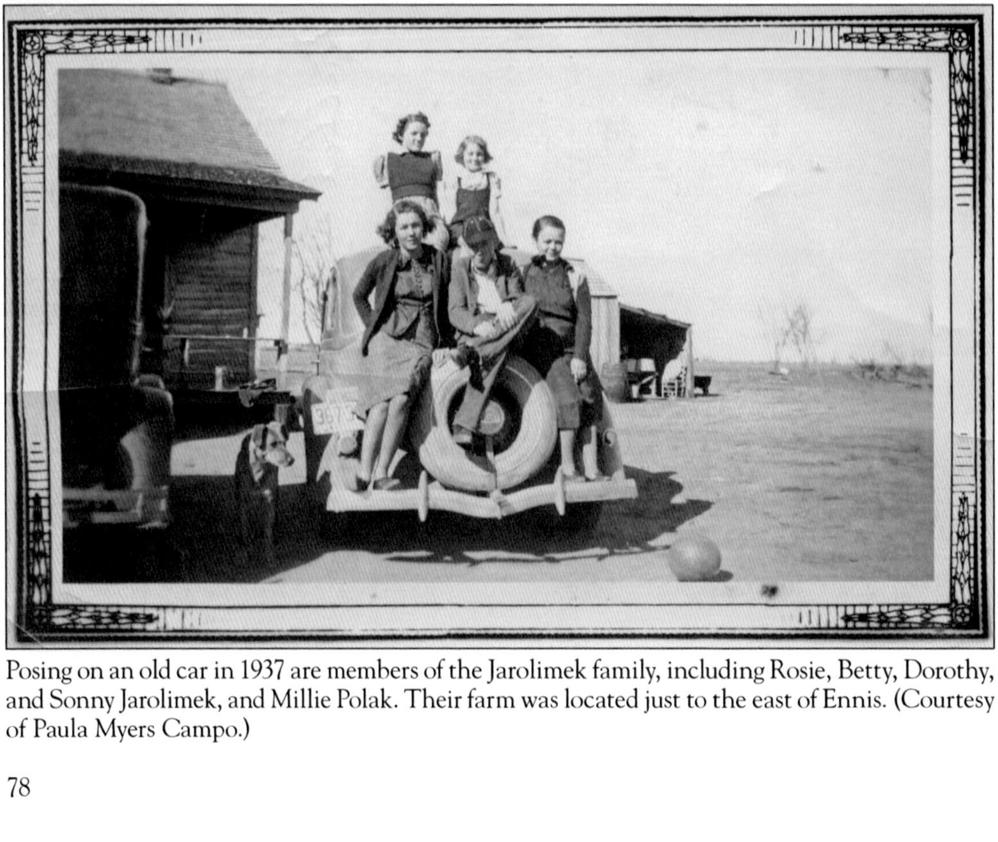

Posing on an old car in 1937 are members of the Jarolimek family, including Rosie, Betty, Dorothy, and Sonny Jarolimek, and Millie Polak. Their farm was located just to the east of Ennis. (Courtesy of Paula Myers Campo.)

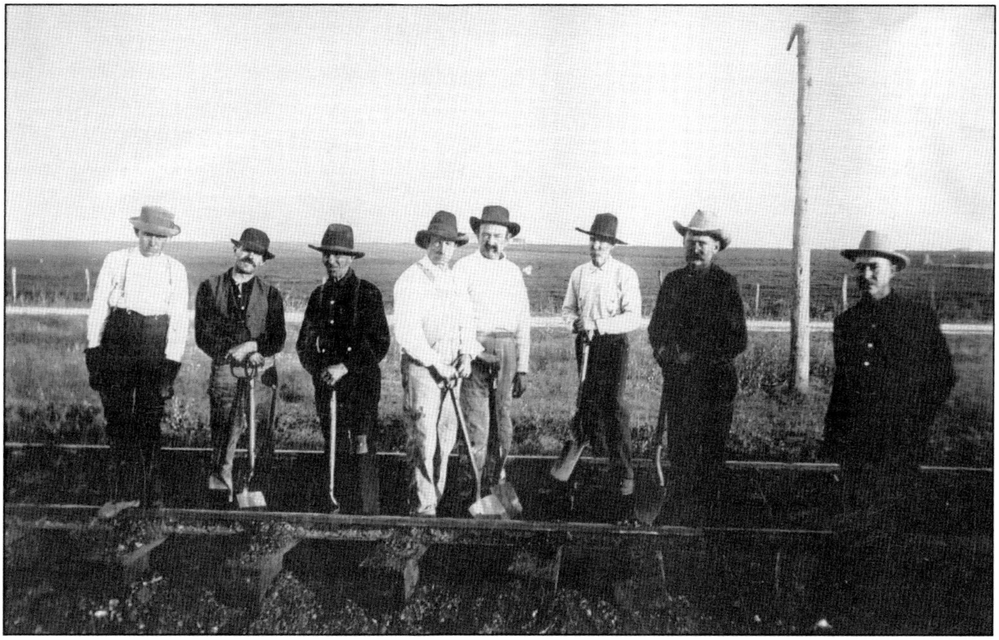

Southern Pacific Railroad section houses, pictured below, were located along the railway to provide housing for the section men assigned to keep the track in good condition. The structures also provided the necessary space to store the tools and equipment needed for these tasks. John Burris, foreman of the section crew pictured above, is at the far right. (Both courtesy of Milton Gallagher.)

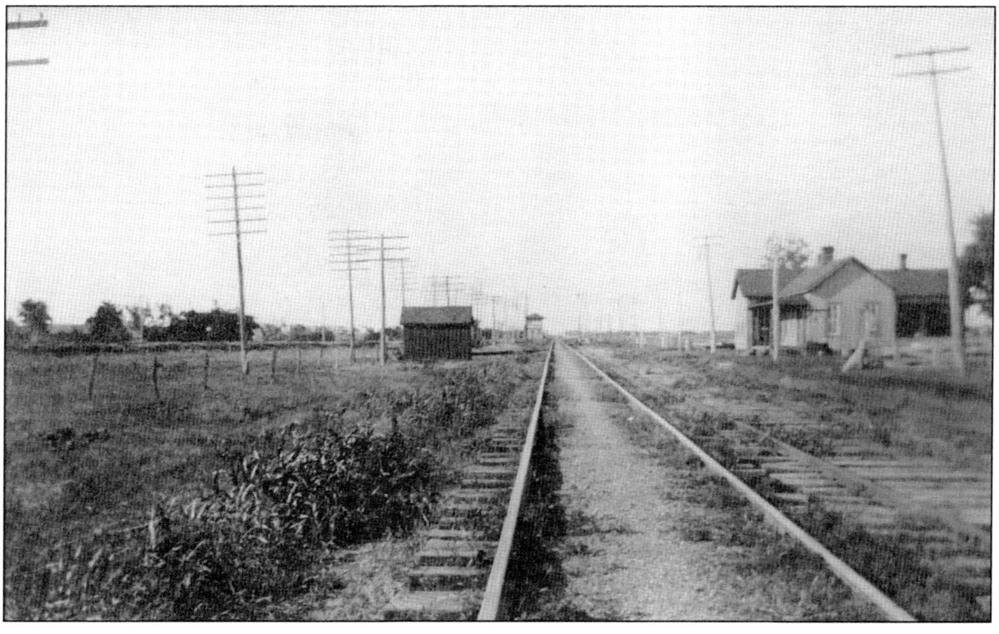

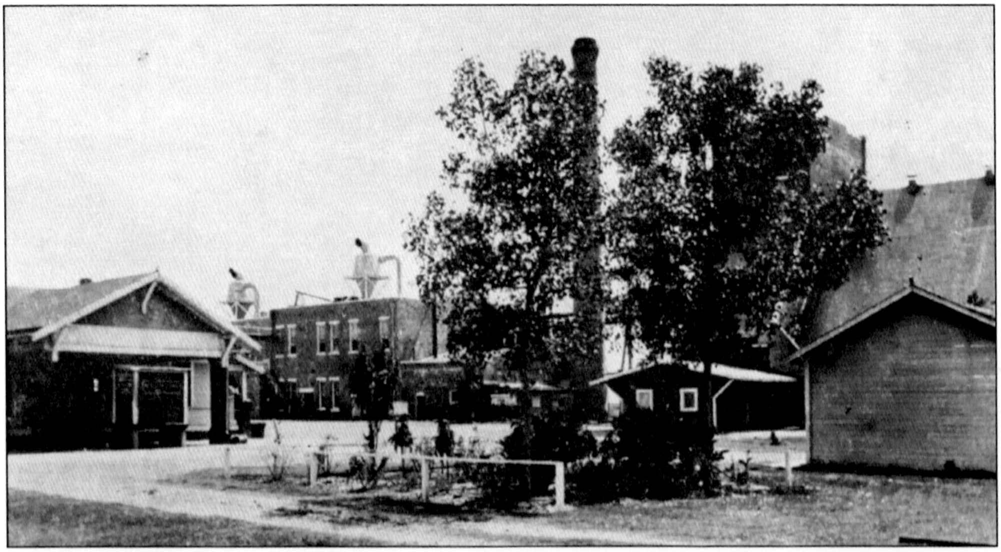

In 1890, Ennis had a cotton compress, three cottonseed depositories, and one cotton gin. By 1914, there was one cotton compress, one cottonseed oil mill, and four cotton gins. The single compress company, Ennis Cotton Compress, was established in 1885 and at that time was located at East Lampasas Street along the east side of the rail. When established, it had the capacity to process over 700 bales of cotton per day. Below is a c. 1910 view of the Ennis Cotton Compress alongside the track. Above is Planters Cotton Oil Company. Once a discarded by-product of the process, cotton seeds were found to provide an additional source of revenue to Ennis's cotton industry. When pressed, the oil from the cotton seeds could be used in soaps and animal feed. (Both courtesy of Ennis Public Library.)

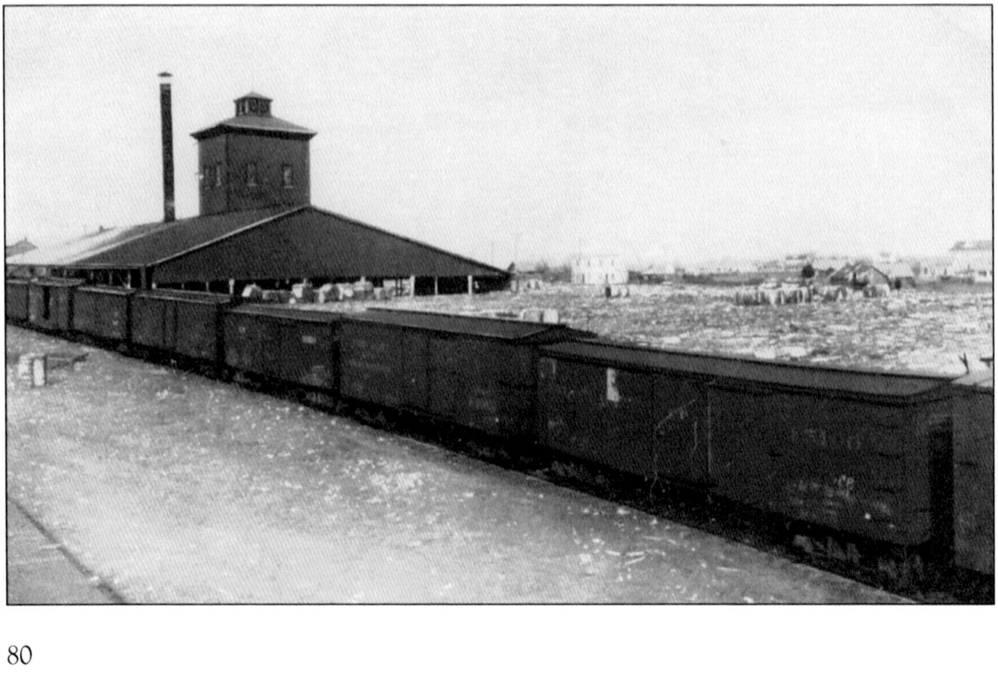

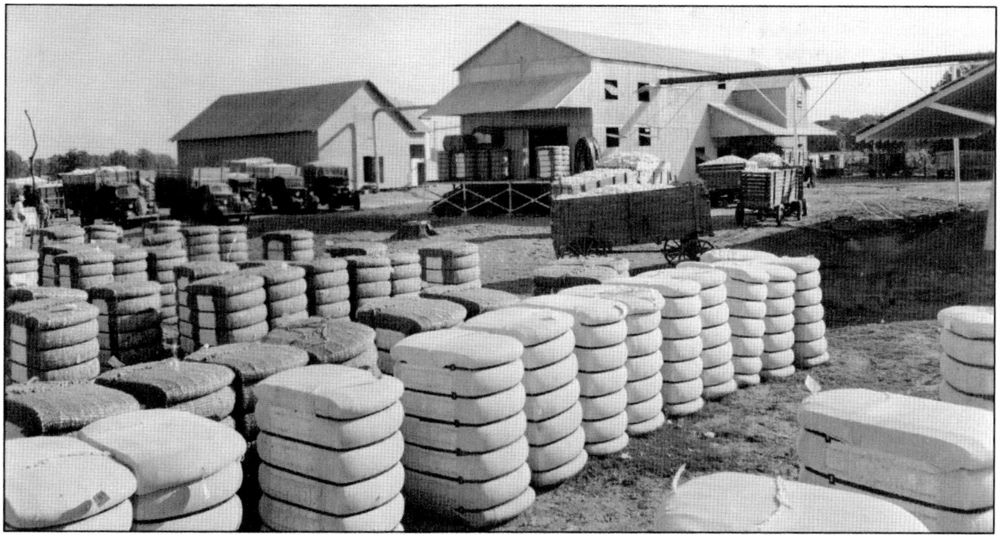

There were many cotton gins in Ennis and the surrounding communities through the years. Farmers would bring their cotton to the local cotton gin, where the cotton fiber would be separated from the seedpods and cotton seeds. Stacks of cotton bales at an unidentified facility are seen above. Pictured below is the Ennis Cotton Co-op Gin. (Above, courtesy of Ennis Public Library; below, Dorothy Betts.)

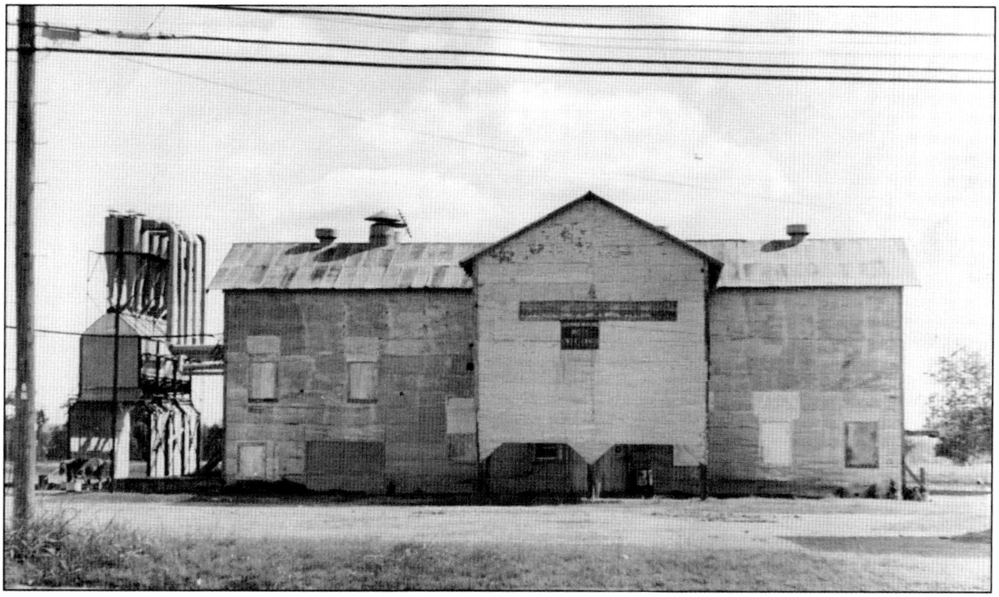

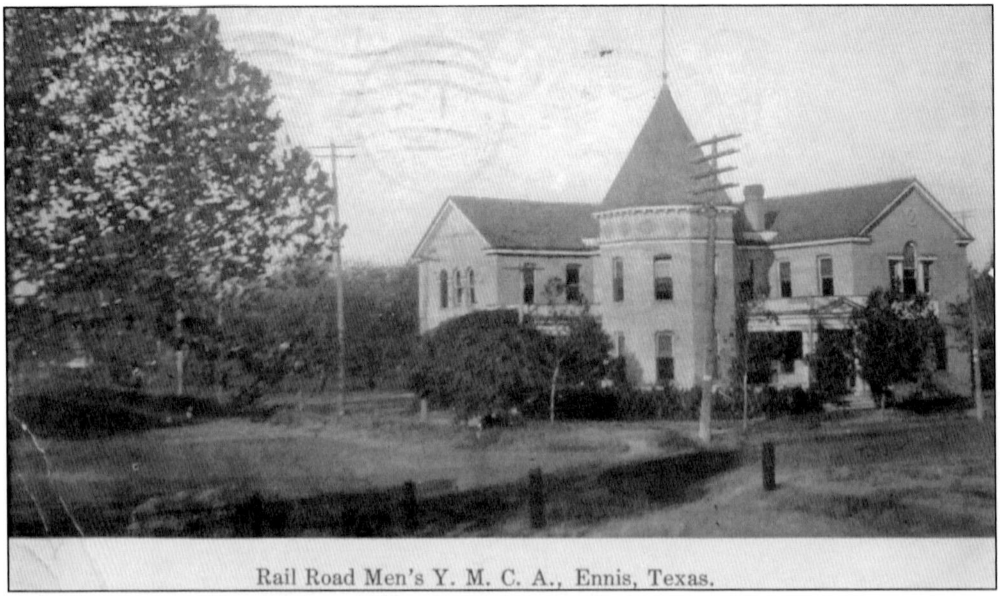

The Rail Road Men's YMCA was located at Southwest Main and Baylor Streets. In 1932, the railroad superintendant and division offices were relocated to the YMCA building after the destruction of the older depot building. The division headquarters remained at this site until they were moved to Dallas in 1965.

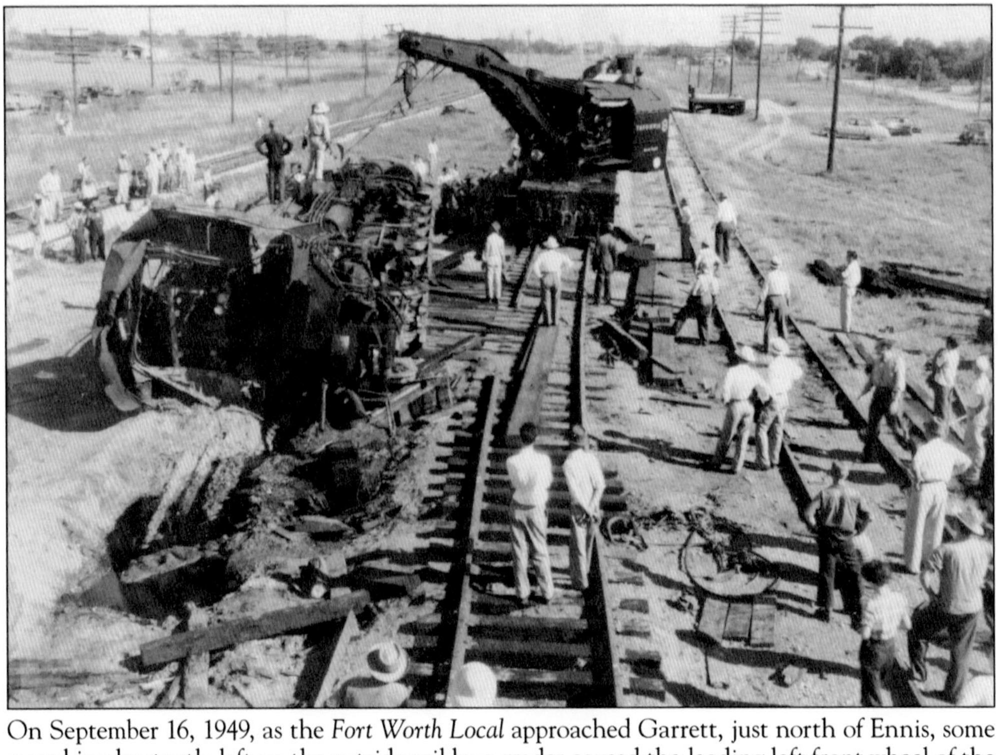

On September 16, 1949, as the *Fort Worth Local* approached Garrett, just north of Ennis, some gravel inadvertently left on the outside rail by a grader caused the leading left front wheel of the locomotive engine to lift off the track. Engineer Archie Crane was fatally injured, scalded by the escaping steam boiling out of the top of the engine. (Courtesy of Ennis Public Library.)

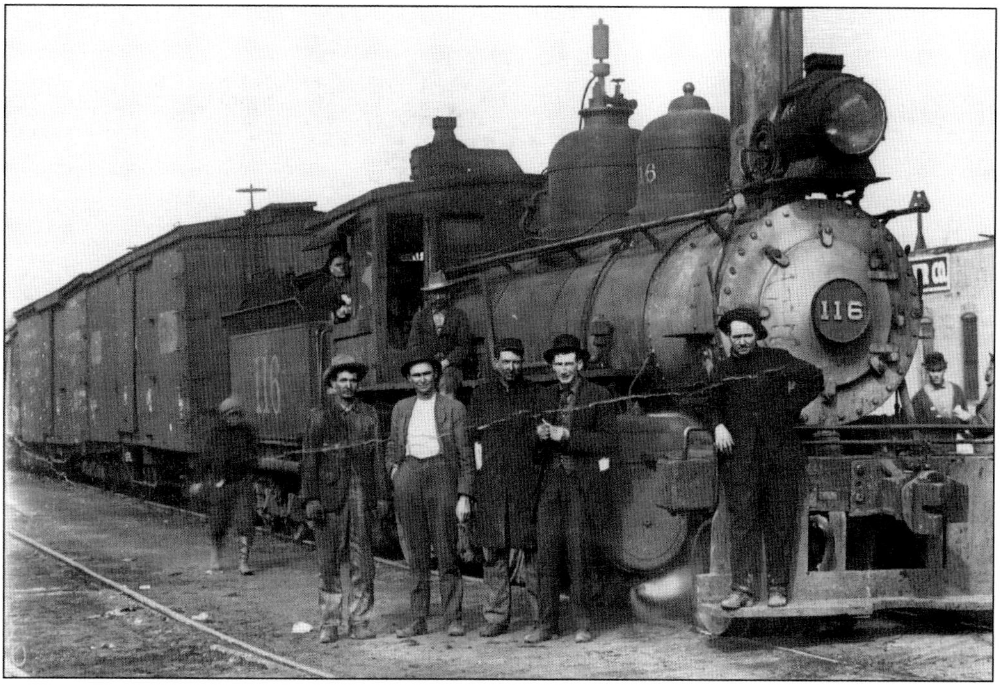

The railroad provided jobs to Ennis residents for decades from the early years to the 1960s. Pat Connolly, pictured above at the far right on the train cowcatcher in the early 1920s, was a brakeman for the railroad. The cowcatcher at the front of the train was meant to deflect and move to the side foreign objects on the track that could pose a danger or impede the movement of the train. Railroad workers gather for a meeting, below, at the roundhouse in the 1940s. (Above, courtesy of City of Ennis; below, Loretta Davis.)

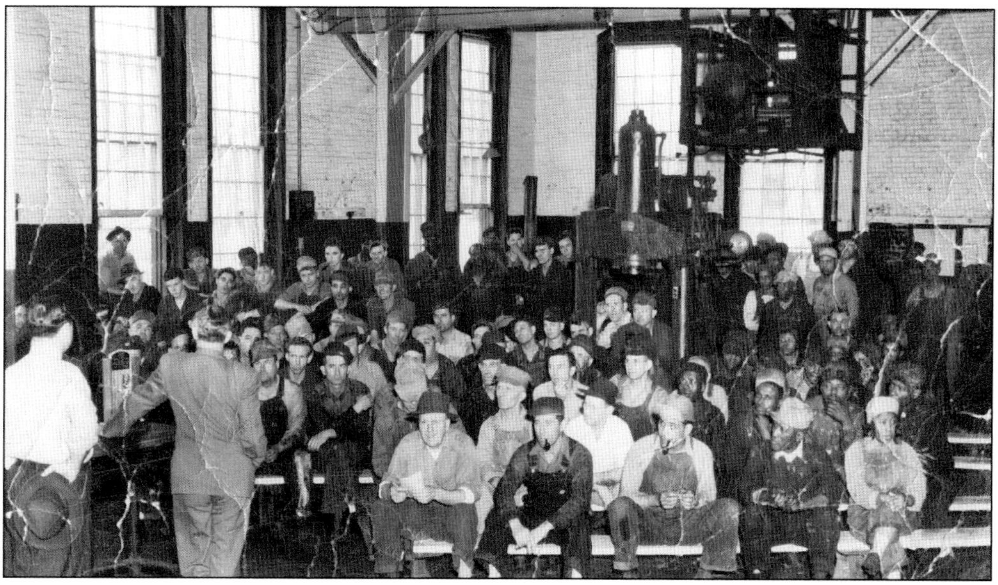

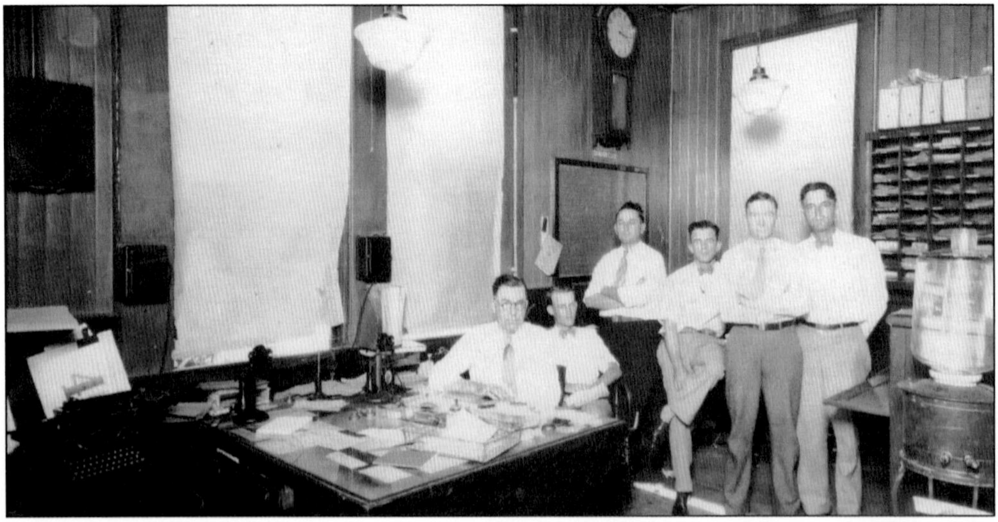

Several men who worked in the railroad office, located at the north end of the platform, are pictured above from left to right: John Rawlings, Joe Adams, dispatcher ? Miller, Caller Maris, Pat Comiskey, and Max Ludwig. Comiskey was the car distributor at the time, and Ludwig was telegraph operator. A. C. Dinkins, pictured below, was another longtime dispatcher. (Above, courtesy of City of Ennis; below, Ennis Public Library.)

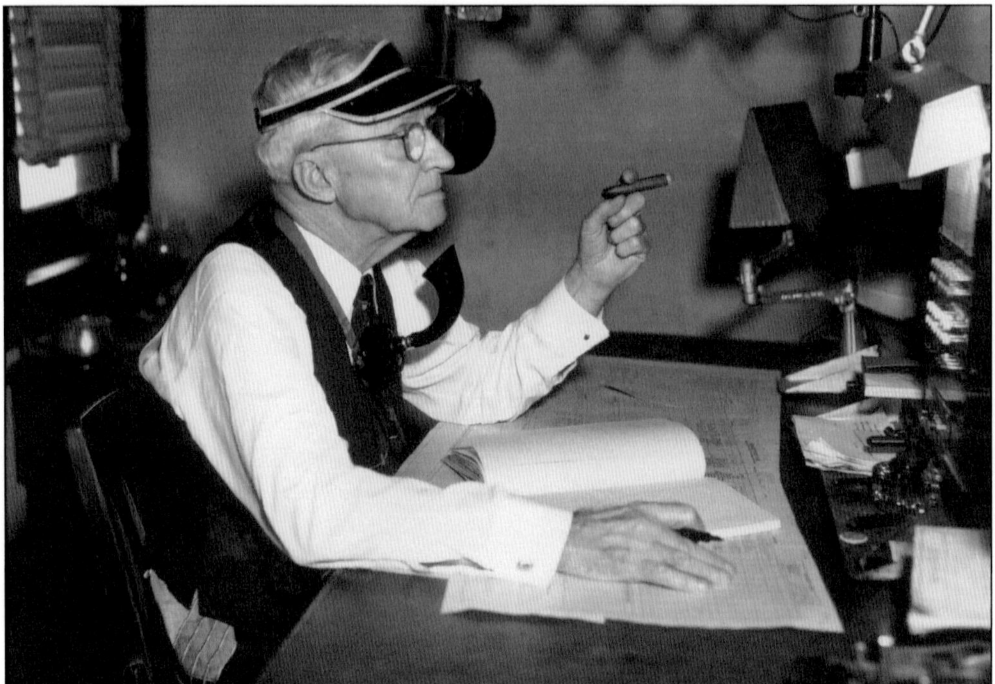

Five

Church Bells

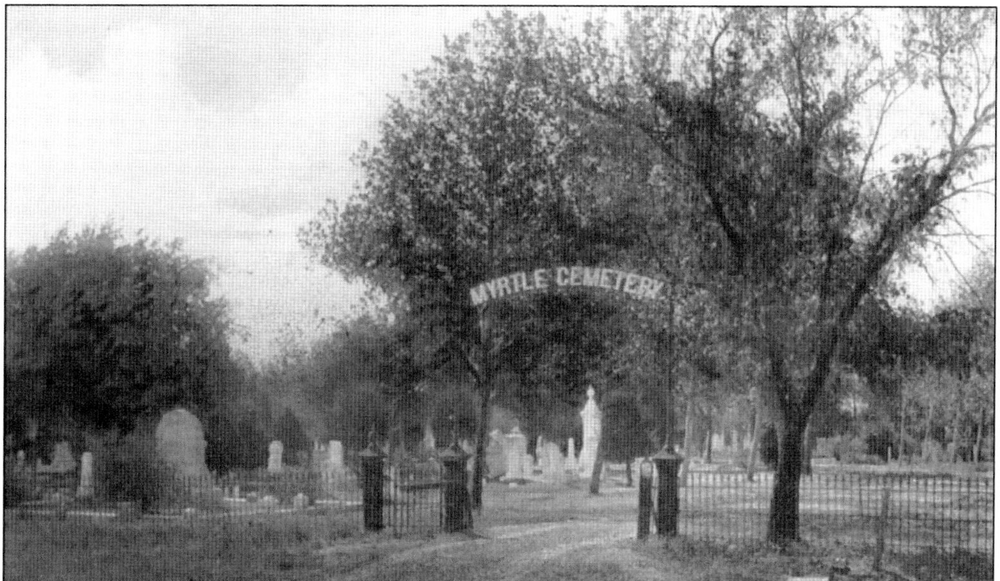

A little girl named Myrtle was the first to be buried in what is now known as Myrtle Cemetery. Not much is known about her other than her family was traveling through the area in a covered wagon in the earliest days of the town when she fell ill and died. What is certain is that when members of the community met around 1875 to buy land for a cemetery, the tract of land chosen included her small grave site. Her grave, then located at the cemetery entrance, was marked simply with her name etched on a wooden marker. The original 10 acres were purchased from Col. W. H. Parsons for $100.

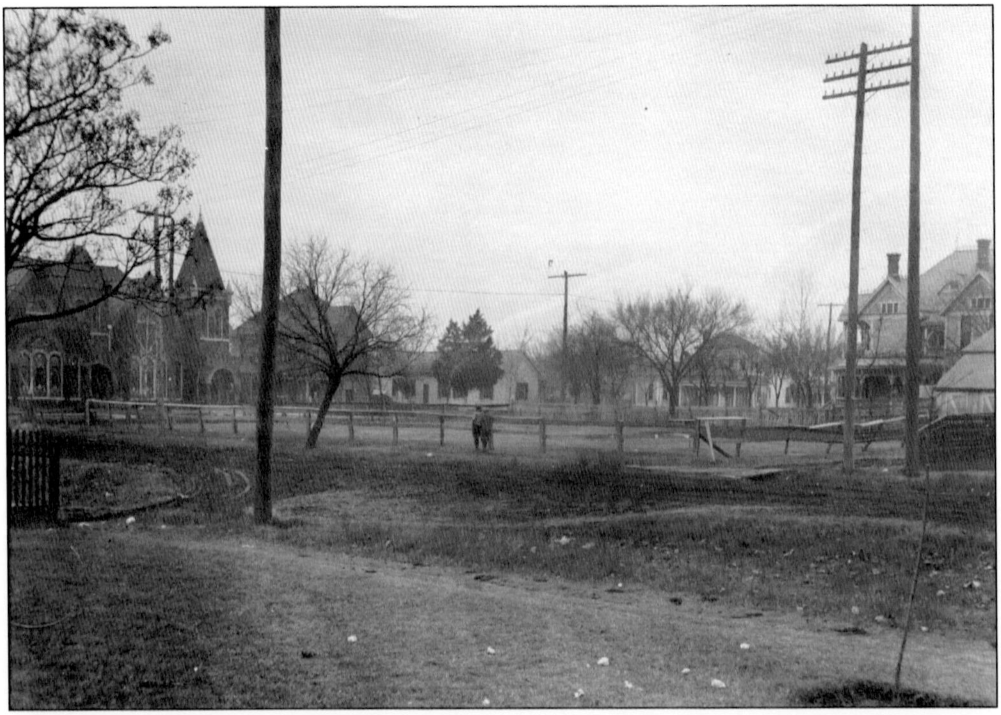

The Rowe Cotton Gin and Grist Mill was once located in the fenced area of these photographs. Pictured above to the left, around 1910, is the Tabernacle Baptist Church, built in 1901 at North McKinney and West Knox Streets. Below at the far right is St. Thomas Episcopal Church, built around 1890 at the northeast corner of the same intersection. The church was destroyed by fire in the 1920s. To its left is the First Presbyterian Church, built in the late 1880s. This church was destroyed by fire on Christmas 1945. An army barrack was purchased from Camp Berkley in Abilene, dismantled, and then rebuilt in Ennis at the same location as the previous First Presbyterian Church, where it still stands today. (Both courtesy of Ennis Post Office.)

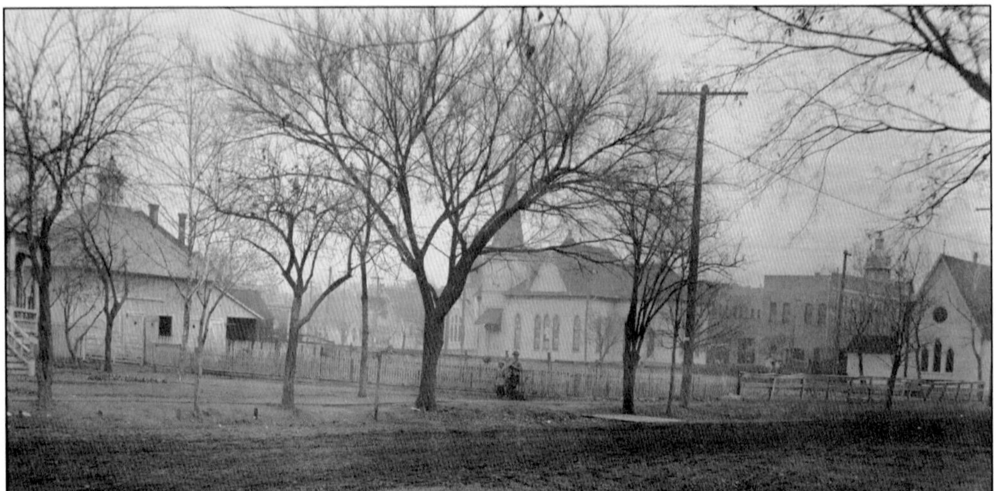

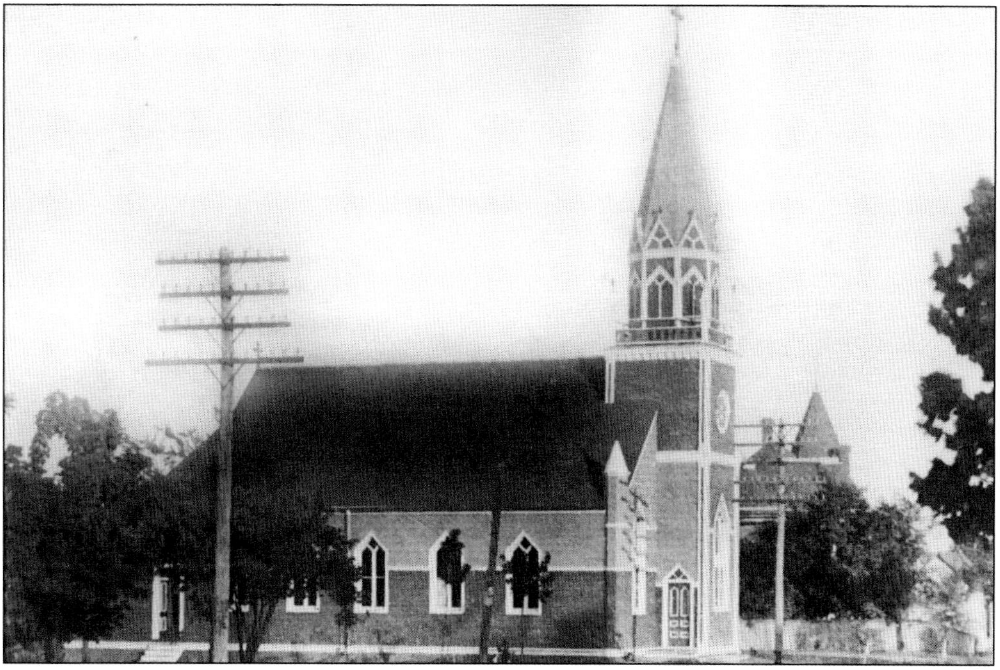

The Holy Redeemer Church was built in 1902 at Preston and Baylor Streets. It sat on the site of what had been St. Joseph's Catholic Church parking lot, where the many parishioners who came in from the country areas would leave their wagons during the services. (Courtesy of Mary Ann Novy Lamkin.)

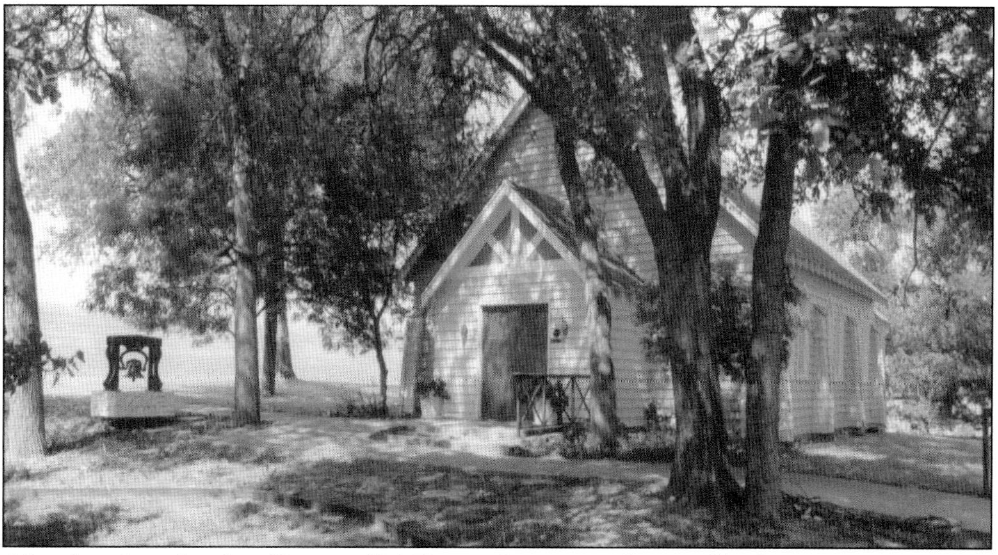

After their first church at Knox and McKinney Streets was destroyed by fire, it was several years before the Episcopalian congregation built a new church at Sherman and Tyler Streets in the early 1930s. In 1987, St. Thomas Episcopal Church, along with the original 1888 cornerstone, was carefully moved to its new position on Park Street across from Old City Lake, where it still stands today. (Courtesy of Ben Tucker.)

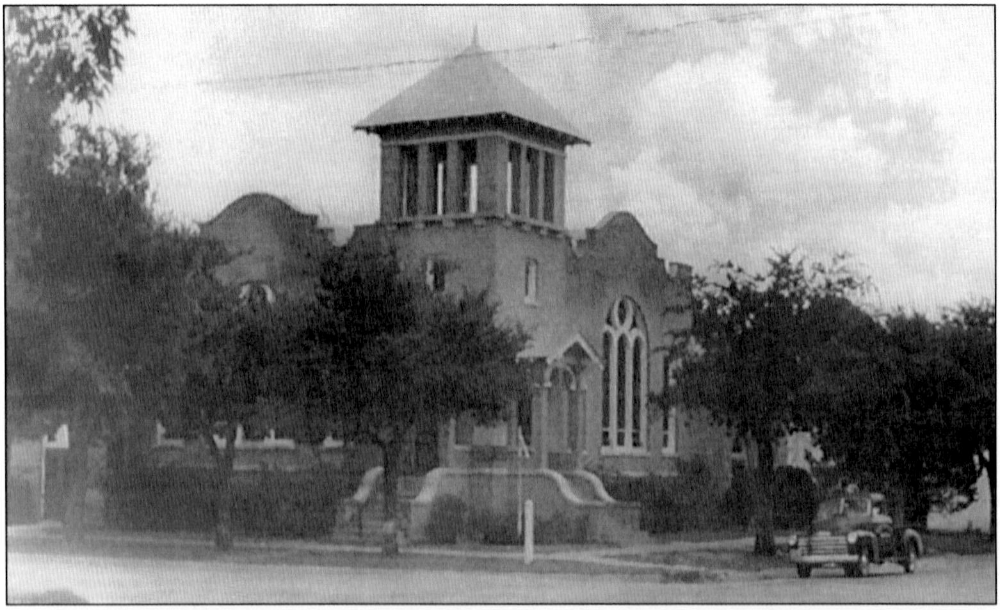

The First Christian Church was organized in Ennis in 1876. They built their first church building at the northeast corner of Ennis Avenue and Clay Street. In 1913, they completed a new church, pictured here, at the southeast corner of Sherman and Baylor Streets, where they worshipped until the 1970s. (Courtesy of Jim and Helen Templin.)

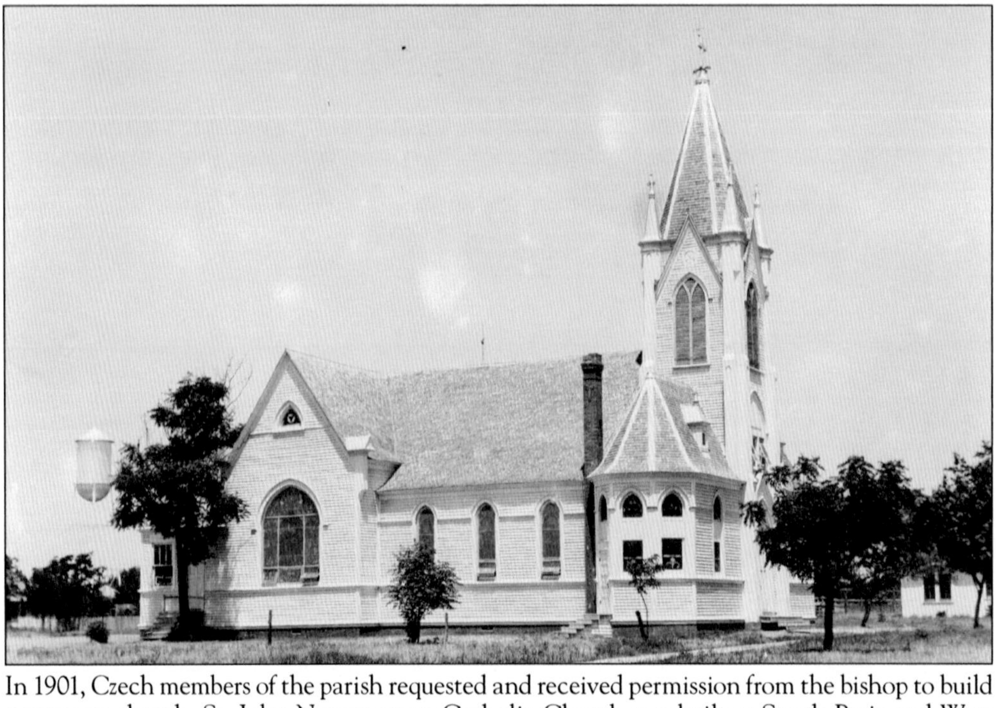

In 1901, Czech members of the parish requested and received permission from the bishop to build a separate church. St. John Nepomucene Catholic Church was built at South Paris and West Lampasas Streets. Through the efforts of many Czech families and area businessmen, $3,600 was raised, and the ground-breaking for the new church took place in 1902. (Courtesy of Mary Ann Novy Lamkin.)

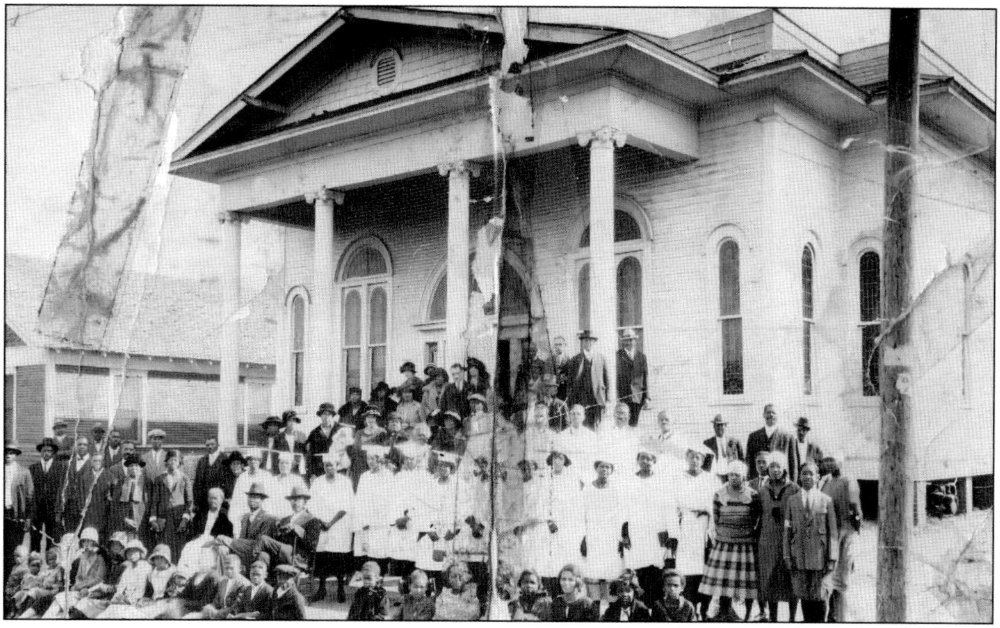

The St. Paul Missionary Baptist Church was founded in 1878. A small church was built at the present site of the Ennis Junior High football field. A larger church built on the same site a few years later was destroyed by fire in 1914. A new church, pictured above, was then built at 909 West Brown Street. Some of the founding members were Doc, Harry, Joe, Robin, and Willie Biggins; Joe Davis; Angelina Richardson; and Tom Templin. Men of the St. Paul Missionary Baptist Church, pictured below in 1920, included David Nero, Henry Thomas, Watson Sherrell, Ralph Battle, Strahmore Akins, L. F. Huckahy, Jake Daffan, Jeff Lister, Ben Biggins, Leroy Russell, Jeremiah Russell, and founding members Doc Biggins and Tom Templin. The congregation still meets at the same location in a new church built in 1965. (Both courtesy of Loretta Davis.)

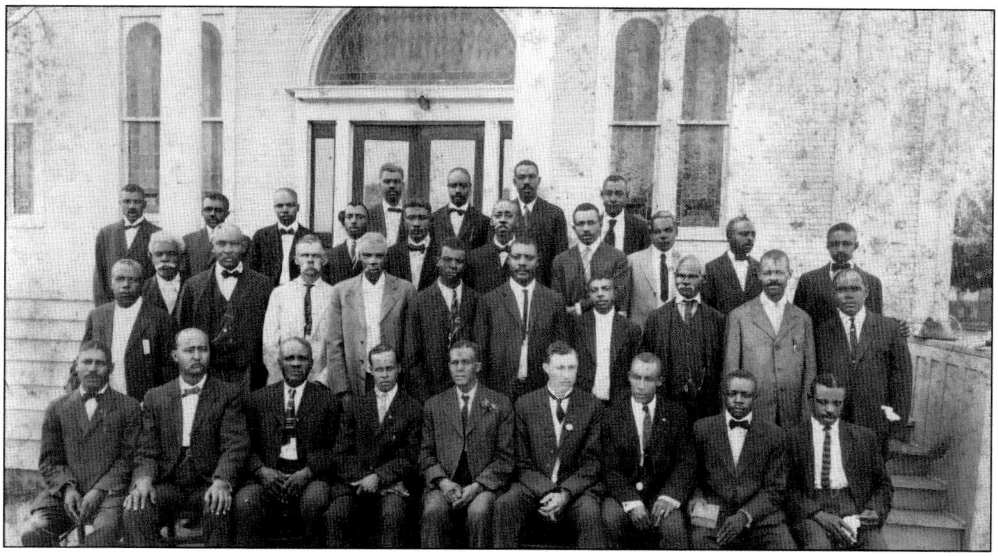

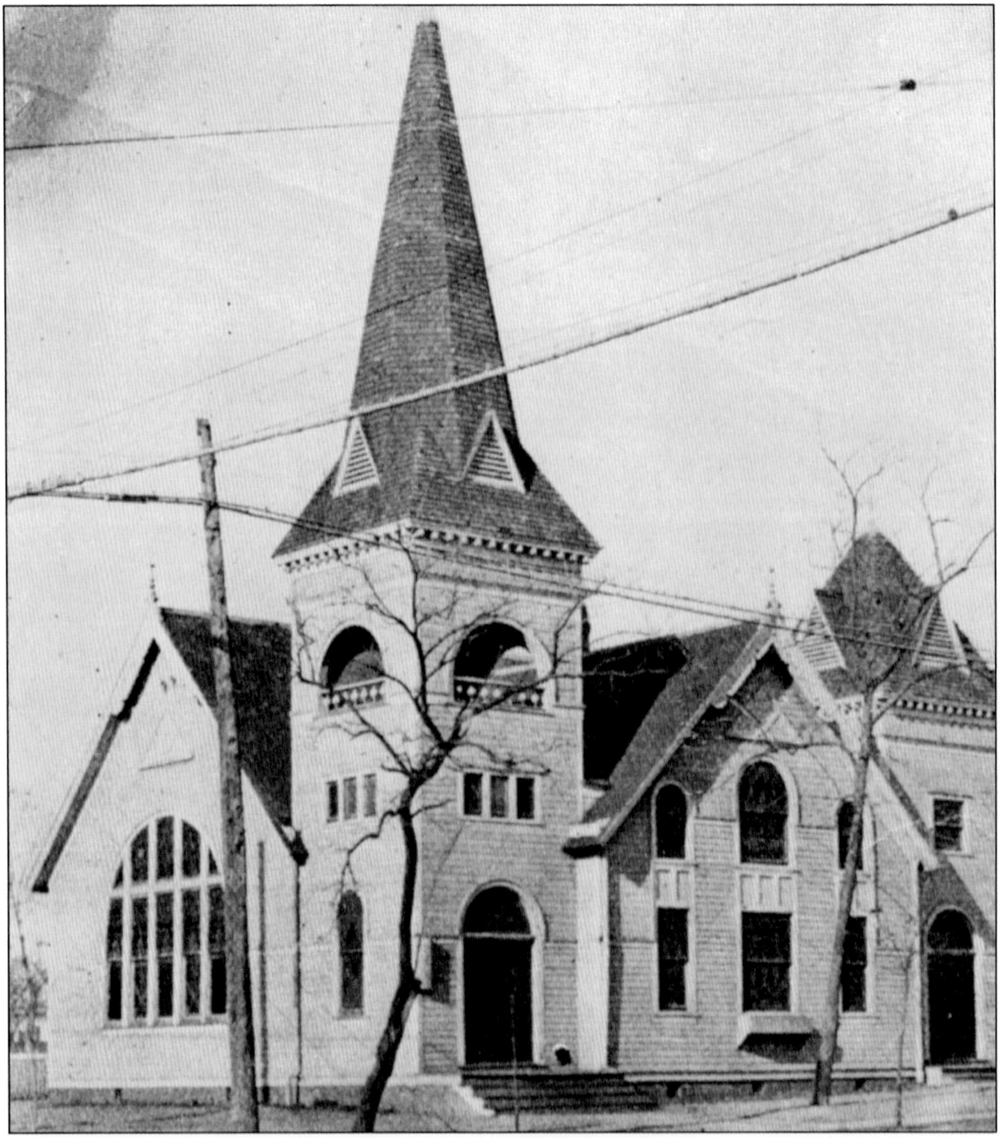

The First Baptist Church of Ennis, pictured around 1920, was organized in 1873. Many of its first members came from Burnham Baptist Church just south of Ennis. Their first services were held in a vacant store on Main Street between Ennis Avenue and Knox Street. Later services were held in the First Presbyterian Church on the corner of South Dallas and West Milam Streets. These services were led by Rev. E. K. Freeman of Corsicana, who was succeeded by Rev. W. H. Parks. Under his tenure, the congregation built their own church at the northwest corner of Dallas and Baylor Streets. Shortly after its completion, it was destroyed when a cyclone hit the city. Church members rebuilt with the assistance of Morris Wright of Bardwell, who had also helped construct their first church.

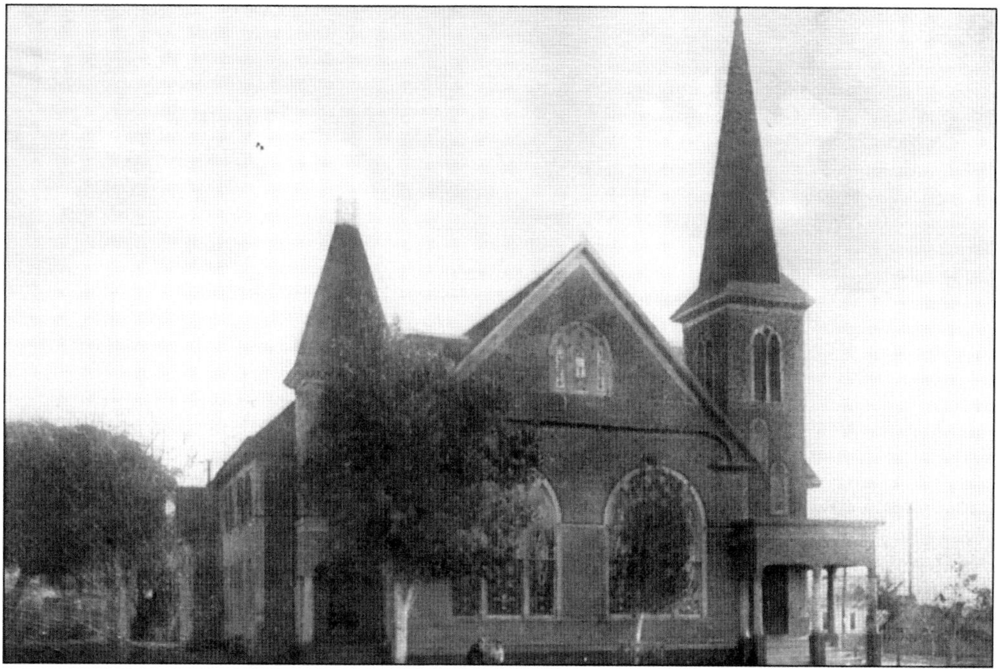

The First United Methodist Church of Ennis was organized in 1872 and held its first services in the store owned by Thomas L. McCarty and G. Blakey. In 1878, the congregation built its first church, pictured above around 1910, located at South Dallas and West Crockett Streets. Sunday school classes were conducted in the building next door, referred to as "the Bungalow," shown below in the 1930s. The church relocated to North Sherman and West Belknap Streets in 1949. (Below, courtesy of Ennis Fire Department.)

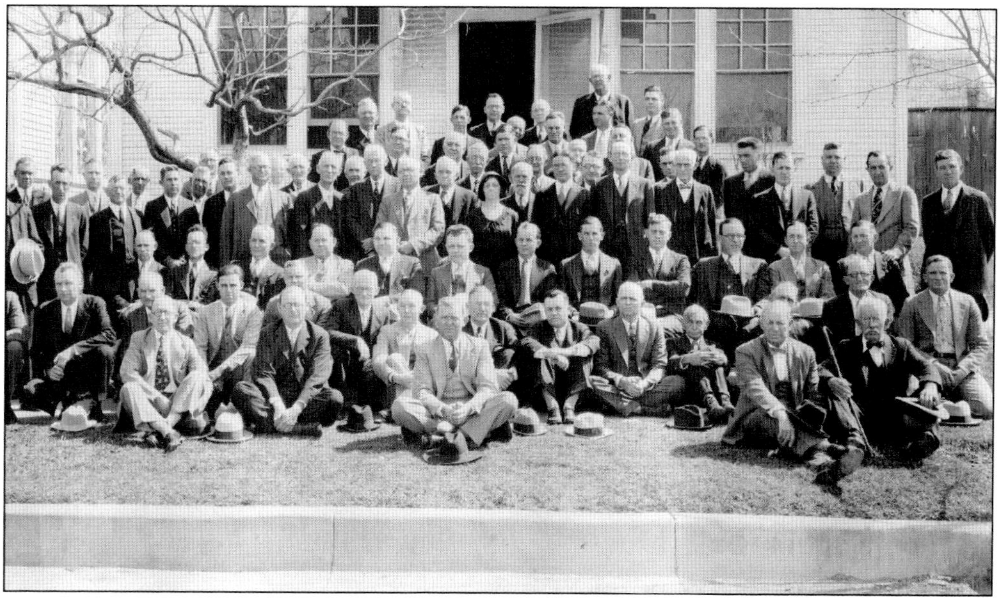

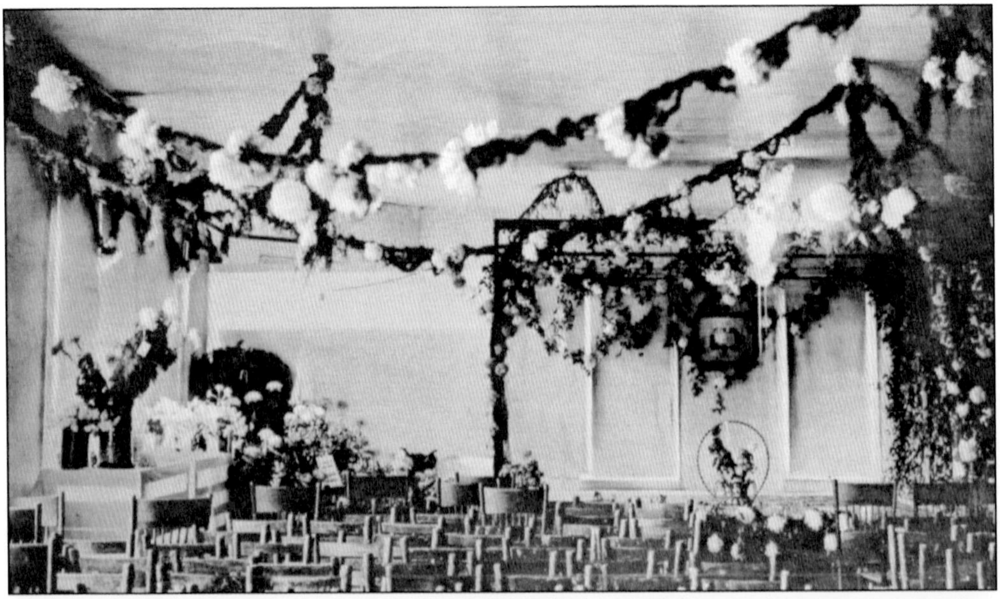

The Myrtle Cemetery Society was formed in 1891 with the mission to support the cemetery. As a group, they raised funds in various ways, including memberships, donations, and benefit functions such as the flower show, pictured around 1909, which was held at the Elk Hall. The organization was founded by a small group of women but grew to over 140 members by 1895.

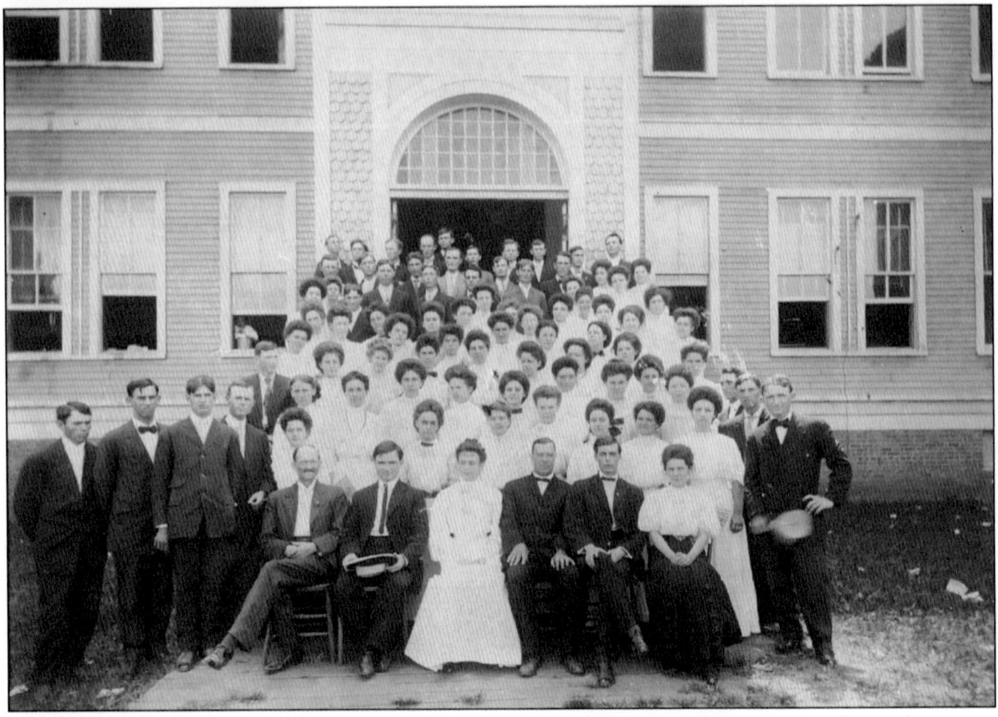

There are early accounts of the various places church members would meet if without their own place of worship. They often met at other churches that opened their doors to them, vacant stores, homes, and, at times in these early years, the schools, as perhaps this group is, posed in front of Ennis High School in the 1890s. (Courtesy of Ennis Public Library.)

Six

SCHOOL DAYS

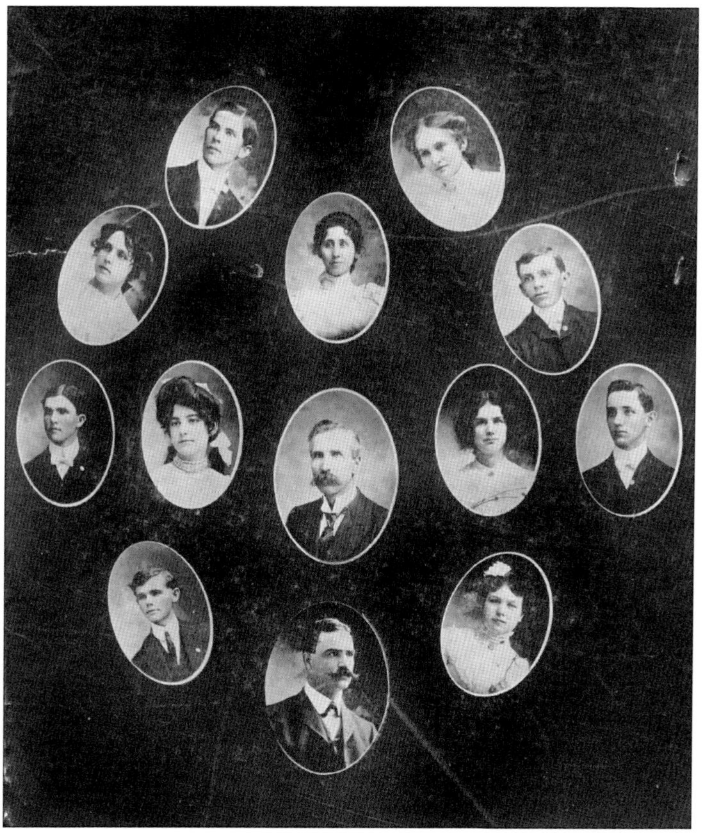

The graduating class of 1902 from Ennis High School, shown here, was a small one and not much larger than the first graduating class in 1886. That year, only seven students made up the first graduating class from Ennis High School. They were Charles Allen, Will Brown, Mattie Crutcher, Dora Davenport, Winnie Loggins, Lula Pace, and B. Thornwell Trewitt. Charles Allen was the first class valedictorian and Mattie Crutcher the first class salutatorian. Dr. J. C. Loggins, one of the early settlers of Ennis, presented the graduates with their diplomas, and Supt. W. B. Sutton gave the closing address at the ceremony. (Courtesy of Ennis Heritage Society.)

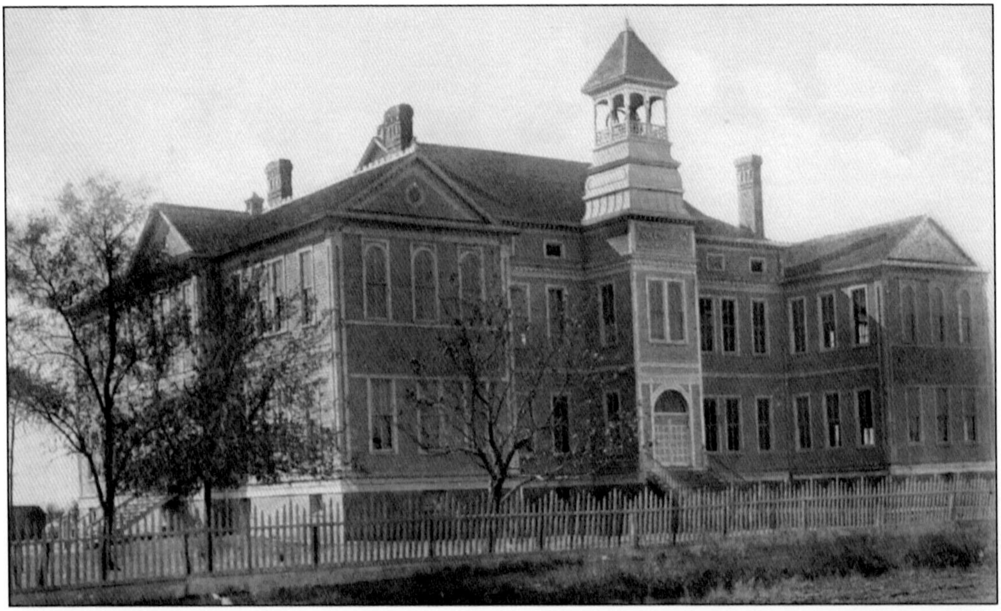

After the first school was destroyed by fire, a new school was built in 1894 and came to be known as "Old Faithful." It was considered a state-of-the-art school for its time and was a reflection of the pride this young community had in its children. It included 10 "recitation" rooms, a laboratory equipped to teach both chemistry and physics, and a library with approximately 2,000 books on its shelves. The new school was also equipped with Star and Steinway pianos in the Conservatory of Music, as well as an auditorium capable of seating up to 700. Above is a view of the school front, and below is a side view on a Field Day in the early 1900s. (Both courtesy of Ennis Public Library.)

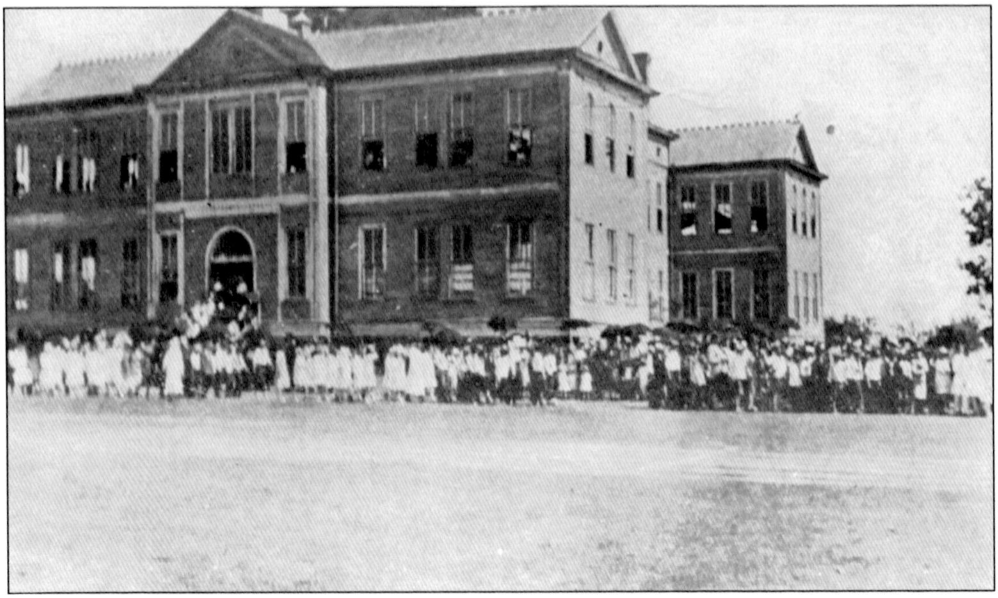

The first school building, located at the North Gaines Street location, was constructed in 1881. The ornate Victorian structure, pictured here, was completely destroyed by fire in 1893. The bell tower, intended to call children to school, stood tall above the nearby residential neighborhood and could be easily seen from the downtown area. (Courtesy of Mary Helen Nowlin Gentry.)

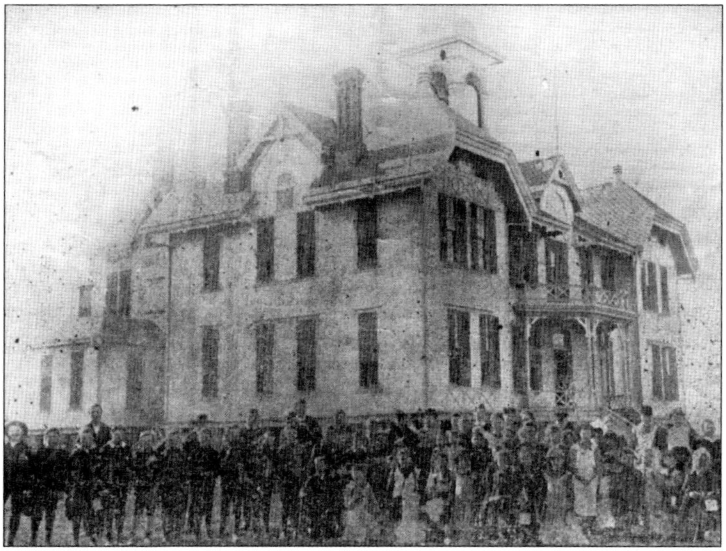

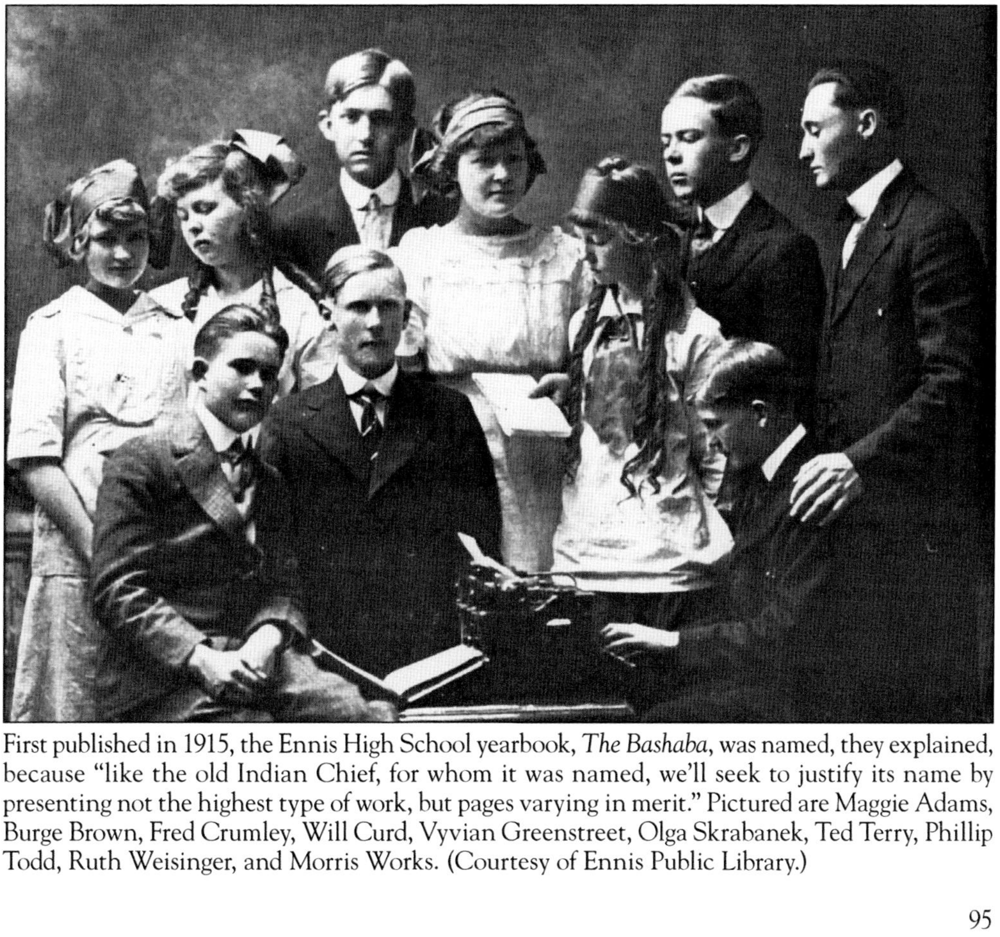

First published in 1915, the Ennis High School yearbook, *The Bashaba*, was named, they explained, because "like the old Indian Chief, for whom it was named, we'll seek to justify its name by presenting not the highest type of work, but pages varying in merit." Pictured are Maggie Adams, Burge Brown, Fred Crumley, Will Curd, Vyvian Greenstreet, Olga Skrabanek, Ted Terry, Phillip Todd, Ruth Weisinger, and Morris Works. (Courtesy of Ennis Public Library.)

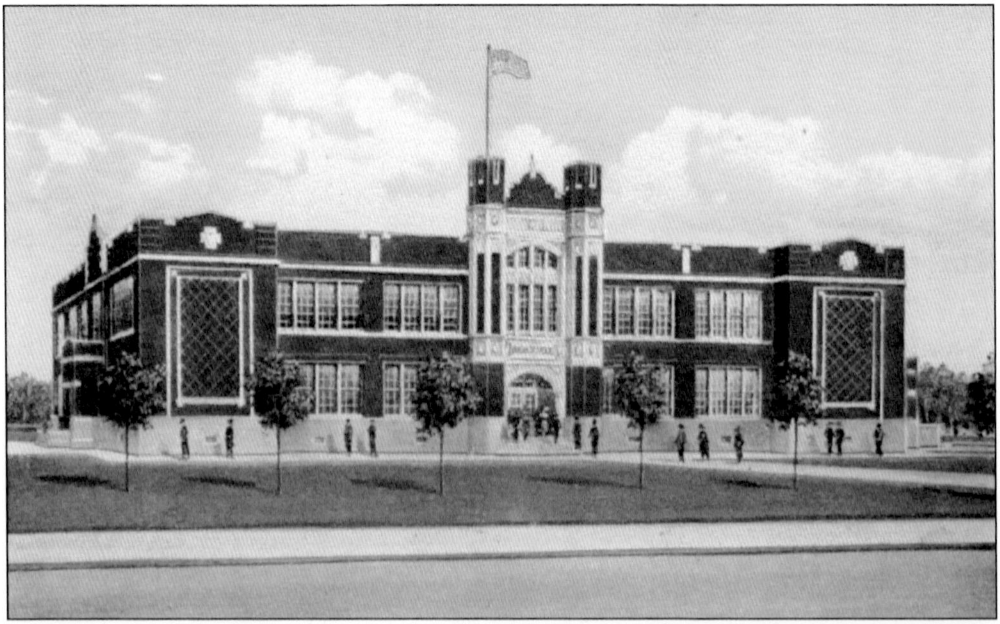

In 1916, the new Ennis High School was completed. The basement housed first and second grades and an eating area that also served as the girls gymnasium. The remaining elementary grades and the boys gymnasium were located on the first floor. An auditorium and high school classes were on the second floor.

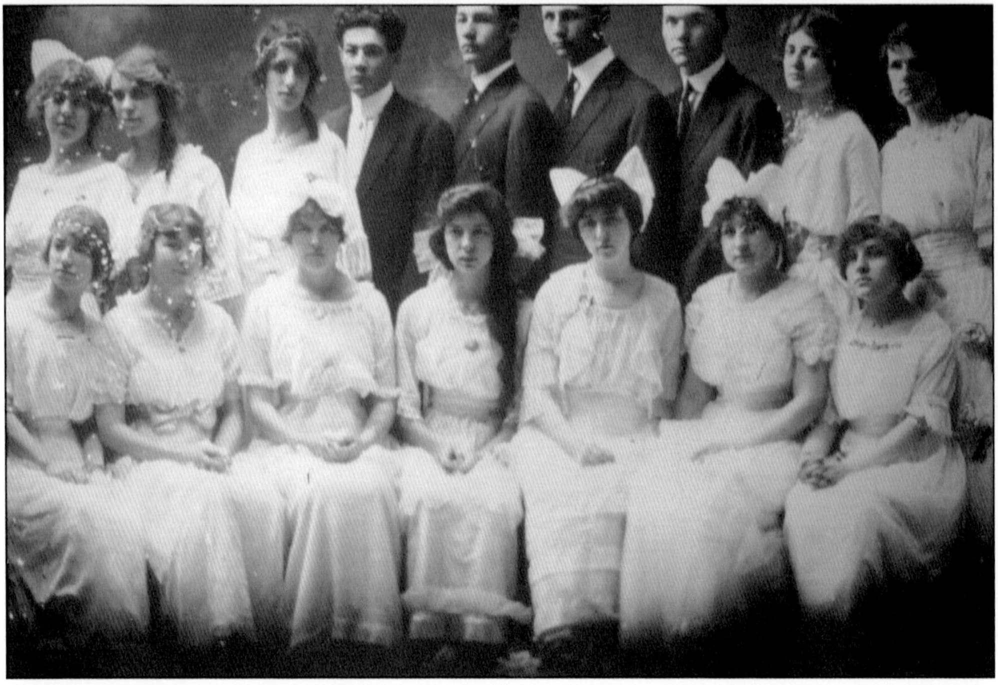

Just months after the end of World War I, members of the class of 1919 gathered for their graduation photograph. While a time of celebration, it was also a time of rebuilding. The city had suffered greatly from the flu epidemic, which made no discrimination between young and old. (Courtesy of Ennis Heritage Society.)

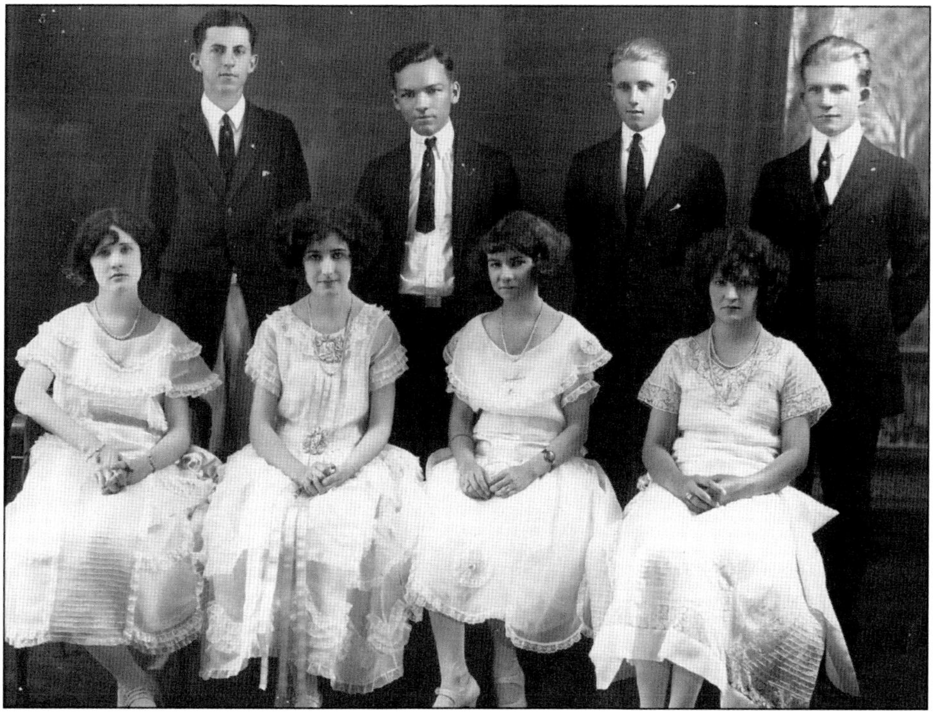

In the Ennis High School class of 1923, eight students shared the distinction of graduating with those they had started school with in the same first grade. Pictured above from left to right are (first row) Margaret Atwood, Blanche Menard, Addlean White, and Jessie Harper; (second row) Ray Telfair, Arthur McElroy, Jack Castellaw (class valedictorian), and Oscar Nelson Allen (class salutatorian). Fifty years later in 1973, members of the class of 1923 came together once again. Pictured below from left to right, they are (first row) Ruth Sims Mims, Virgie Cox Stewart, Lila Mai Whittington Fitzgerald, Ray Telfair, Esta Bufkin Stringer, and Hulette Jones Nabors; (second row) Blanche Menard, Annie Laurie Whittington Wahrmund, Cecelia Kelly McNally, Felix Wright, Addlean White Bennett, Lorene Sullivan Marchbanks, and Rev. John Collier. (Both courtesy of Telfair family.)

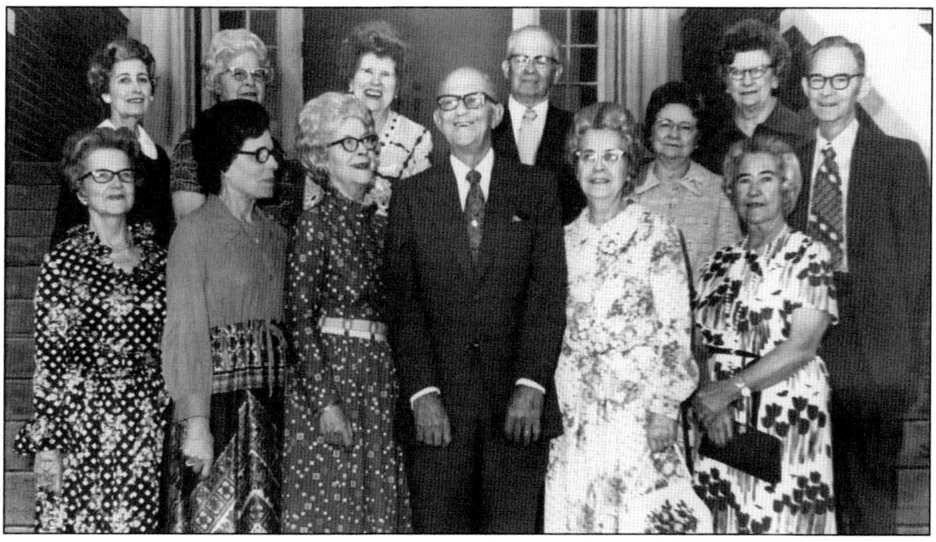

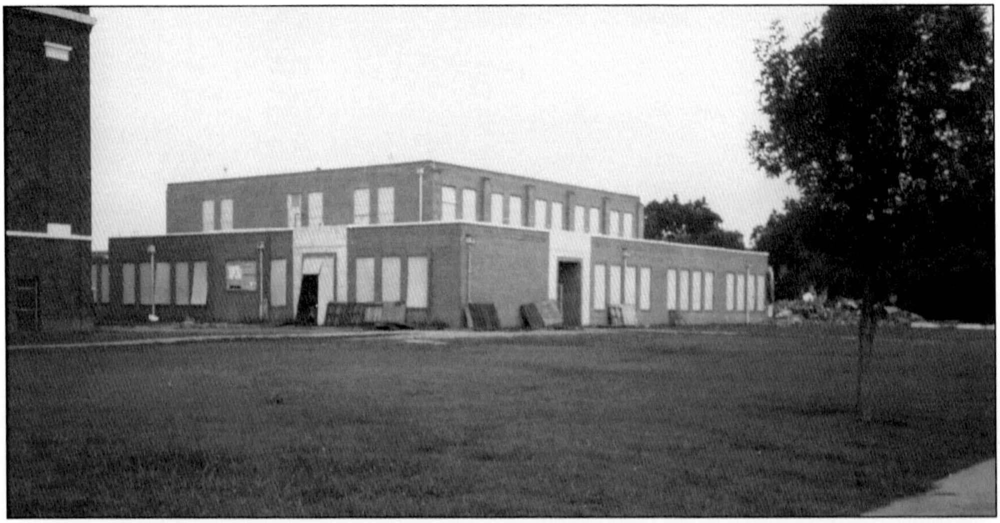

The David Crockett School was completed in 1937. Work on a gymnasium began in 1941 but wasn't completed for several years because construction was halted at the beginning of World War II. (Courtesy of Chad Spence.)

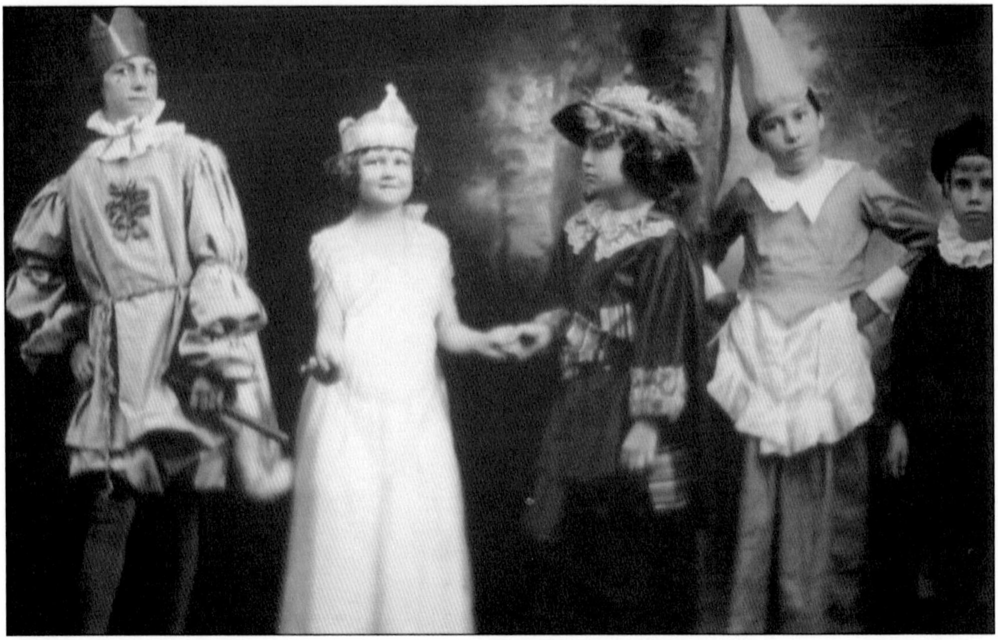

Whatever school they attended, children have always enjoyed the arts in Ennis schools. Since the early years of the school system, students have participated in orchestras, bands, and plays, as pictured here. (Courtesy of Ennis Heritage Society.)

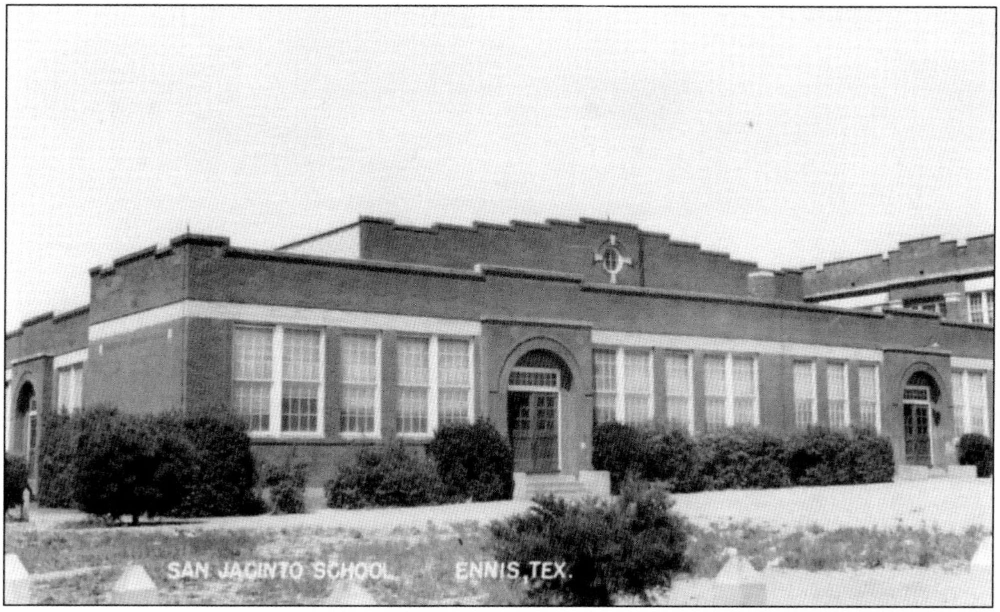

Plans for San Jacinto Elementary School began in 1923. Located at the northwest corner of North Gaines and Belknap Streets, it was built just south of the high school. When it was constructed, the school had nine classrooms for the primary grades, an auditorium with a balcony, an office, and a book room. (Courtesy of Ivan and Judie Goodwin family.)

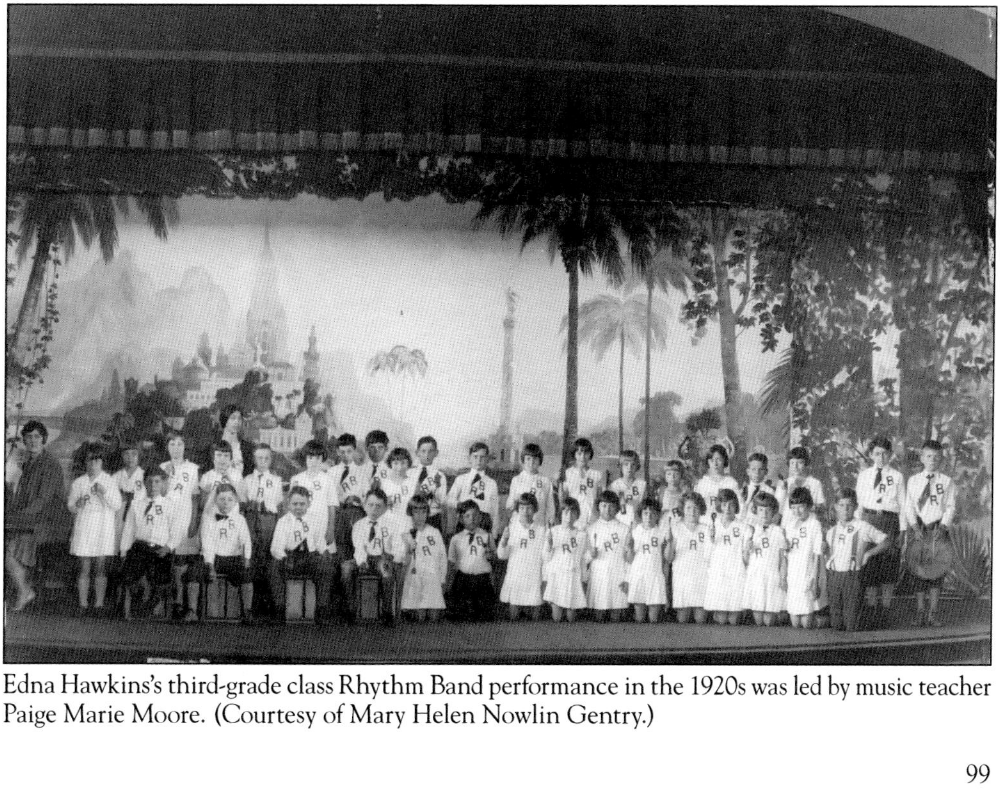

Edna Hawkins's third-grade class Rhythm Band performance in the 1920s was led by music teacher Paige Marie Moore. (Courtesy of Mary Helen Nowlin Gentry.)

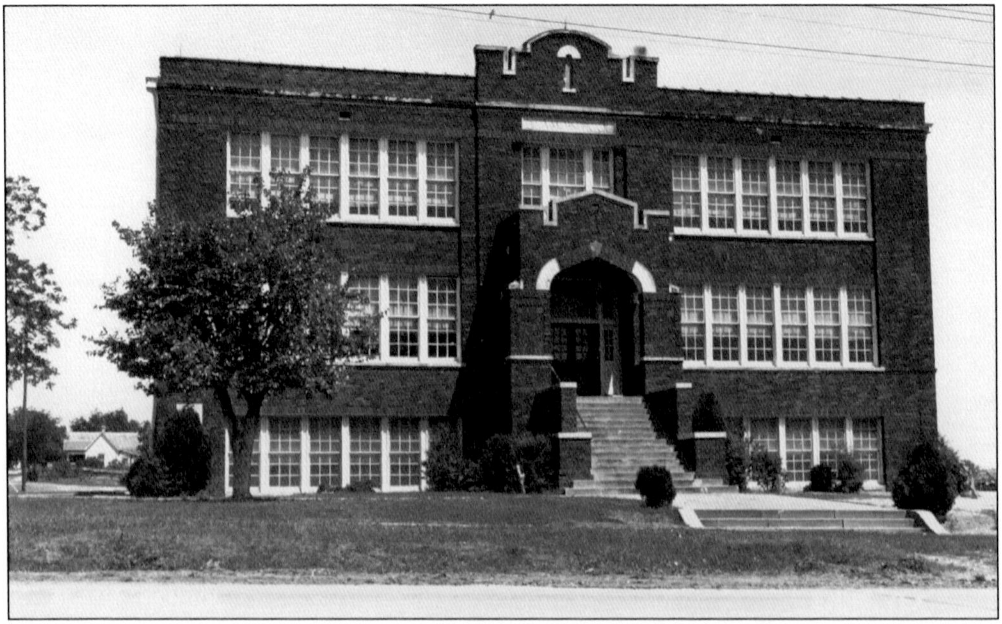

The Alamo Elementary School was built in 1915. It replaced the original Ward School building, located at the same site since the late 1800s at East Ennis Avenue and North Shawnee Street. Pictured below is a first-grade class at Alamo during the 1950s. (Above, courtesy of City of Ennis; below Chad Spence.)

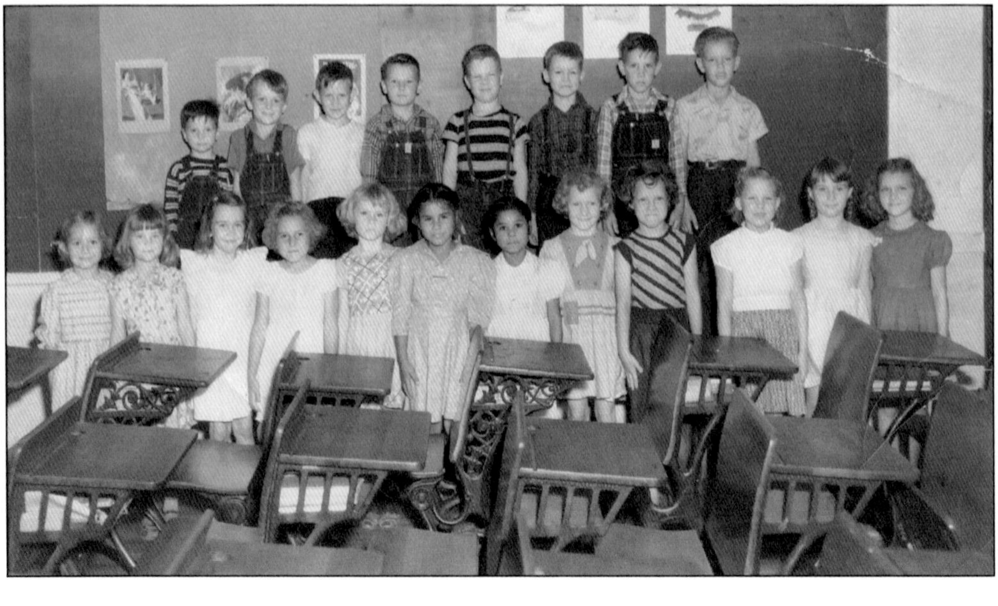

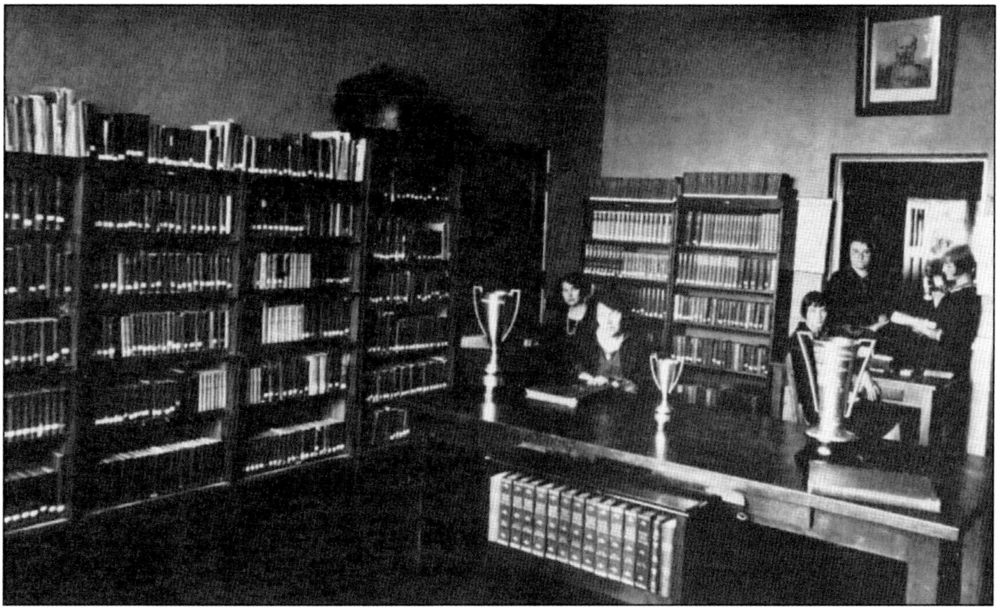

J. C. Watkins was an early superintendant of Ennis schools and an active advocate for a strong library. In 1893, when the library and over 2,000 books were destroyed by fire, the school board took the lead in purchasing 1,200 books for a new library. Pictured in the 1920s, the new J. C. Watkins Library implemented the Dewey Decimal System in 1924. (Courtesy of Ennis Public Library.)

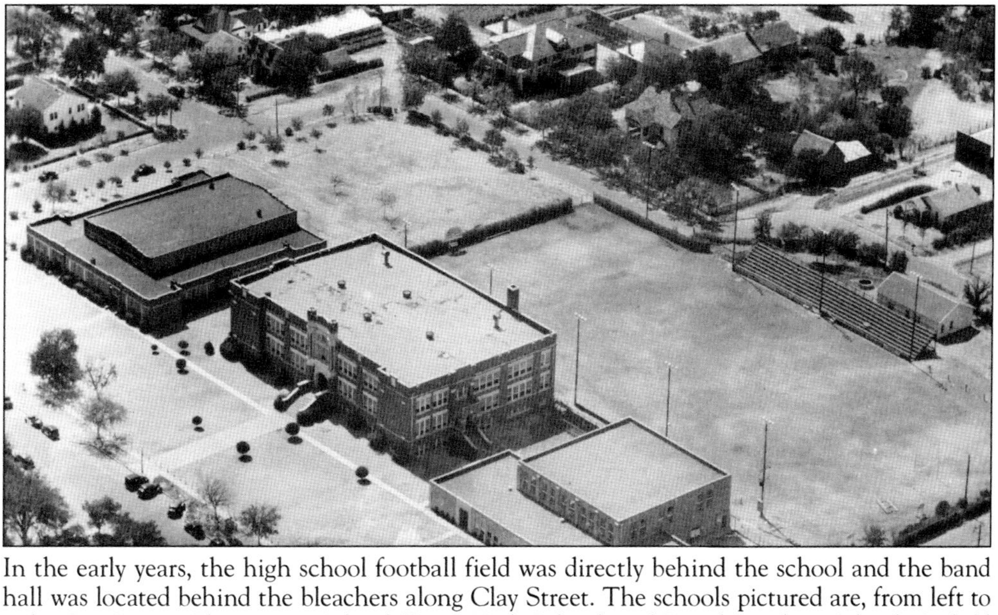

In the early years, the high school football field was directly behind the school and the band hall was located behind the bleachers along Clay Street. The schools pictured are, from left to right, San Jacinto Elementary School, Ennis High School, and David Crockett School. A child could complete his entire education in Ennis during those years without ever leaving the block. (Courtesy of Mary Ann Novy Lamkin.)

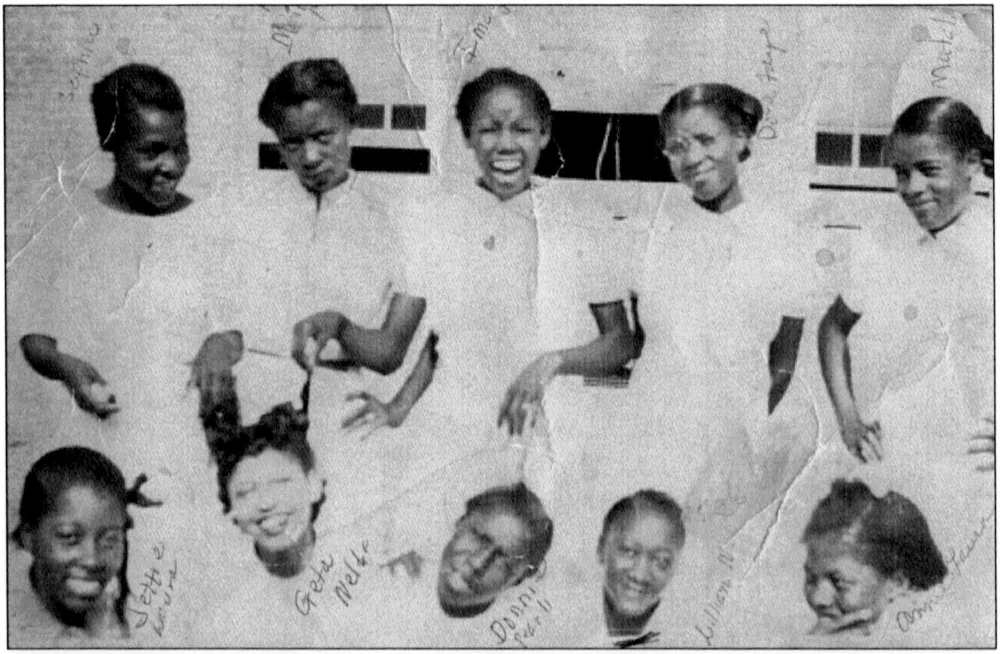

Members of the Colored High School class of 1940 gathered for this photograph in the late 1930s. From left to right are (first row) Jettie Coleman, Greta Nelda Kane, Donnie Pearl Jackson, Lillian Nell Lewis, and Anna Laura Robinson; (second row) Sophia Lucille Jackson, Mary Lucille Flowers, Imogene Stell, Dora Jones, and Mataline Coleman. (Courtesy of Woody Lewis family.)

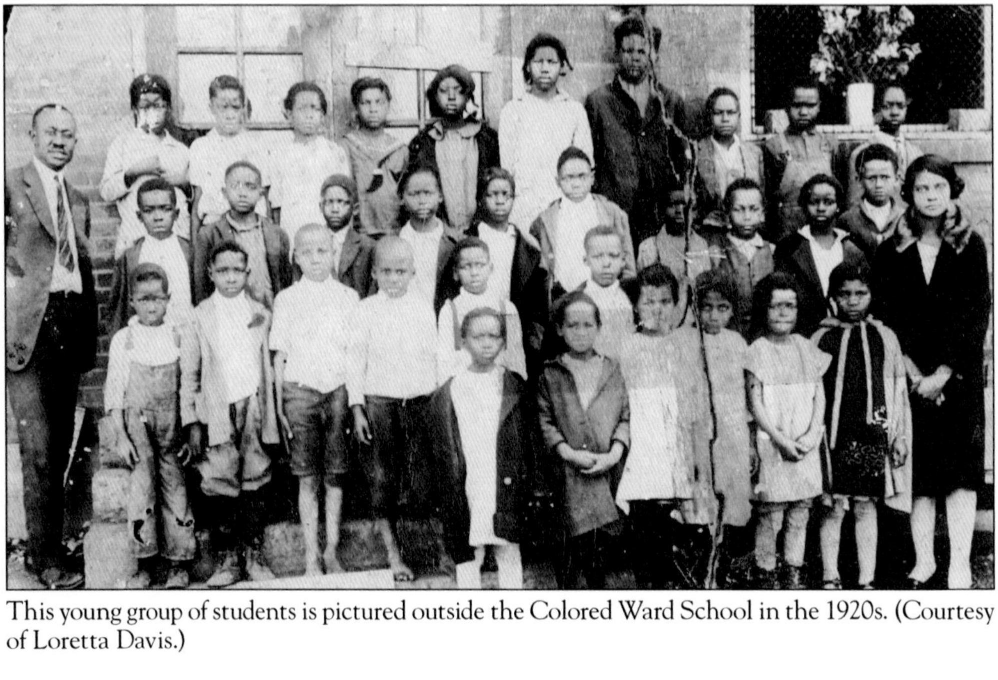

This young group of students is pictured outside the Colored Ward School in the 1920s. (Courtesy of Loretta Davis.)

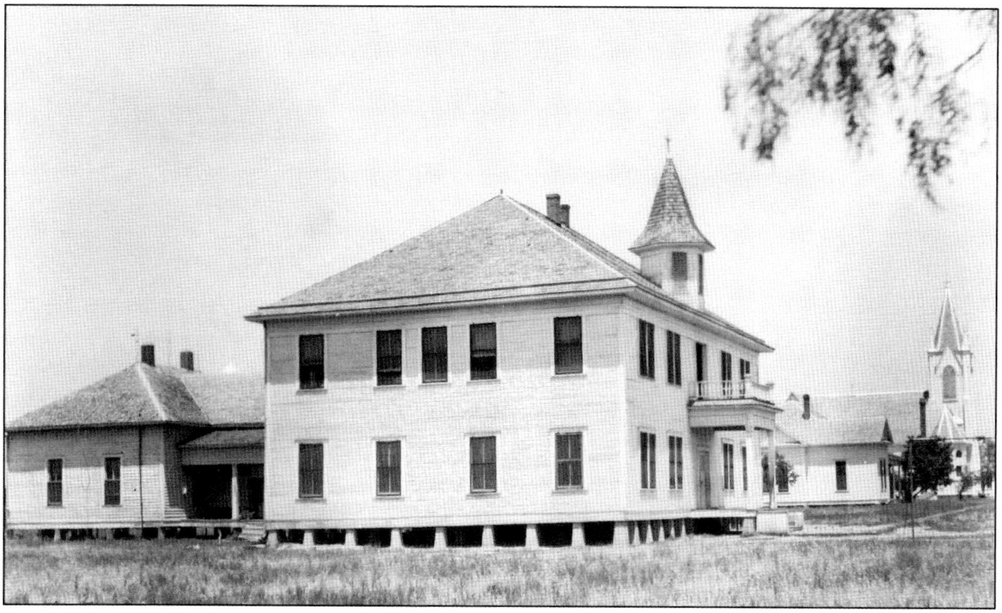

In 1912, Fr. Francis Kowalski founded the St. John Elementary School in a small two-room house. In 1917, a new school, pictured above, was built on St. John property. The classrooms were on the first floor and housing for the Sisters on the second floor. (Courtesy of Mary Ann Novy Lamkin.)

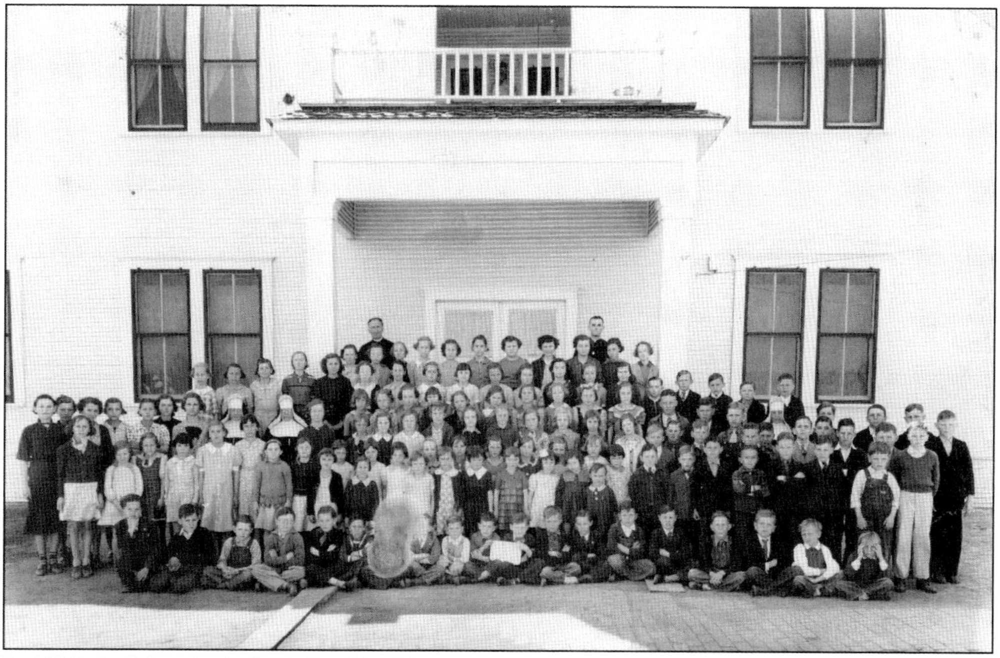

In 1930, St. John Catholic School had been providing students with an education for almost 20 years. Gathered in front of their school are students and teachers, including, from left to right (at the rear on each side of the door), Fr. Francis Kowalski, founder of the school, and Fr. Vincent Micola. (Courtesy of Adell Valek.)

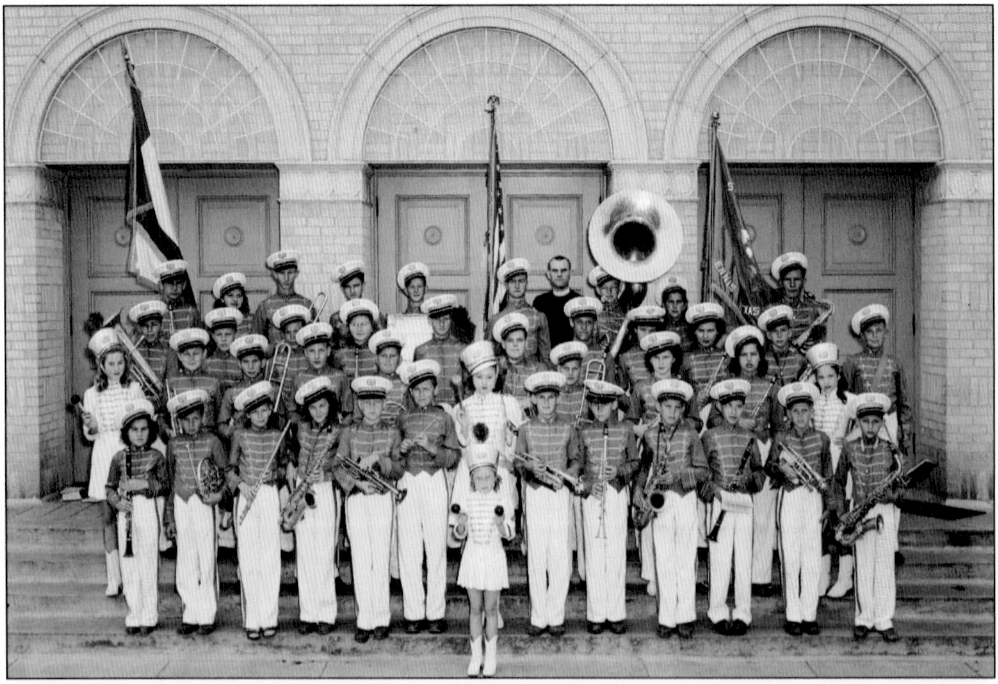

Under the guidance of Father Micola, St. John's School began a school band in the early 1940s. Father Micola, pictured in the fourth row among band members, played the violin but taught all the instruments played by band students. (Courtesy of Mary Ann Novy Lamkin.)

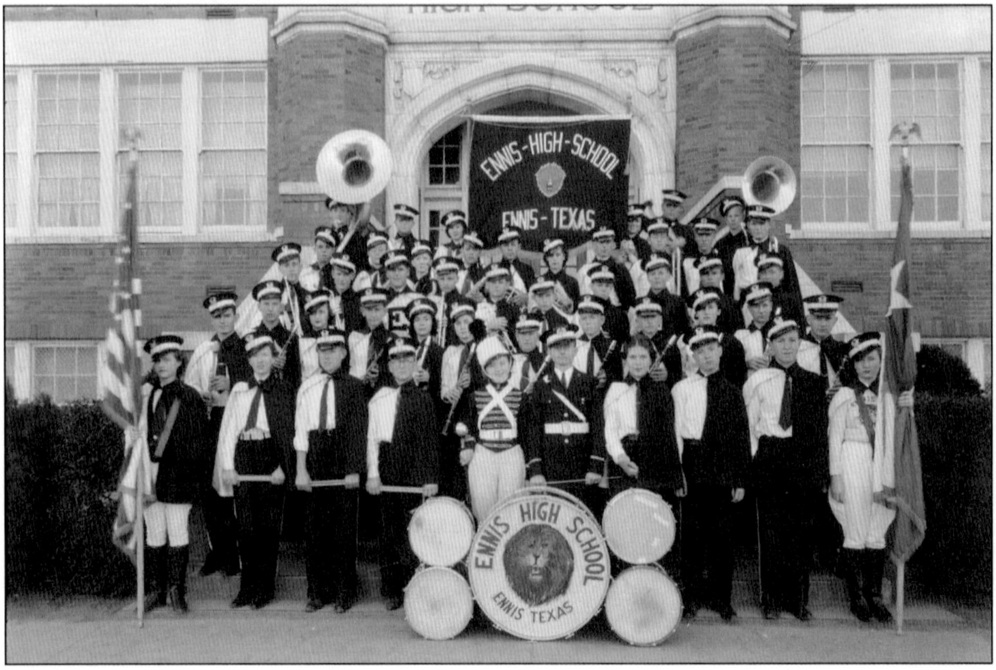

The Ennis High School Band has been a long-standing tradition since its inception. The Ennis High School Band of the mid-1930s was conducted under the leadership of J. D. King. (Courtesy of Mary Helen Nowlin Gentry.)

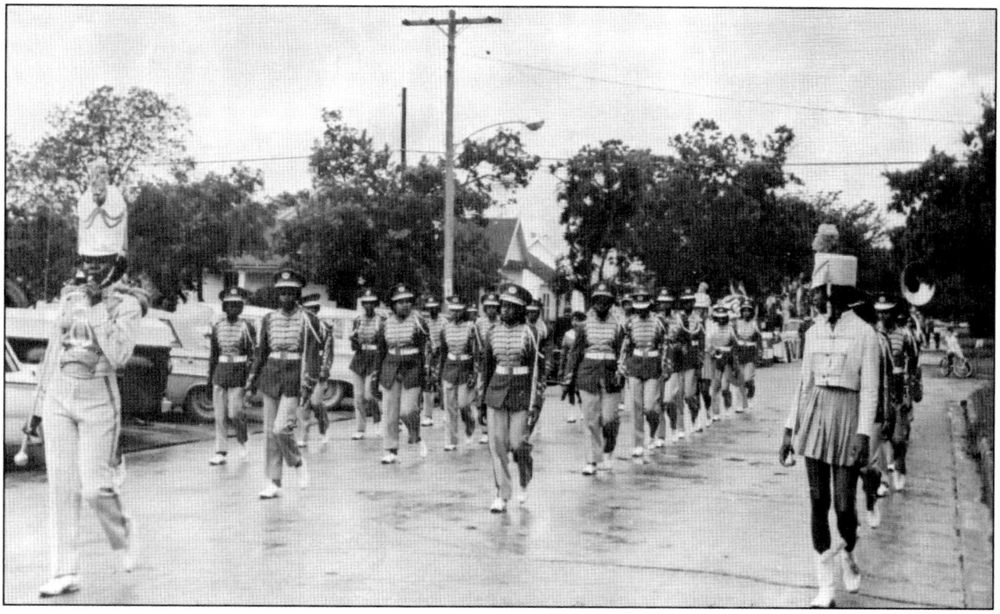

Recognized as an integral part of school life for many students, the Carver High School dedicated their 1964 yearbook to the Carver High School Band, pictured here in 1964 at an unidentified event. (Courtesy of Carver Alumni Association.)

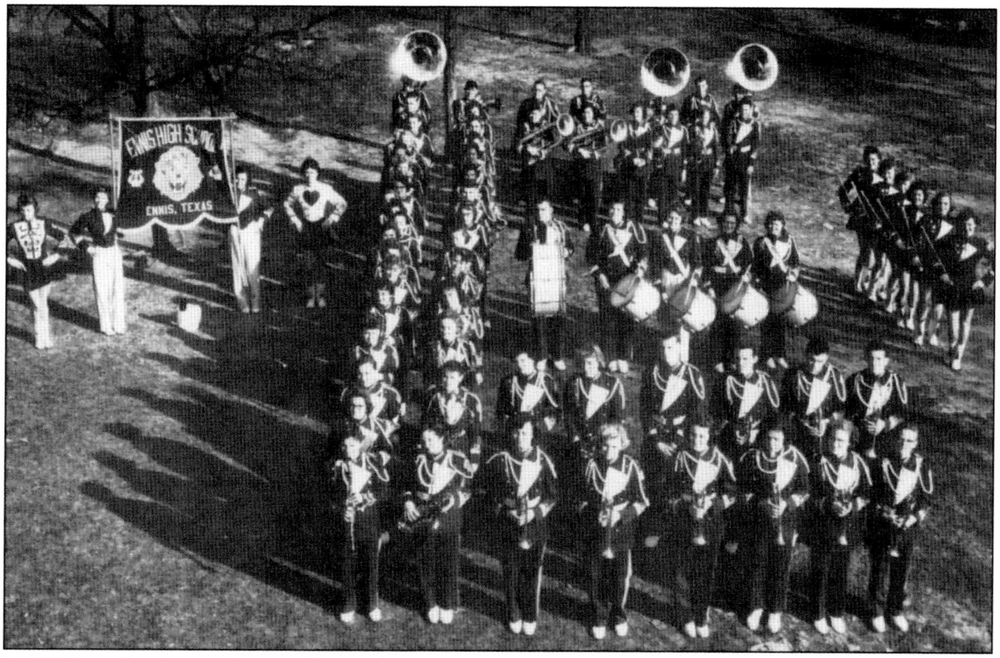

In 1956, under the guidance of band director Ivan Goodwin, the Ennis High School Band adopted the "E" for Ennis formation, referred to as the "Flying E," pictured above. In the following years, graduating classes also adopted the "E" formation for the class graduation picture. This tradition has endured to the present day. (Courtesy of Ivan and Judie Goodwin family.)

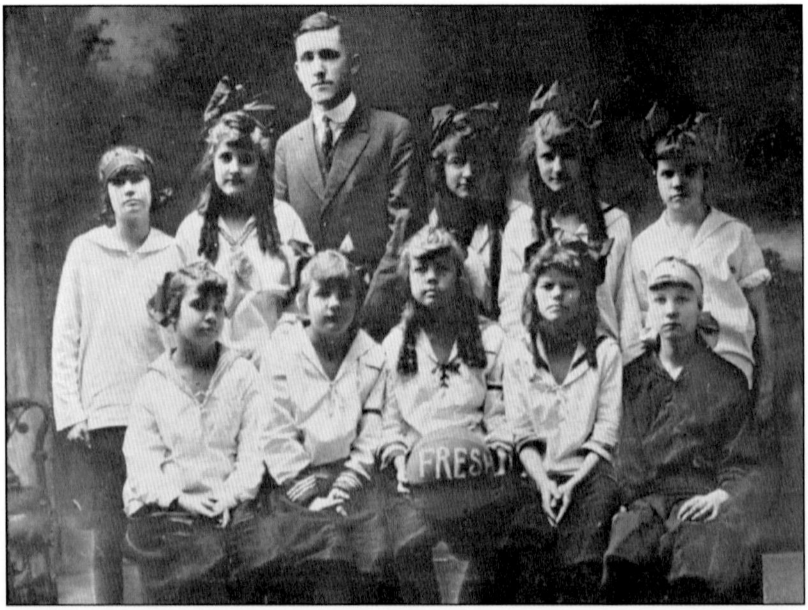

In the 1914–1915 school year, Ennis High School had both a girls and a boys basketball team. Seen above, the girls team included, from left to right, (first row) Early Blakey, Johnnie Long, Eugenia Blakey, Frances Allen, and Olga Skrabanek; (second row) Viola Emerson, Loraine Kelley, coach Frank Story, LaRue Sweatman, Cammie Cook, and Marguerite Burkhead. Below, from left to right, the members of the boys team are (first row) Osborne Fuqua, forward; Bill Curd, forward; Lon Howard, captain; and Si McClain, guard; (second row) Claire Rooker, substitute; Burge Brown, center; and Luther Howard, guard; (third row) coach R. H. Brister and Clifford McCullough, substitute guard. (Both courtesy of Ennis Public Library.)

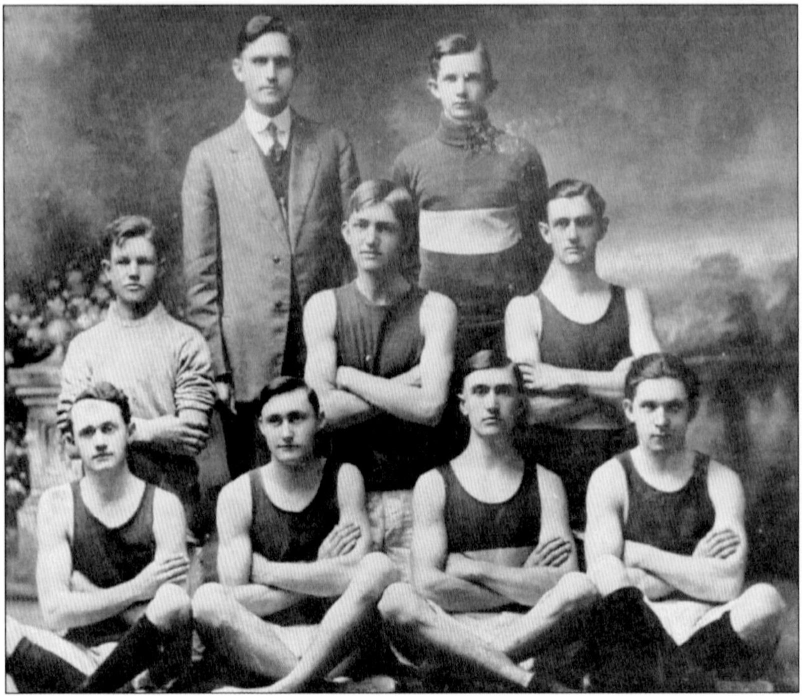

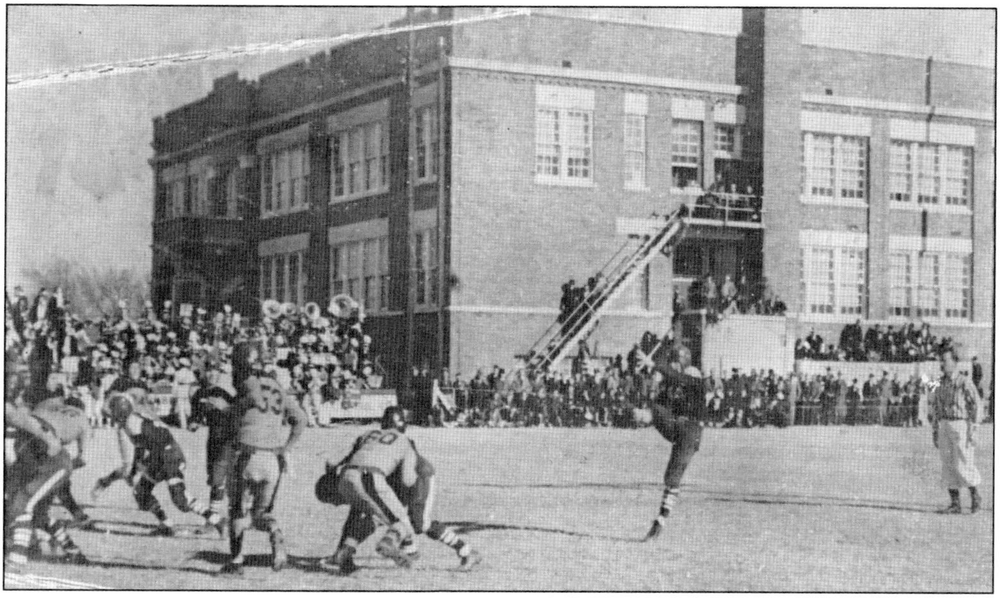

Football has been played at Ennis High School since the early 1900s. Before the new stadium was built to the west of Clay Street, the game was played in the field directly behind the high school, pictured above in the mid-1930s. During those years, coach Frank Blair (below, standing, second from left) and coach "Chaddy" Davidson (below, standing, second from right) led the team. (Both courtesy of Mary Helen Nowlin Gentry.)

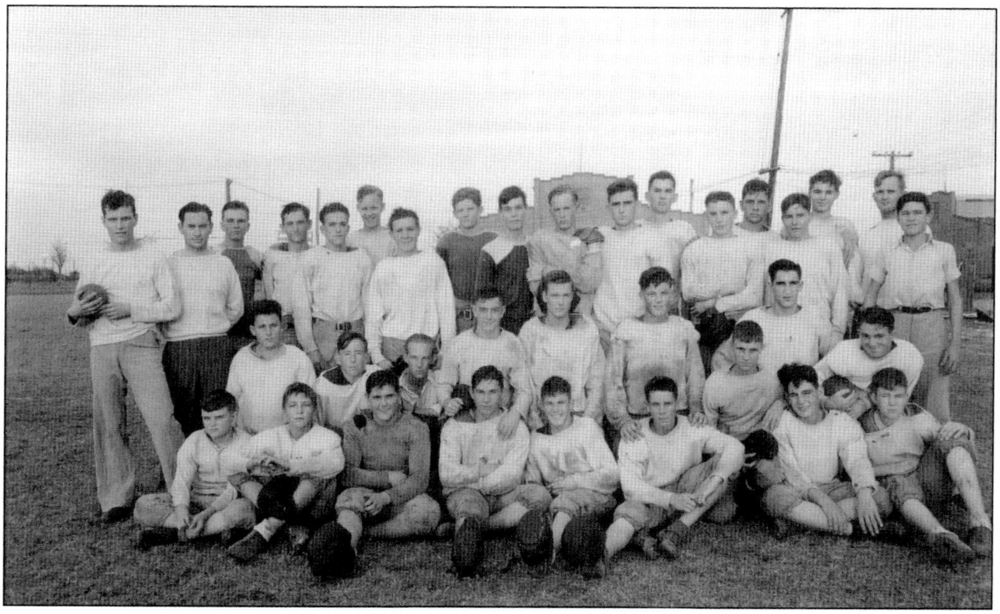

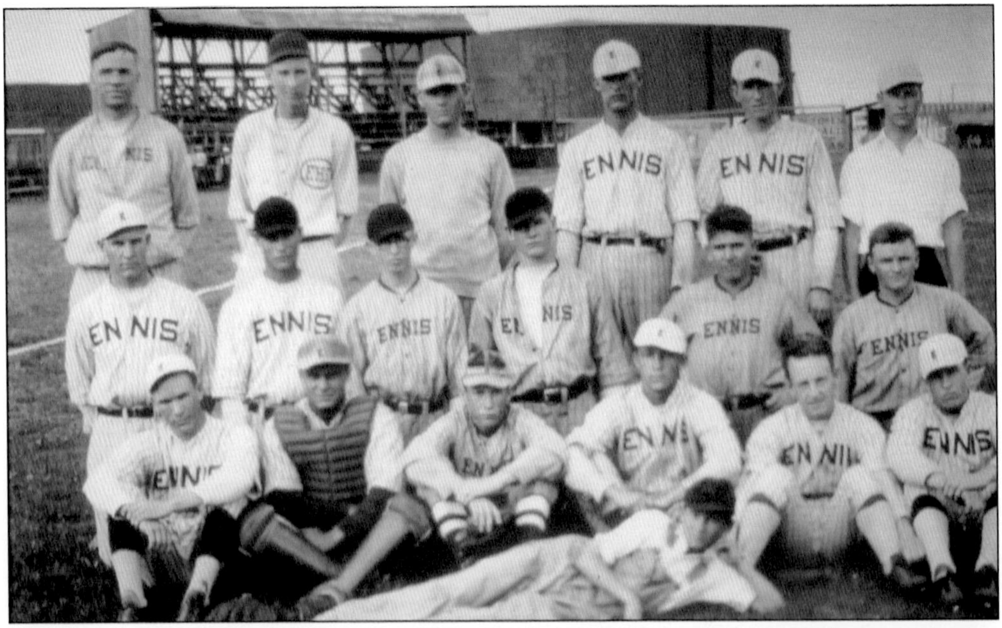

To better prepare his high school baseball team of the 1920s, coach R. B. Neilson, pictured at the far left of the third row, would often have them play against the Southern Pacific team, a semiprofessional ballclub at the time. (Courtesy of Ennis Heritage Society.)

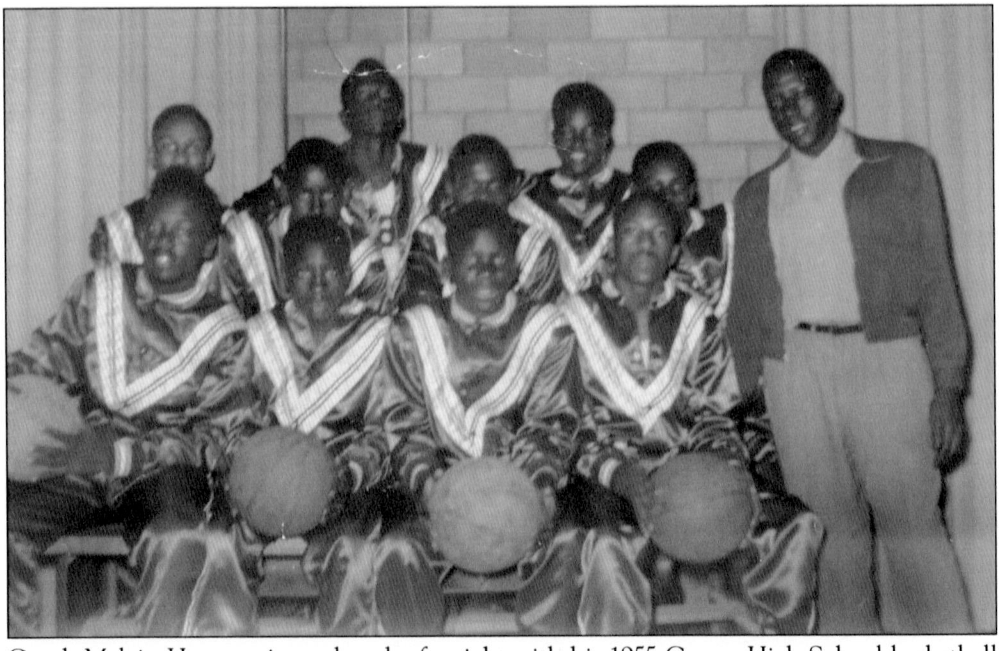

Coach Melvin Hunter, pictured at the far right with his 1955 Carver High School basketball team, was joined in later years by assistant coach William Stell, a former student and one of the first Carver athletes to receive a full athletic scholarship . (Courtesy of Melvin Hunter.)

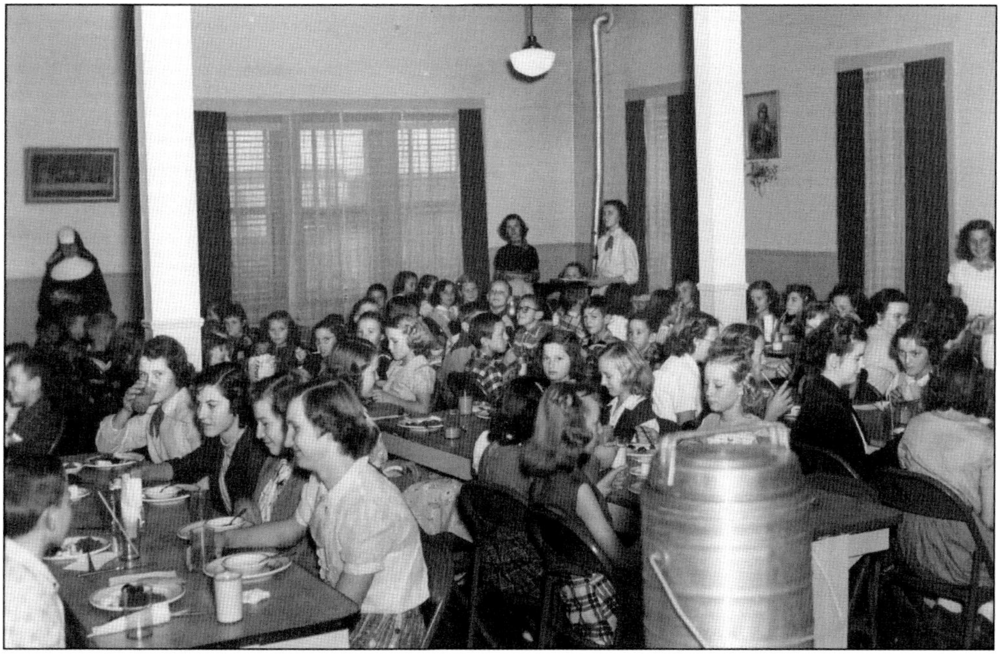

The St. John cafeteria, pictured in the 1950s, was located in the old school gymnasium. Built from the wood of the original church, it was the location of numerous school functions over the years. (Courtesy of Mary Ann Novy Lamkin.)

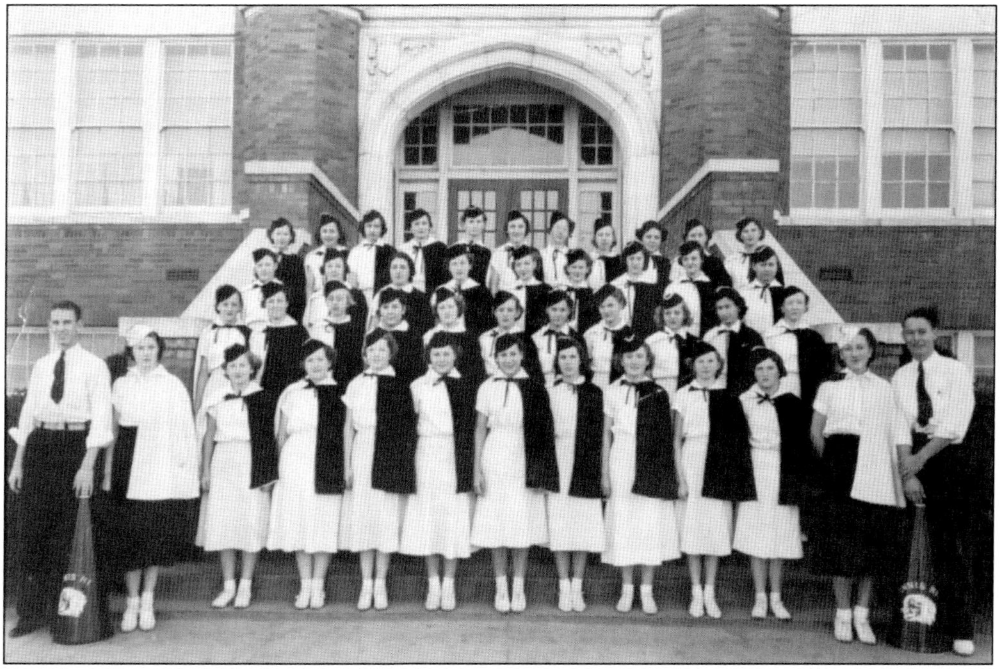

The Ennis High School drill team was first organized in the 1935 school year under the guidance of teacher Katherine Maxson. Ennis High School was one of only a few high schools in the state at that time that allowed boys on the drill team, as seen in this 1936 photograph. (Courtesy of Mary Helen Nowlin Gentry.)

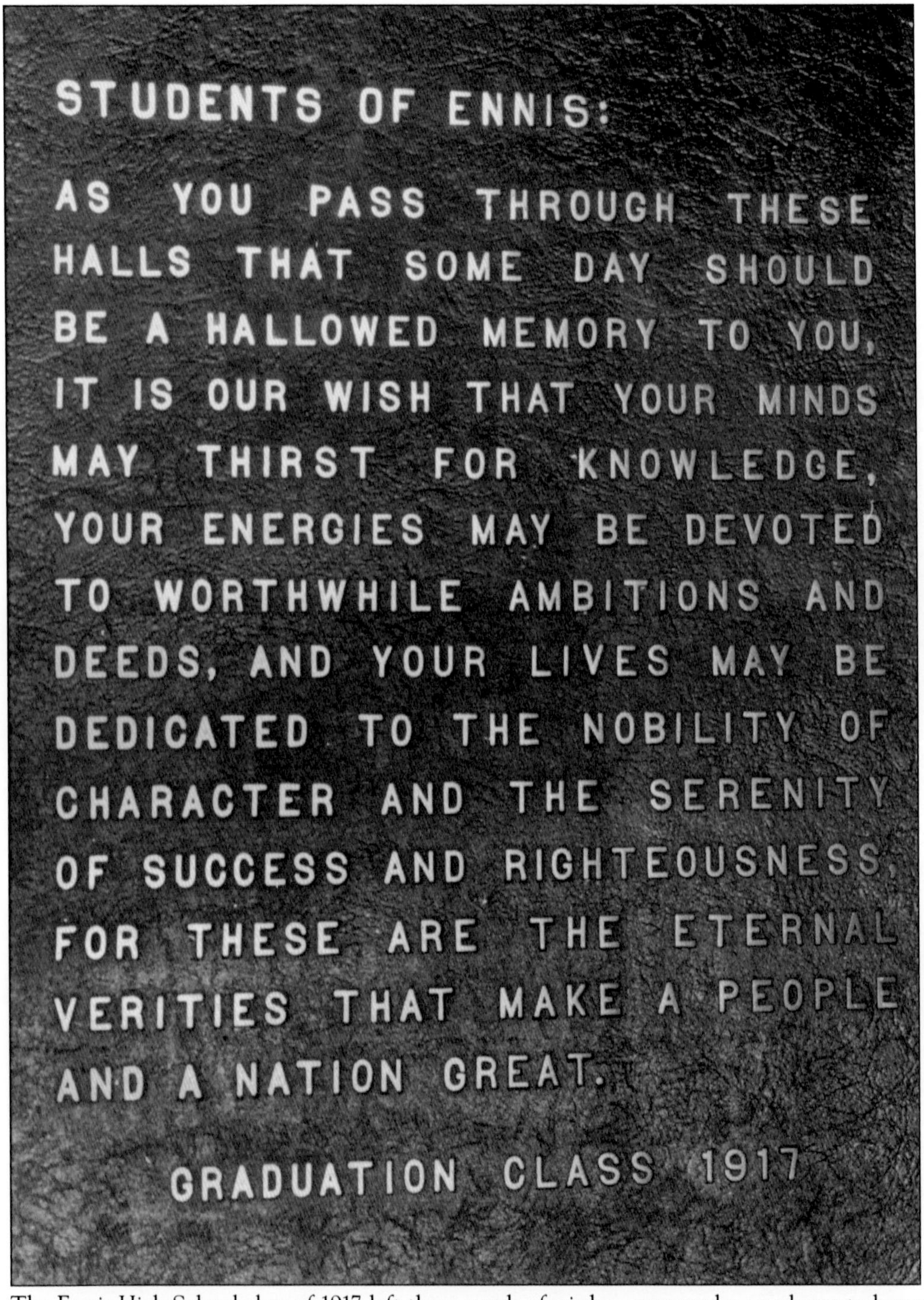

The Ennis High School class of 1917 left these words of wisdom engraved on a plaque to hang in their alma mater for all those students who would come after. These students graduated at a time their country was entering the "War to End All Wars." Their words exemplify their acknowledgment of the seriousness of the world events surrounding them and that which they deemed to be of consequence. (Courtesy of Ennis Public Library.)

Seven

Stories We Tell

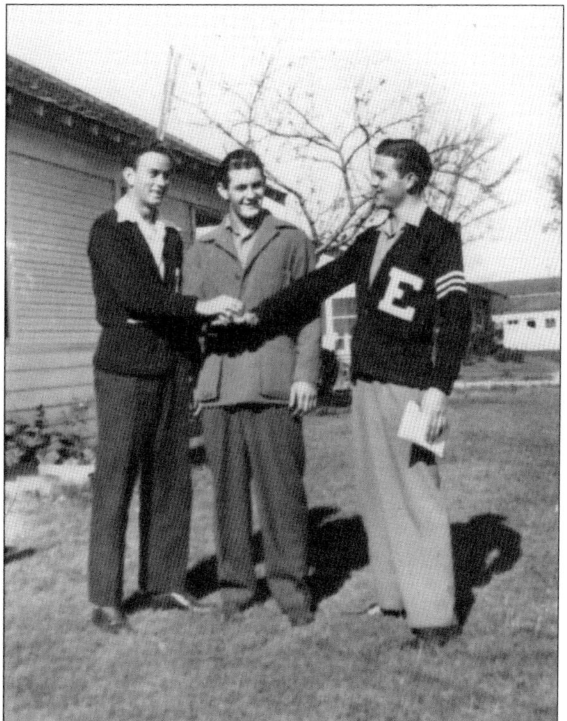

Seven young men from Ennis fought in the Battle of Iwo Jima in World War II. Joe Riley Crow, James Wesley "Airdale" Goodwin, George M. Lucas, Jack Lummus, William Thomas "Dooney" Pierce Jr., Raymond Forest Rickert, and James Vinson Head were all part of the Marine Corps that stormed the island. In the first 23 minutes of the assault on Iwo Jima, 9,000 marines gained the island, including Jack, Dooney, George, and Ray. Of the seven men, Joe Crow was the first casualty on February 20, 1945. Jack Lummus was killed by a land mine on March 8, and on that same day, Airdale Goodwin was shot and later died aboard a hospital ship. Dooney Pierce was killed on March 13 by a sniper. Goodwin, Crow, and Pierce, pictured from left to right outside Pierce's home after a farewell party given by his mother, were best friends, classmates, teammates, and fellow marines. (Courtesy of Ginger Crow Boon.)

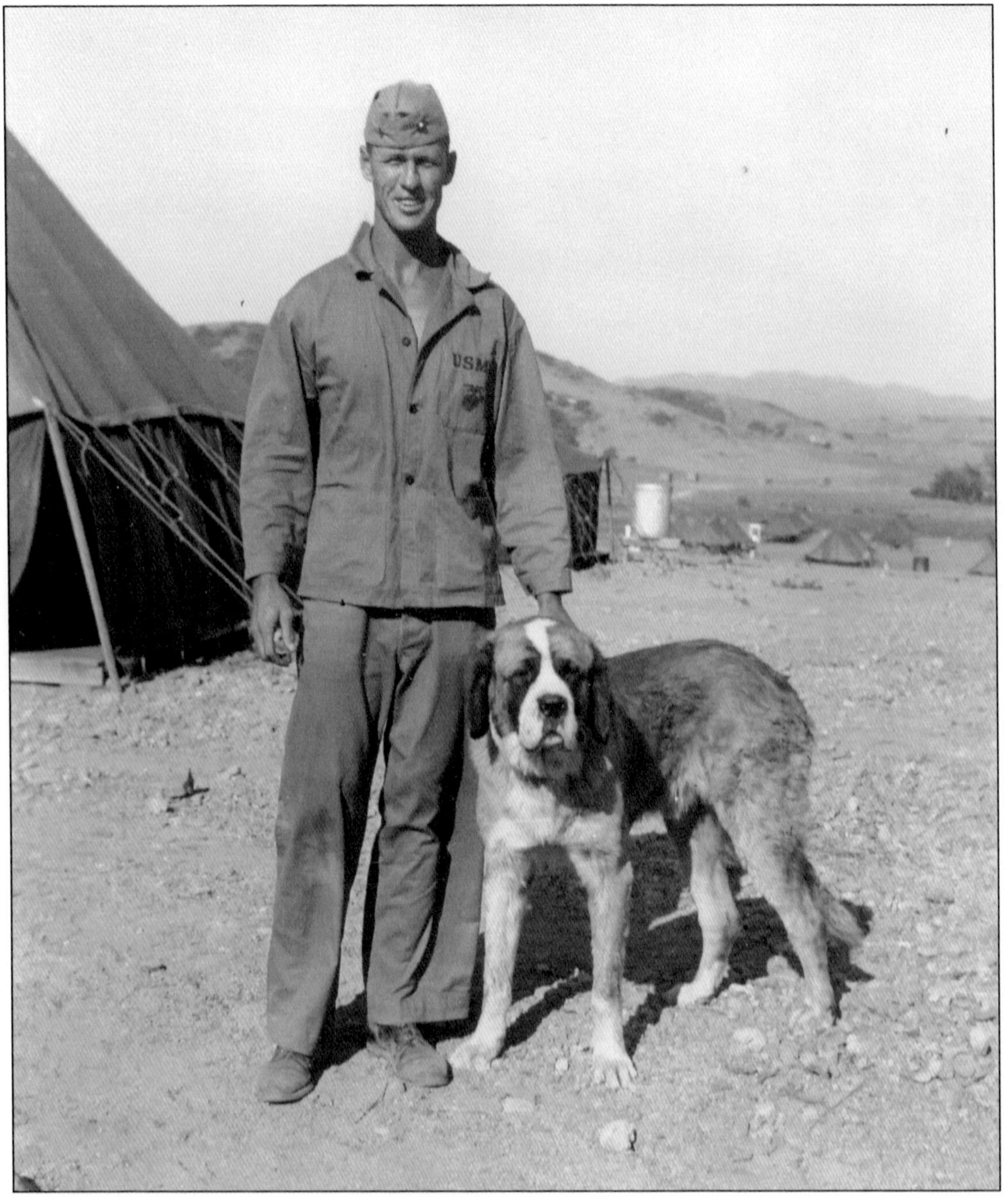

Jack Lummus was 12 when he and his family moved to Ennis. The year he graduated from Baylor University in 1941, he also signed a contract with the National Football League's (NFL) New York Giants. After the first season and just weeks after the attack on Pearl Harbor, Jack joined the U.S. Marine Reserve in January 1942. On February 19, 1945, he was with the 5th Marine Division as it landed with the first wave of assault troops on Iwo Jima. On March 8, he led the charge that breached General Kuribayashi's defensive line. During that charge, Jack stepped on a mine, shredding his leg and sending shrapnel into his abdomen. He was posthumously awarded the Congressional Medal of Honor, one of two players in the NFL to have received it. On February 22, 1986, a Maritime Prepositioning Ship was christened the *1st Lt. Jack Lummus*. He is pictured in July 1944 at Camp Joseph Pendleton with the St. Bernard given to the 27th Marines, 5th Marine Division by Col. James Roosevelt, son of Pres. Franklin D. Roosevelt. (Courtesy of www.jacklummus.com.)

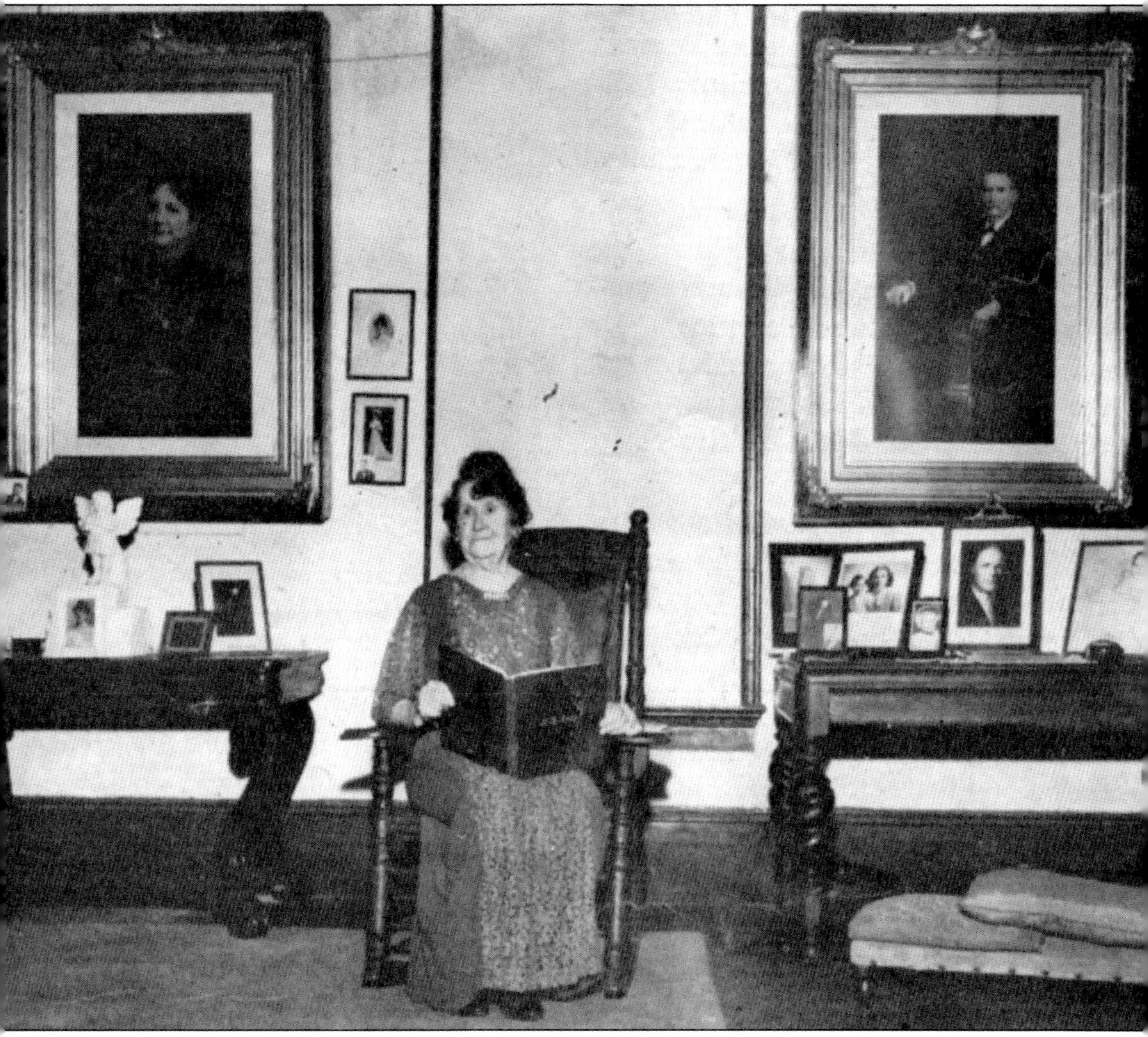

Katie Daffan was the daughter of Lawrence and Mollie Day Daffan, a member of the Hood's Texas Brigade of the Confederacy and the Ennis division railroad superintendant. Katie served five terms as the president of the Texas Division of the United Daughters of the Confederacy. She wrote several books, including two textbooks adopted by the Texas State Textbook Commission in the early 1900s. She ran for Texas governor and in 1911 became the first woman in Texas to head a state institution. She later served as the first president of the Texas Historical Society and was state historian for the Daughters of the American Revolution. She worked as a literary editor for the *Houston Chronicle* and was a Houston Public Library trustee. She spent most her final years in Ennis teaching at local schools, writing a column for the *Ennis Daily News*, and being involved in many civic organizations. Seated between portraits of her parents in her Ennis home, she is captured by photographer Ford Curry in one of the last photographs taken of her before her death. (Courtesy of Ennis Public Library.)

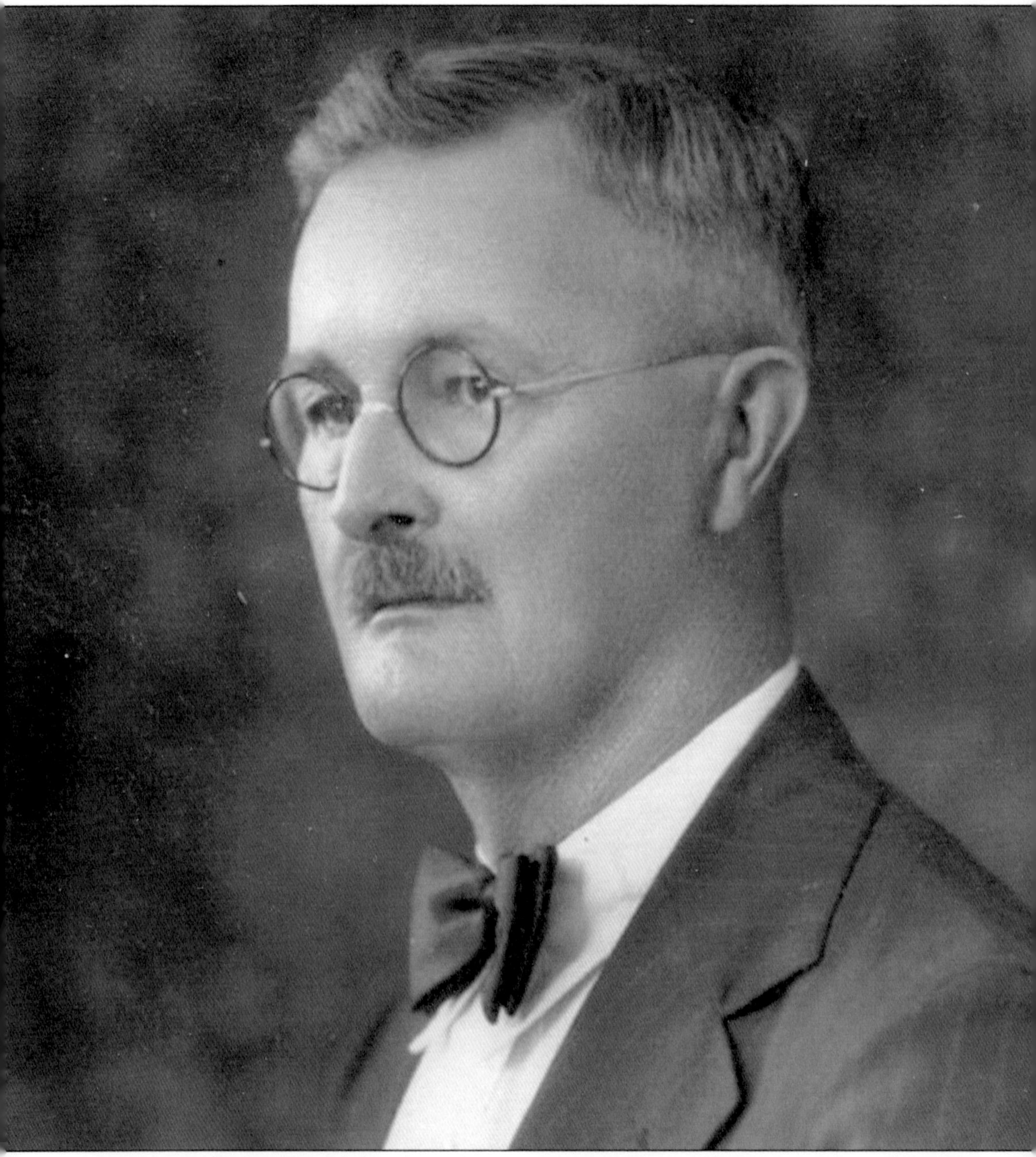

Hix McCanless was an early resident of Ennis, moving to the city from Tennessee in the 1880s. He married Mary Watkins, daughter of Prof. J. C. Watkins, who was one of the early Ennis School System superintendents. Hix served as city engineer for several years. He designed many early structures in the city, including the first major hospital completed in 1924, but what created his legacy are the many buildings, both residential and commercial, that still stand today. His architectural style is recognizable and can be seen at city hall, the Ennis Daily News building (the Ennis Lodge), and many other downtown structures. The very first of the many residential homes he built can still be seen at North Gaines Street in the area north of downtown that now carries his name, the Templeton McCanless Historic District. (Courtesy of Ennis Public Library.)

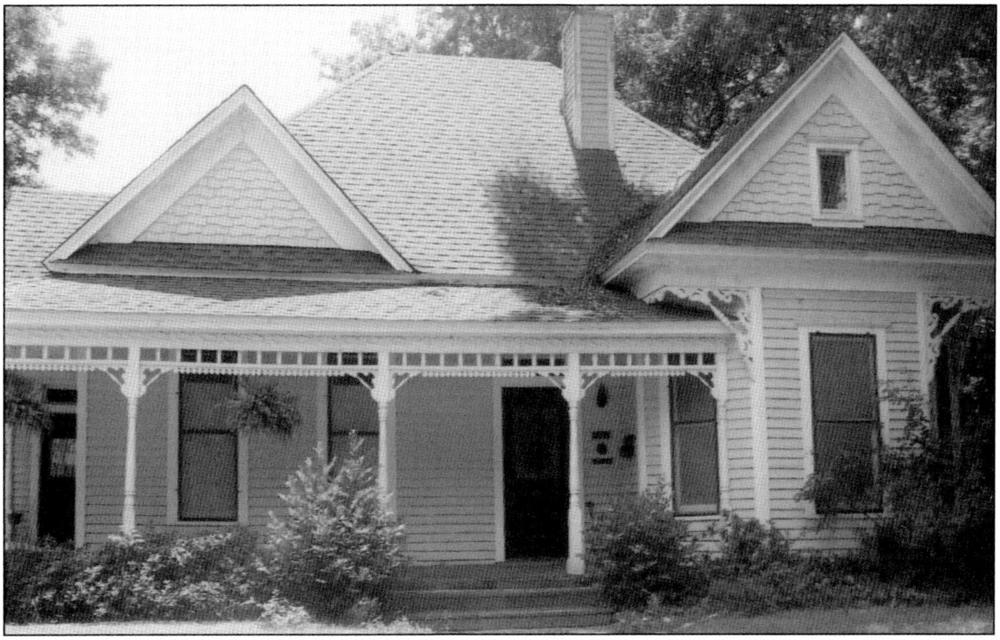

The first house built by Hix McCanless in Ennis is believed to be the Meredith McDowell House, pictured above, at 701 North Gaines Street. He built numerous homes still standing today and many located in the Ennis Historic District. McCanless was also the architect of many downtown buildings as well, including the city hall building, pictured below, which was constructed in 1915. (Above, courtesy of Bill and Suzanne Rhoten.)

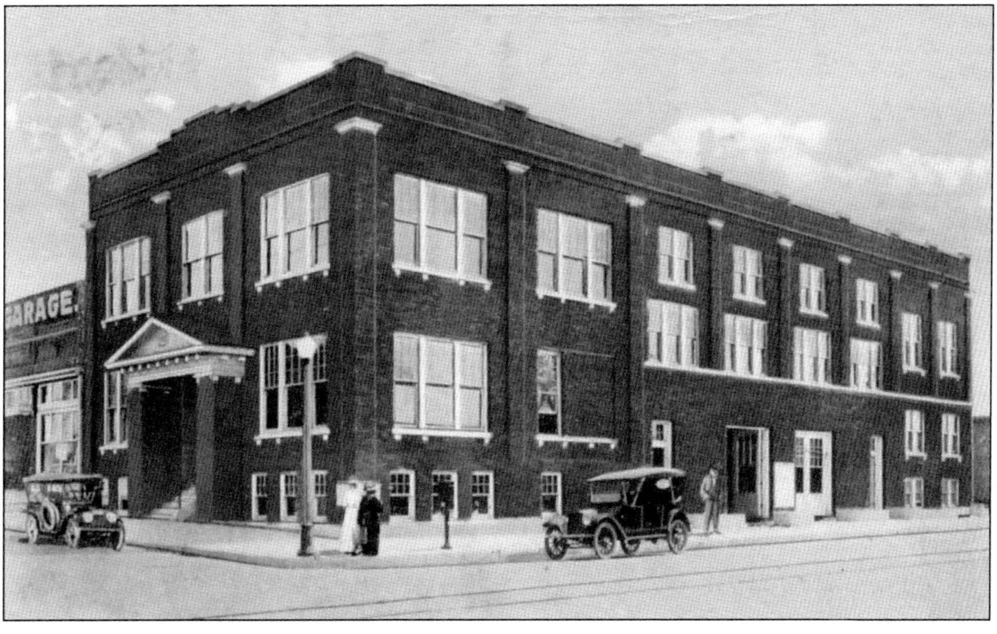

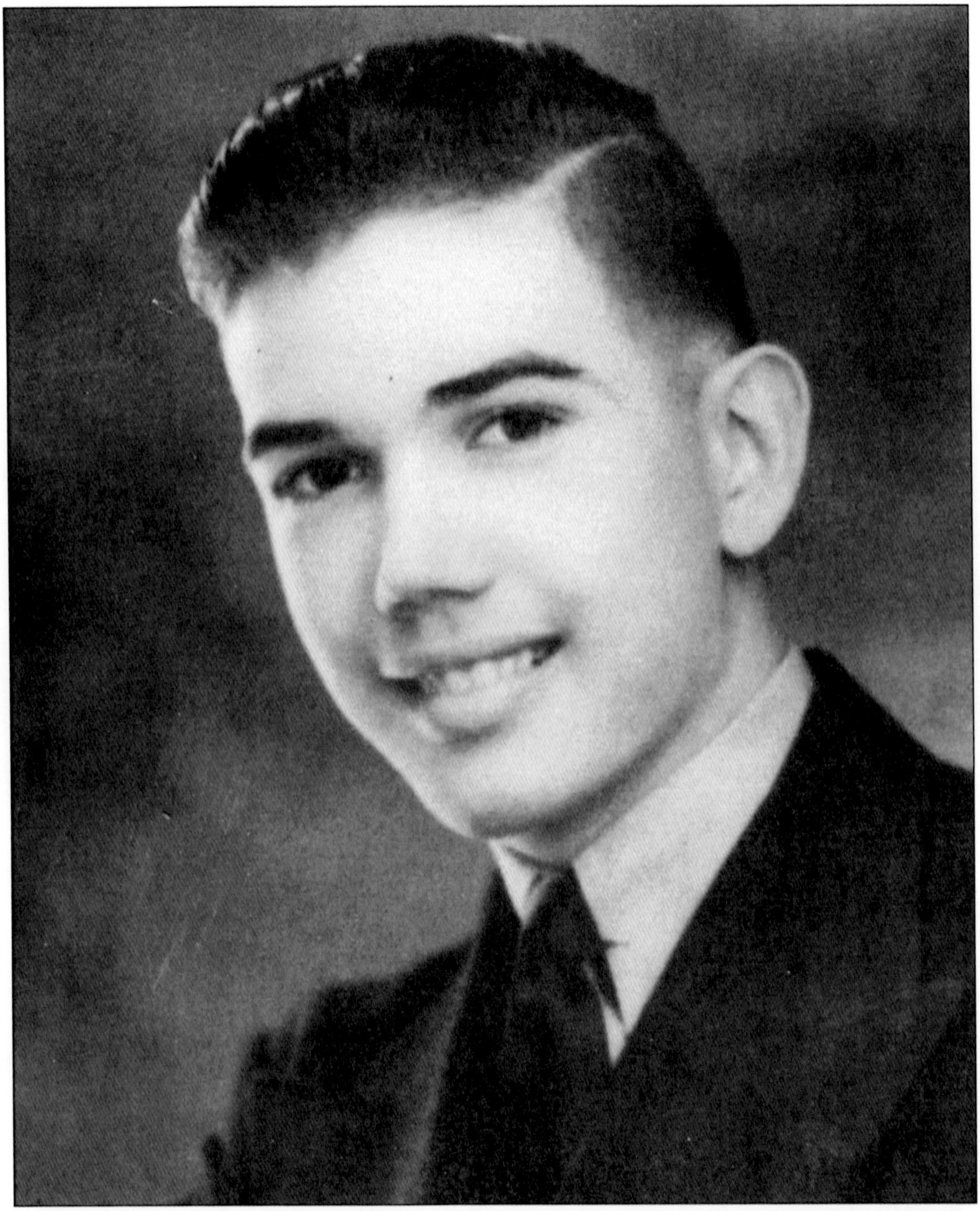

Bob Banner, the well-known director and producer, has many credits to his name. He has produced and/or directed numerous television shows, specials, and movies. He has won an Emmy Award and been nominated for many others. He is an icon to many and a role model to others. But long before anyone knew of Bob Banner the producer and director, he wrote the lyrics for the Ennis High School song, which is still sung today at many school activities. Bob Banner was born and raised in Ennis, Texas. His grandfather, C. M. Banner, was one of the city's earliest settlers and the founder, along with his son, Bob Sr., of Banner Insurance, one of the first insurance companies in the city. (Courtesy of Ennis Public Library.)

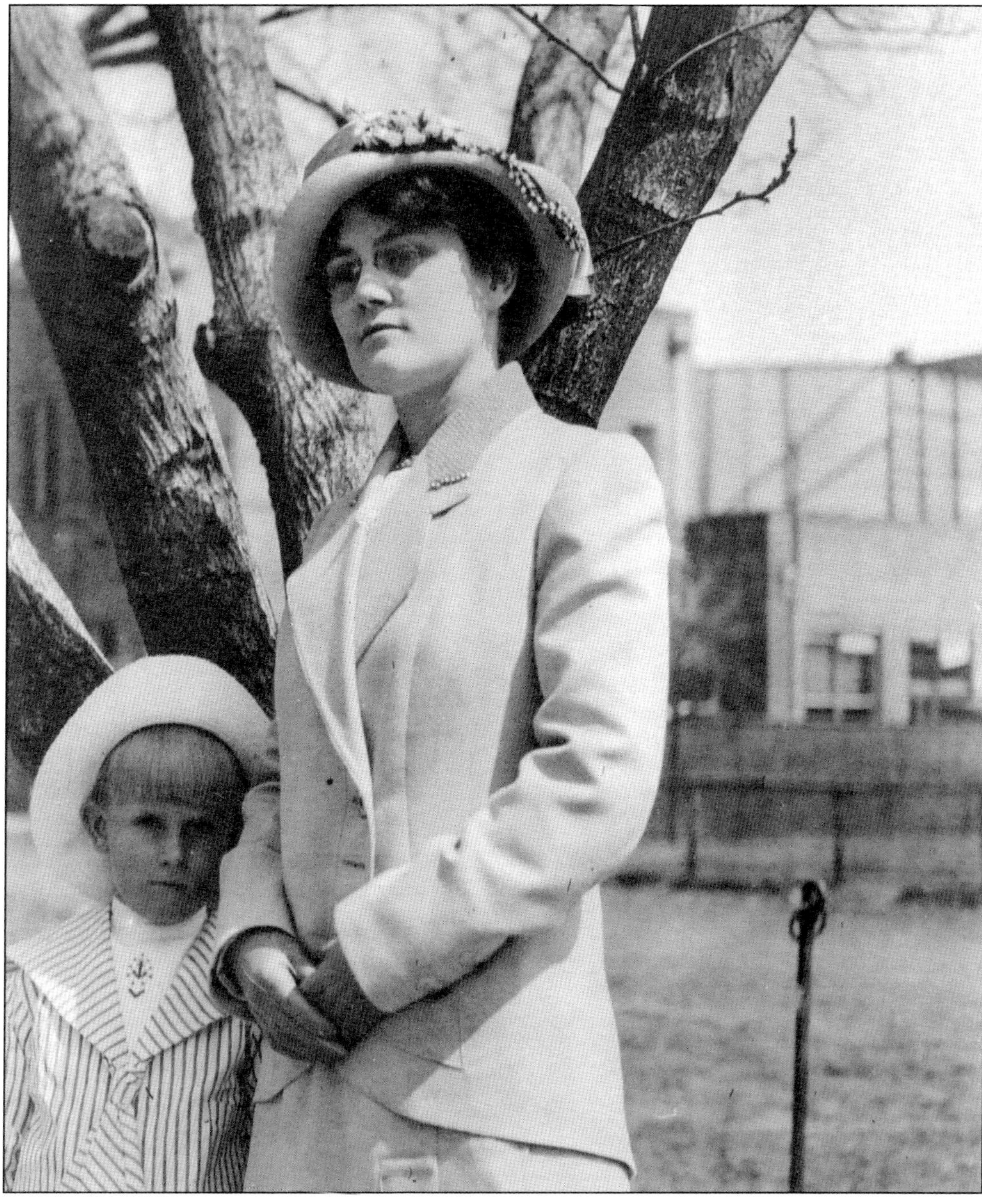

Jack Pender Castellaw is pictured with his mother, Janie Pender Castellaw, around 1910. His father, Jack, owned Castellaw Drug Store in Ennis for over 50 years, and his uncle Jelks Castellaw owned Castellaw Department Store. Young Jack was class valedictorian and planned to go to law school. On January 22, 1927, on a weekend he was supposed to have come home to Ennis to attend a Masons ceremony, he instead travelled with his Baylor University basketball team to Austin for a game against the University of Texas. It was rainy and visibility was poor. In Round Rock, he and nine others on the bus died when the vehicle was hit by an oncoming train. Their deaths brought about state legislation that eventually resulted in railroad crossing overpasses. A memorial service is held every fall to remember those who died. They have come to be known as the Immortal Ten of Baylor University. In 1968, his mother donated almost $700,000 to Baylor University, and today the Castellaw Communications Building still stands as a memorial to her only child. (Courtesy of Ennis Public Library.)

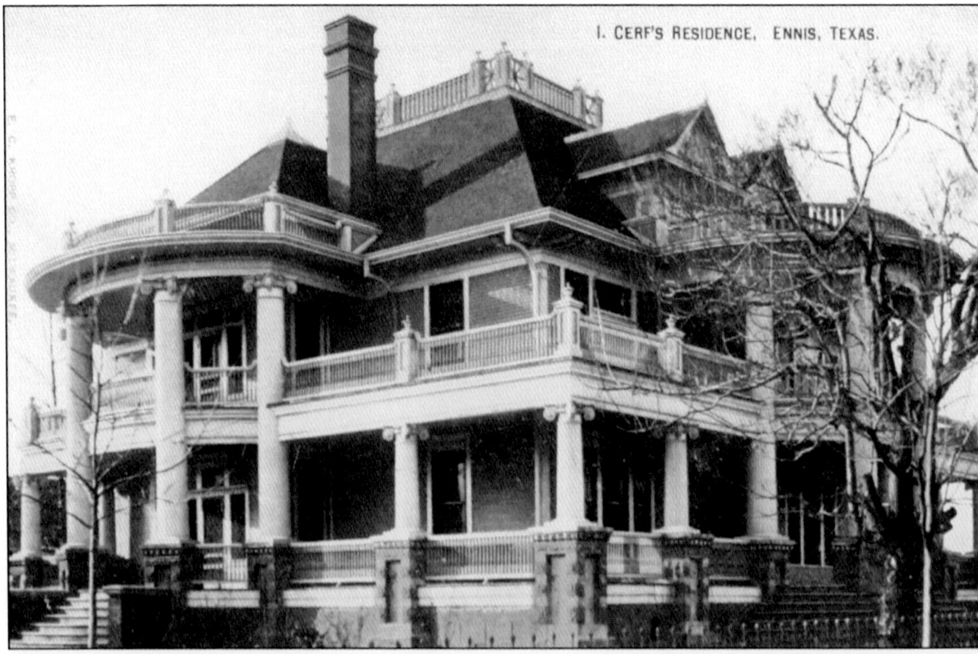

There were numerous wonderful homes built along Ennis Avenue but none that stood out quite like the Cerf home did. Built by Isidore Cerf, a prosperous merchant from France, it was located at the southwest corner of Preston Street and Ennis Avenue. Its Preston Street entrance, pictured to the left, was every bit as impressive as its front entrance on Ennis Avenue, seen to the right.

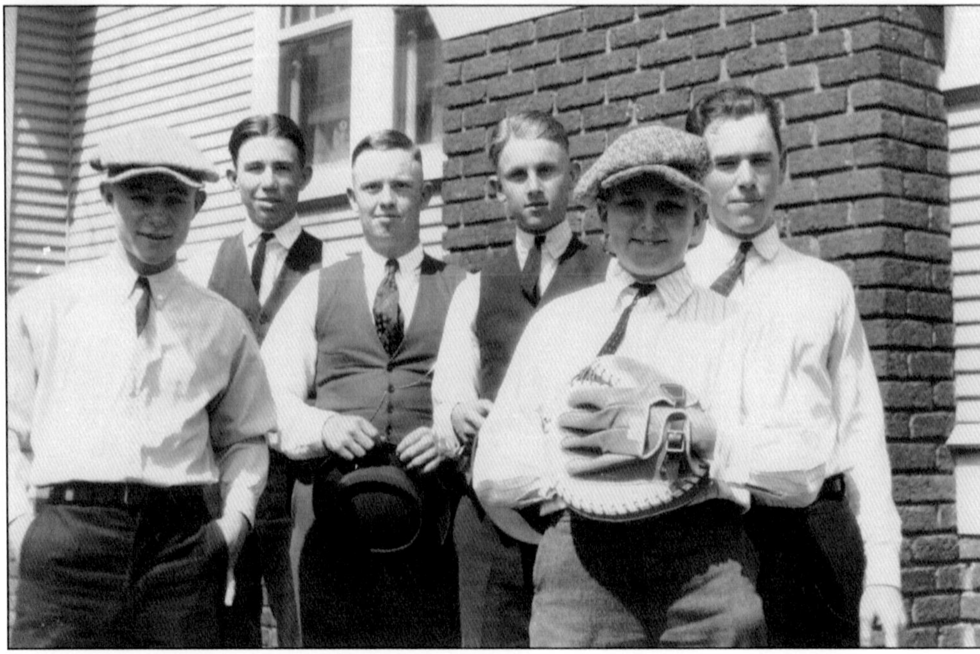

Here is a group of Ennis boys around 1915. As evidenced by the baseball glove, they have plans for their day and perhaps aspirations to set a record similar to that of a decade earlier in Ennis. In July 1902, the Corsicana team defeated Texarkana by a record-setting score of 51-3. Nig Clark, catcher for Corsicana, hit eight home runs during the game. (Courtesy of Ennis Public Library.)

Eight

THEN AND NOW

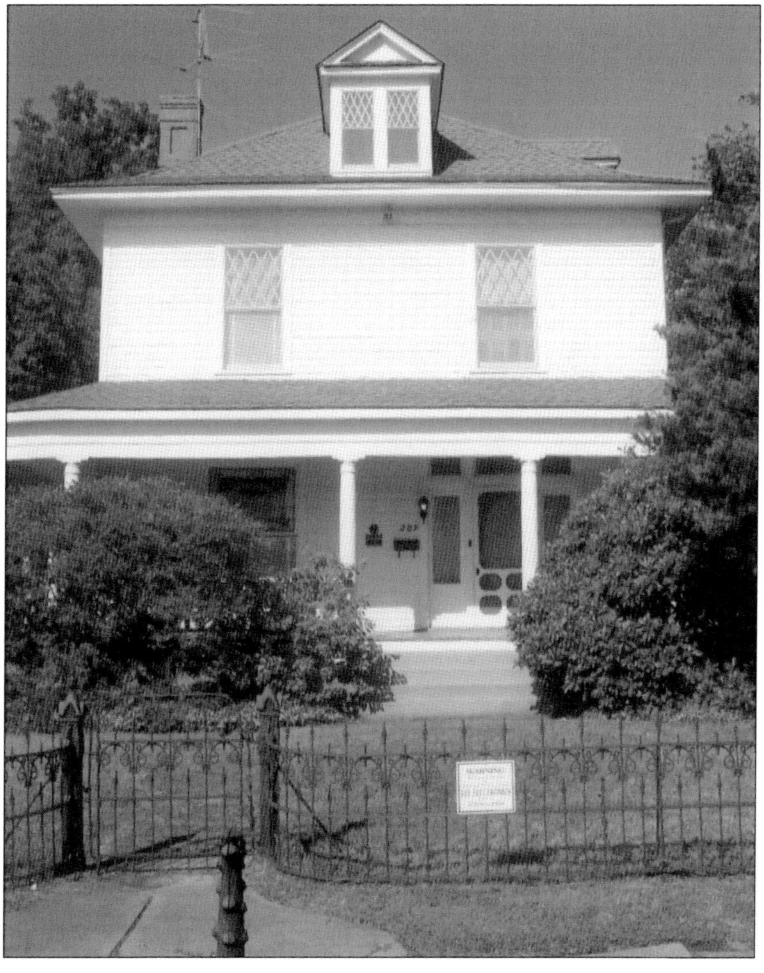

The Telfair Home at 209 North Preston Street was built in 1902 by John Spier Telfair. For over 100 years, it has been owned and carefully preserved by the Telfair family. It has been the location of many community events during those years, including the Centennial Tea hosted by Ray and Jessie Mae Beasley Telfair in 1972, celebrating the 100-year anniversary of the city.

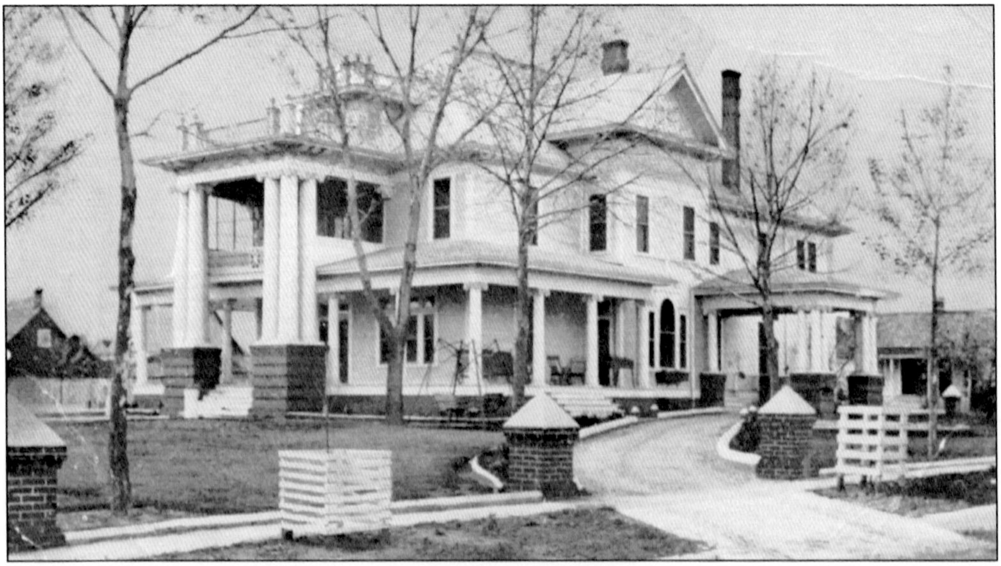

The Moore House at 400 West Denton Street was built in 1905 by Hardin T. Moore and his wife, Malinda Farrar Moore. Moore was a partner in Moore and Fannin Insurance Company, located in the Moore Building. Malinda was considered to be an exceptional businesswoman of her time, and she managed much of the significant estate of her first husband, J. R. Farrar. The home as it is today, pictured below, is still very much as it was around 1910, as seen above. (Both courtesy of Sam and Joanne Ventura.)

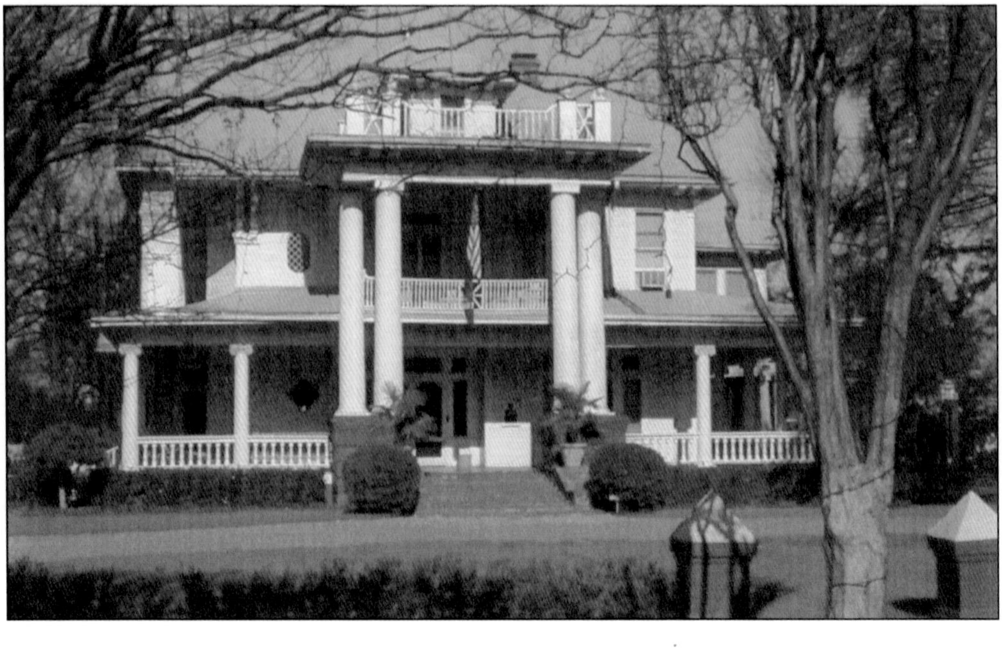

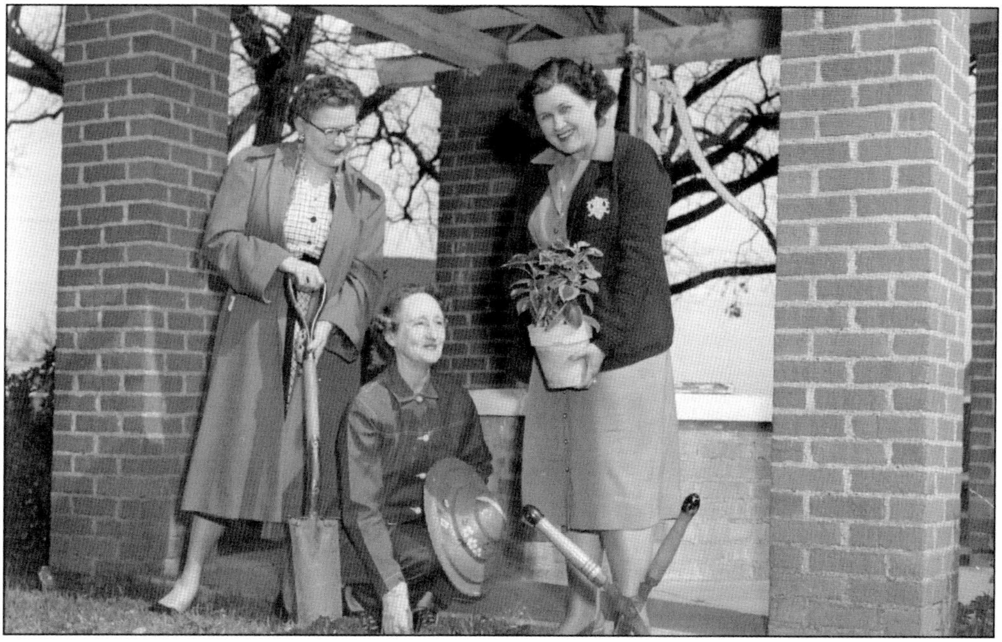

Since its inception, the Ennis Garden Club has served the community through the beautification of its surroundings. In the early 1950s, the group took on the project of landscaping the grounds of the Ennis Municipal Hospital, organized by its landscaping committee, pictured above from left to right, Alleyne Fitzgerald, Mabel Thomas, and Helen Kirkpatrick. Through the decades, they have provided landscaping for many areas of the city, including the Ennis Public Library and Ennis schools. They were instrumental in the preservation of the Kachina Prairie, a local native-grass blackland area, through a conservation easement. They organized both the Bluebonnet Trails and the Bluebonnet Festival, which continue today. Current members of the Garden Club are pictured below on a visit to the Thyme Center. (Above, courtesy of Ennis Public Library; below, Ennis Garden Club.)

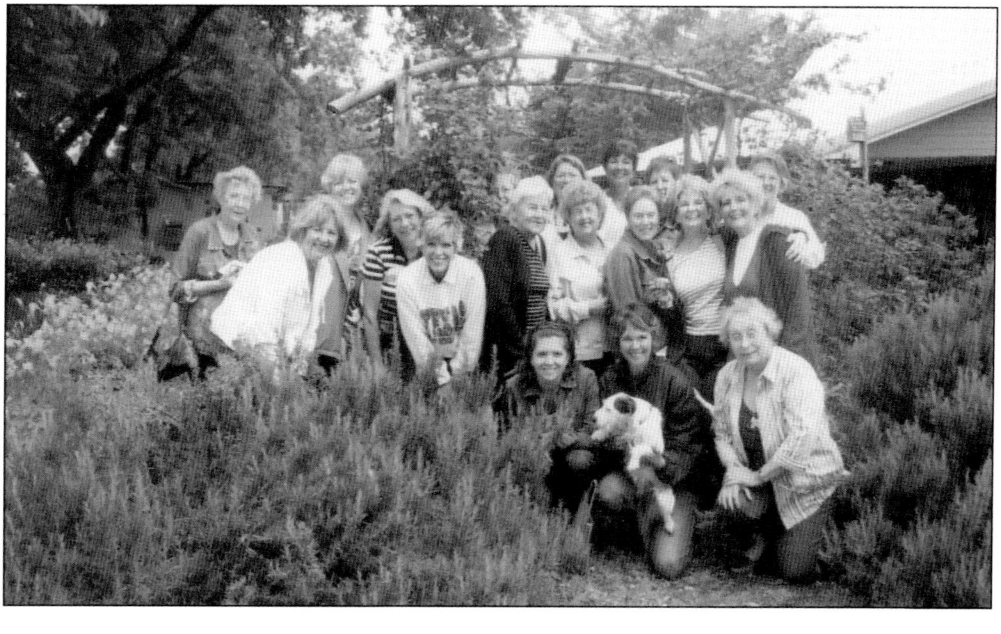

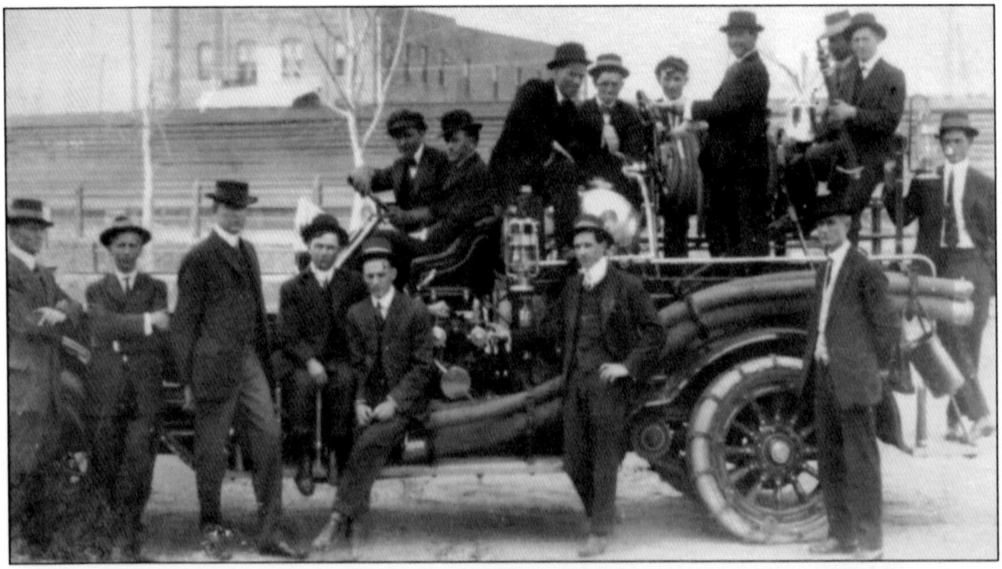

The fire department moved into the new city hall in 1915. That year, members of the department included (in front of the fire truck) Chief Joe Hillyer, Ross Crumley, B. Pittman, Dr. ? Perry, Rupert Blakey, C. Cunningham, and F. Abrams; (on the fire truck) H. Estes, C. Lewis, P. Ransome, B. House, D. Anderson, Sam Estes, John Mayfield, and Allen Disharoon. (Courtesy of Ennis Public Library.)

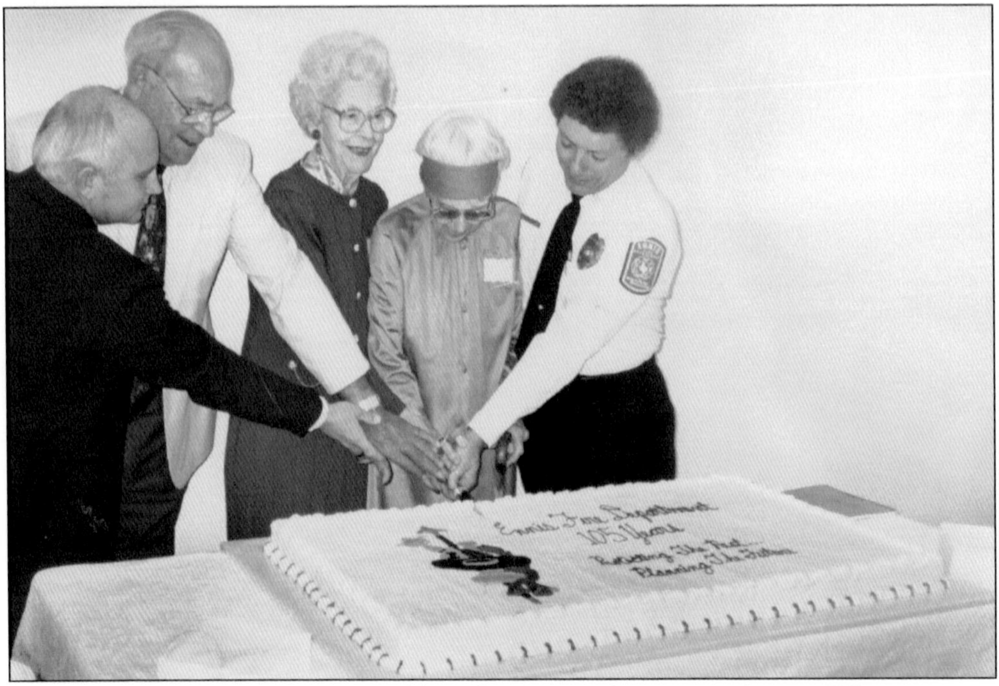

In 1989, the Ennis Fire Department celebrated 105 years of protecting the city. What represents now over 80 years of fire chiefs serving Ennis gathered are, from left to right, Chief Rocky Harber (1981–1985), Chief D. D. Day (1960–1981), Lila Mai Fitzgerald (widow of Chief Hugh Fitzgerald, 1925–1949), ? Lightsey (widow of Chief Jack Lightsey, 1950–1960), and Chief David Hopkins (1986–present). (Courtesy of Ennis Fire Department.)

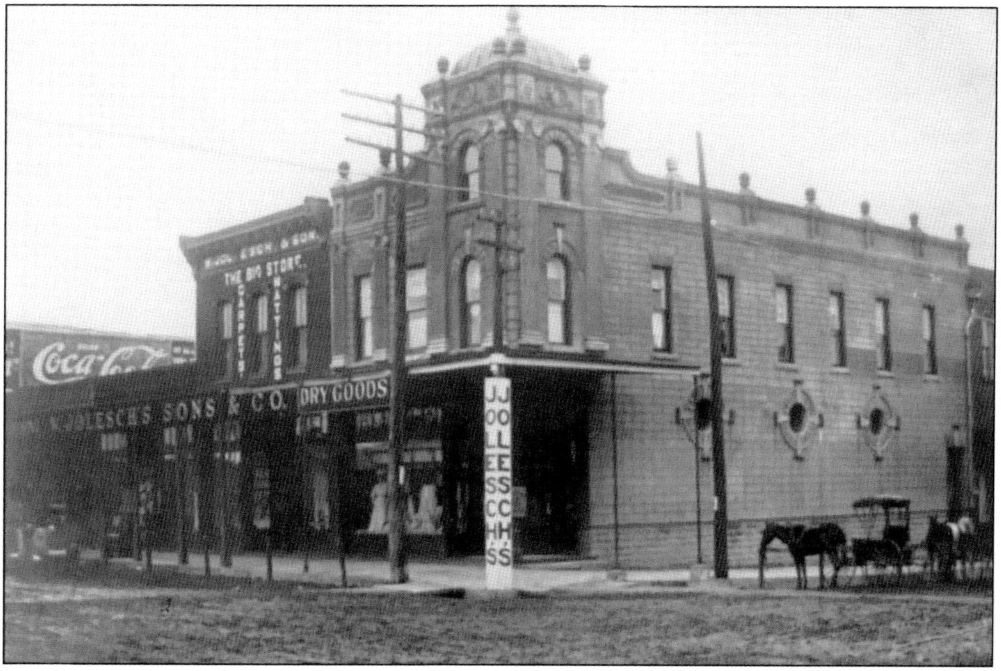

Throughout the years, there has been an effort to retain as much of the historical architecture as possible in both the downtown and residential areas. There have been losses, many of them because of fire. Pictured above is the exterior of Jolesch's at the southwest corner of Ennis Avenue and Main Street in the late 1880s. Ennis was a new and fledging town with many pioneers determined it would grow and flourish, including Joseph Jolesch. Over 100 years later, the building that once housed Jolesch's Sons and Company Dry Goods remains. It has faced many changes over the century but has weathered them, and its foundation still stands strong. (Above, courtesy of Harriett Adams; below, Paula Myers Campo.)

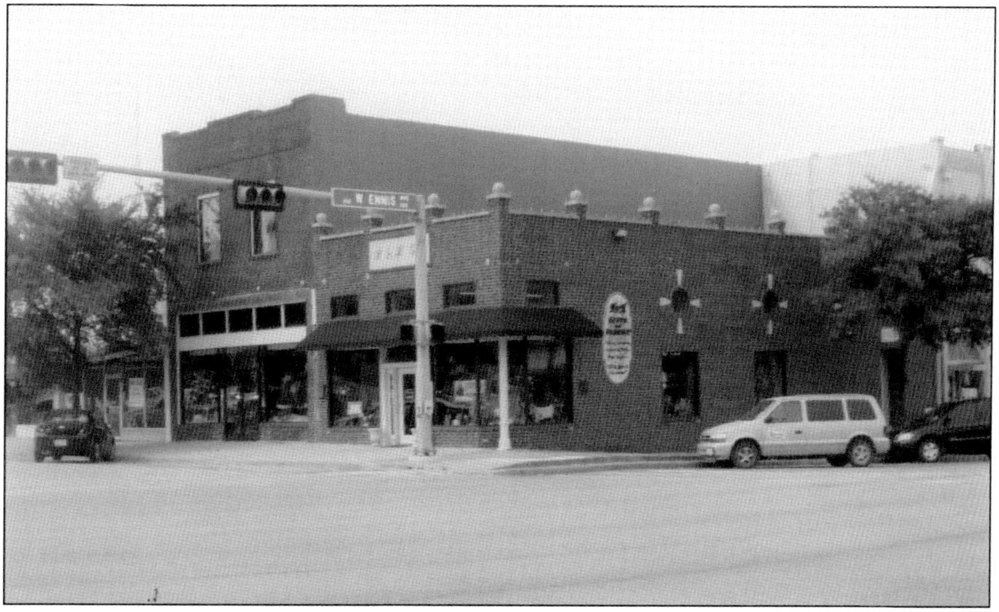

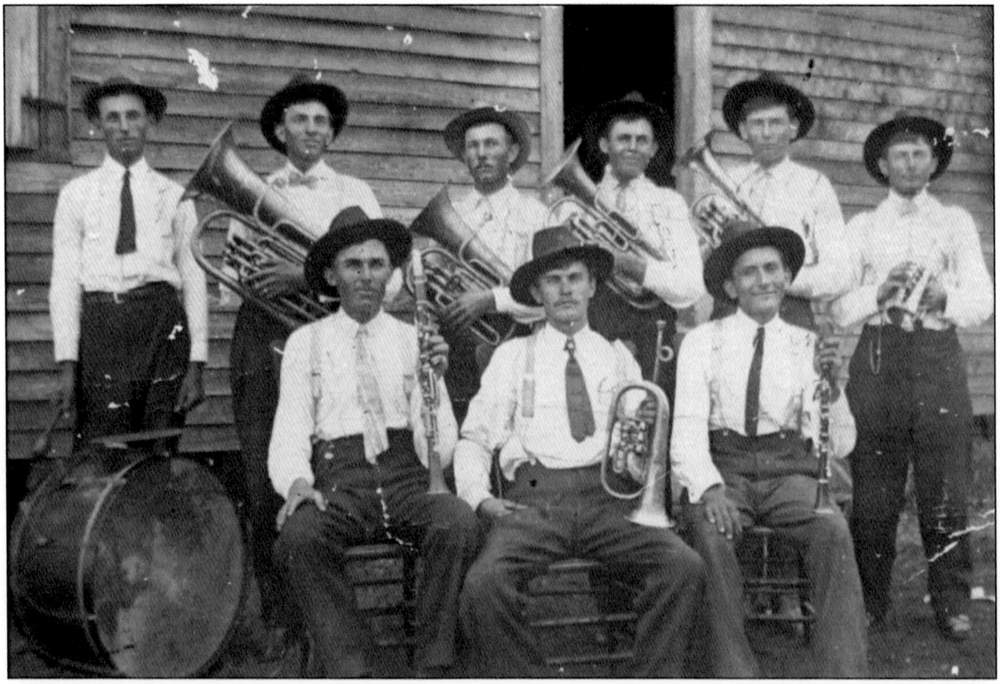

A lasting part of the Czech heritage has been the music, which in over 100 years in Ennis has never lost its appeal. Family bands have remained a strong tradition and kept the music playing strong from one generation to the next. The Martinec Band pictured above around 1915 beside the old KJT Hall included, from left to right, (first row) Frank Honza, ? Martinec, and Joe R. Slovak; (second row) Frank J. Slovak Sr., Frank Kubin, Joe L. Slovak, Joe Honza, Joe Kriska, and Charlie Kovar. Fifty years later, the Music Masters are pictured below performing at the Knights of Columbus Hall. From left to right are Charlie Patak, Raymond Zapletal (Polka Festival founder), Edward Rejcek, Eddie Miller, Daniel Barto (on the drums), Mike Redford, and Edward Muehlstein. (Above, courtesy of KJT and Georgie Honza Kubala; below, Ennis Public Library.)

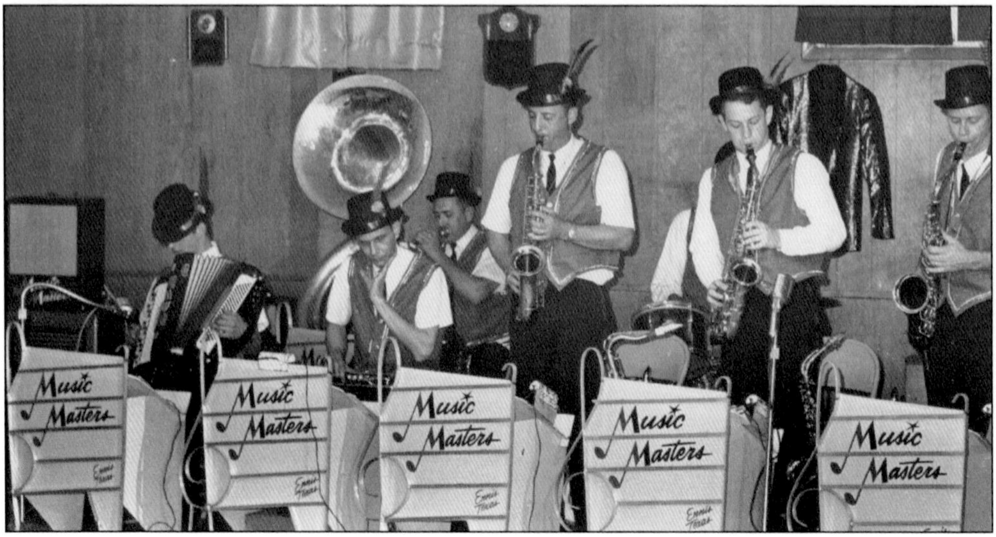

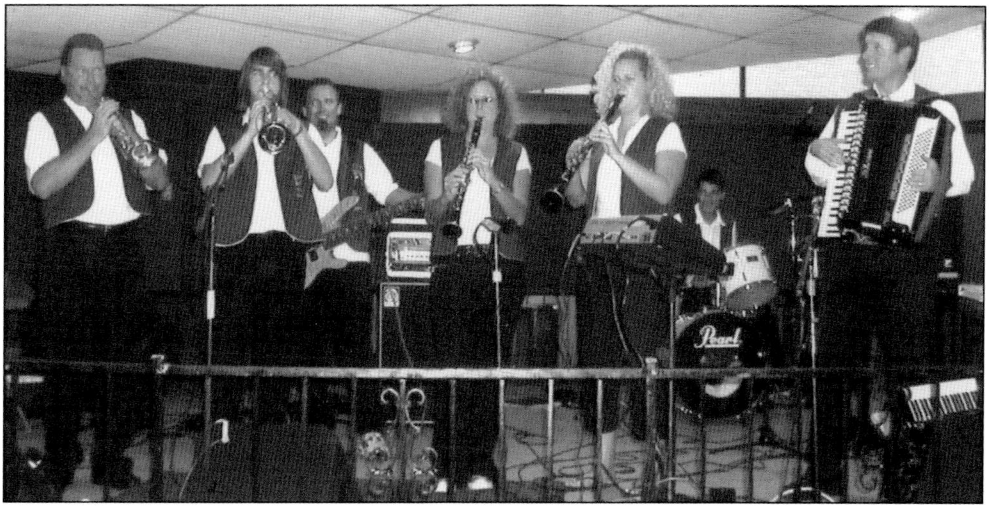

In 1997, descendants of the Martinec and Music Masters Band members came together to carry on the traditions of family and Czech music alike. Brother and sister David Slovak and Jennifer Marek are the grandchildren of Martinec Band member Frank Slovak Sr. Joe L. Slovak and Frank Honza were their great-uncles. Brother and sister Danny Zapletal and Michelle Slovak are the children of Music Masters bandleader Raymond Zapletal. Edward Muehlstein is their uncle. Czech and Then Some band members, pictured above from left to right, are Danny Zapletal, Aaron Schumacher, John Schumacher, Jennifer Marek, Michelle Slovak, Zeke Martinez, and David Slovak. And for over 40 years, Johnnie Krajca, pictured below in his radio broadcast booth, has brought polka music directly to Ennis homes with his *Sunday Morning Polka Show* broadcast from KBEC. (Below, courtesy of Johnnie I. Krajca family.)

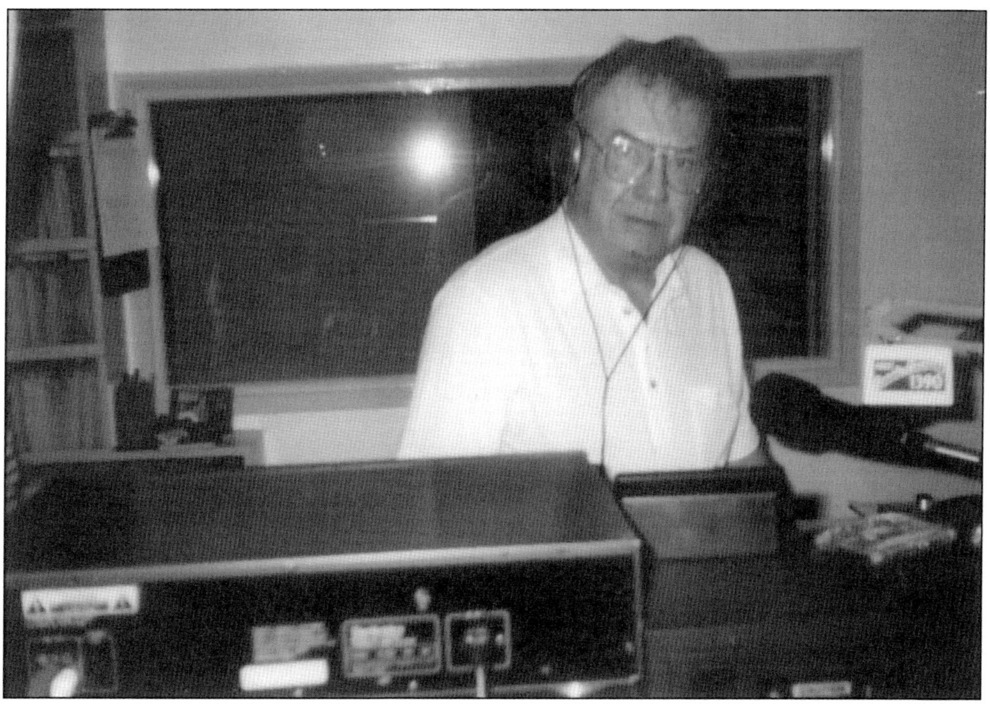

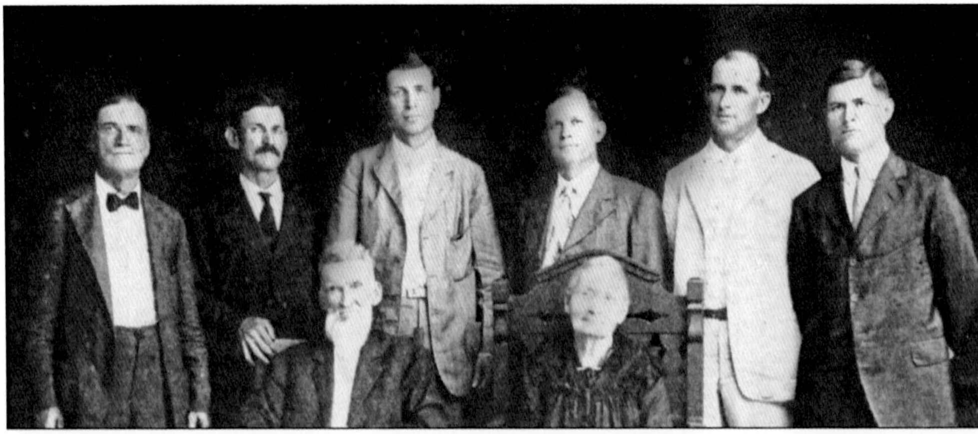

Enoch Marvin Thomas came to Ennis in 1901 to establish the Thomas Shoe Store. In 1915, he and a partner built the first sewer system in the city, which was so successful the city soon purchased it from them. Thomas later served as mayor of Ennis through the early 1920s. Eighty years later, Mayor Russell Thomas has followed his great-uncle in choosing to serve his community. Mayor E. M. Thomas is pictured above with his parents and brothers at a 1916 reunion. From left to right are (first row) Buck Thomas and Susan; (second row) Will, Jim, Bascom, Enoch Marvin Thomas, Mack, and Hubbard. Mayor Russell Thomas is pictured below with his wife, Nancy, in front of a portrait of their daughters, who are from left to right Rebecca, Anna, and Katherine. (Both courtesy of Russell and Nancy Thomas.)

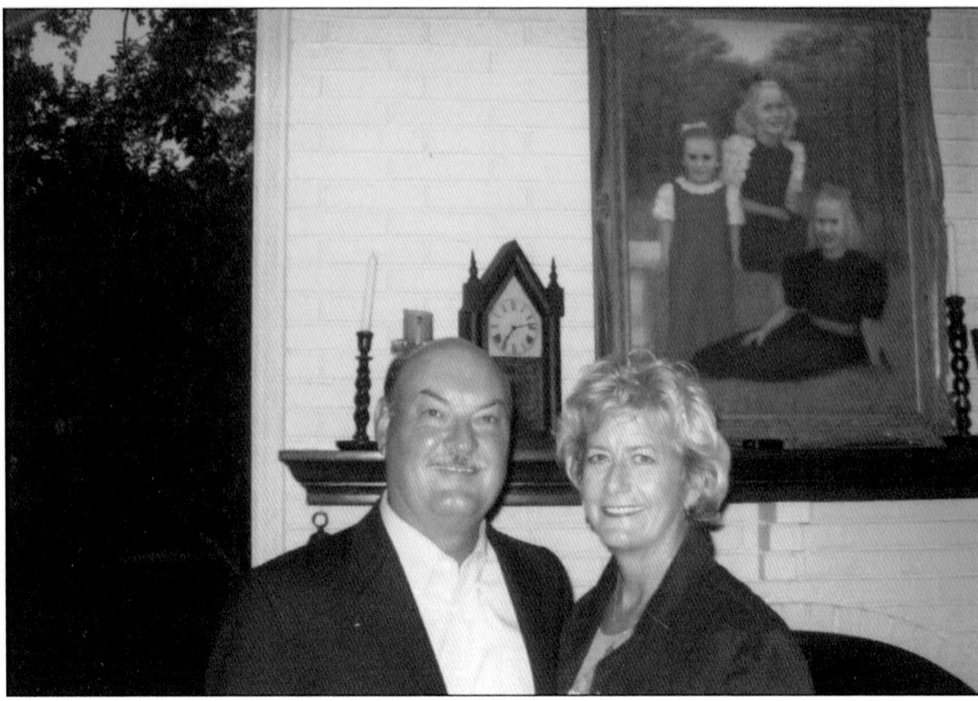

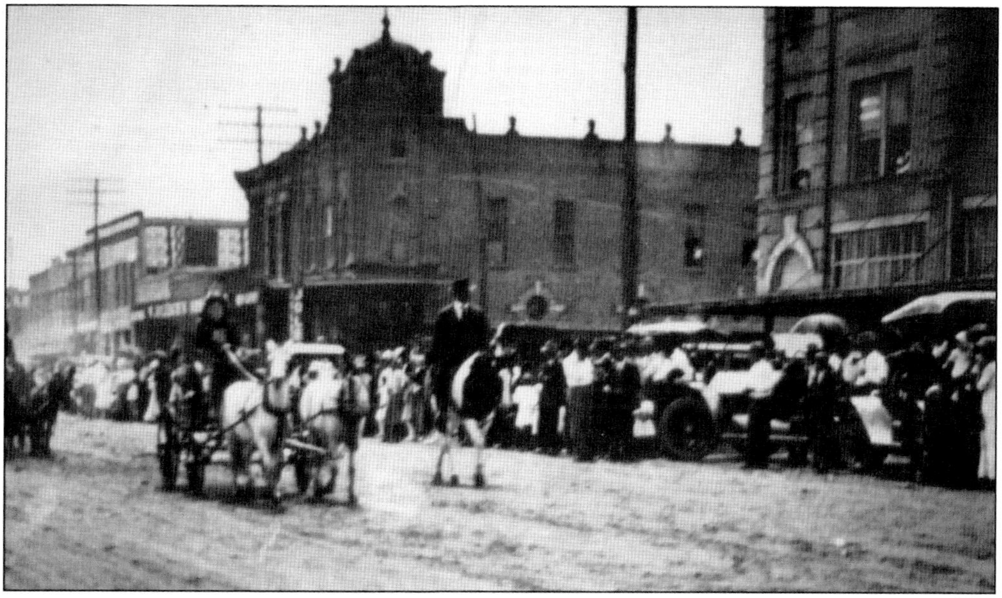

Ennis residents have always gathered along Main Street, whether for a parade or other occasions that call for the town to come together. In 1901, in a letter to his family, future mayor Enoch Thomas wrote of a parade the day before: "There were 40 to 50 fine floats, 25 or 30 decorated bicycles, and three brass bands." Pictured above around 1900, crowds can be seen lined along Main Street. Horse-drawn carriages make their way down the still unpaved street. A scene from a similar perspective is pictured below in 2001 as Ennis again lines up along Main Street and Ennis Avenue for the Polka Festival Parade as they have and will continue for years to come. (Above, courtesy of Ennis Public Library; below Ennis Visitors Bureau.)

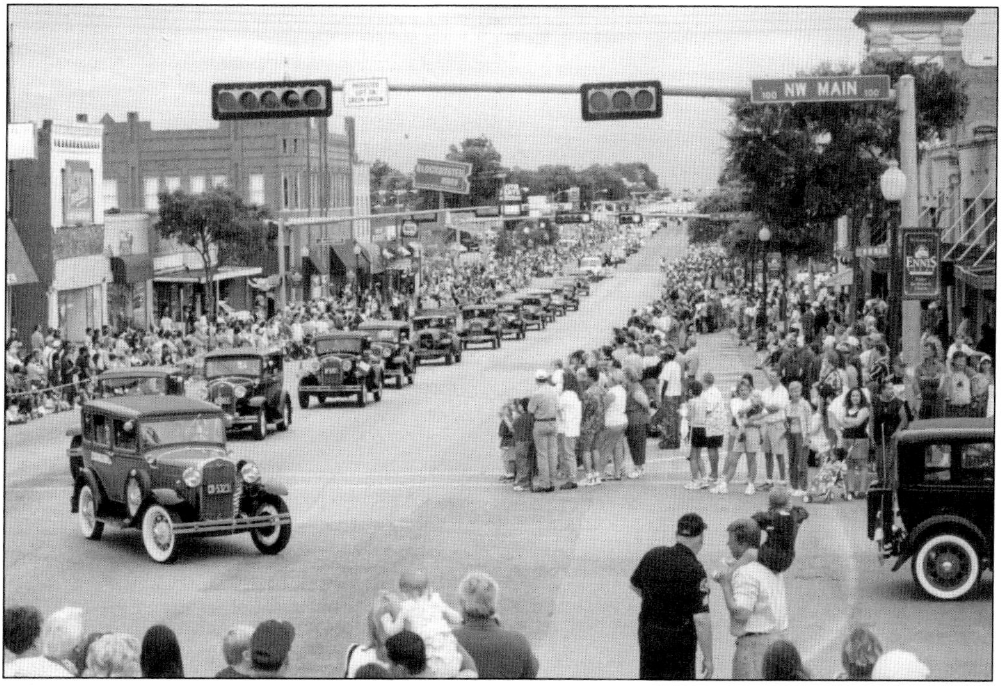